The Author

Sara left Edinburgh, her birthplace, to make the dangerous 20,000 mile overland journey in a car across Africa with her new husband Ross. This trip is described in Appointment in Zambia her first book, which provoked worldwide interest.

They stayed in Zambia for a total of five years, where Sara took up her first teaching post, she finally learned to drive and they increased their number with three daughters. Malachite and Mangoes is an account of this time in her life, and an insight into the social history of that time.

Later, Africa kept calling them back, not least with Ross's job during the nineties which took them to Nigeria, Kenya, Zanzibar, Mauritius, Seychelles and Zimbabwe. At this time they received the honour of being made chiefs of the Yoruba tribe in Nigeria. Later self-funded trips took them around South Africa, Egypt, Botswana and Namibia on a shoestring budget, where they experienced more adventures waiting to be told. Their wanderlust was still unsated, however, and extensive travel in Europe, Asia and the Americas followed when time and money allowed.

Now retired, Sara divides her time between Berkshire and Cyprus. She enjoys writing, gardening, and playing in a band. They continue to travel to new places, but now she prefers it to be in comfort.

Previously by the author

Appointment in Zambia

'Incredible story, ...fascinating new book' (Daily Express)

Malachite and Mangoes

Five years in the Zambian Copperbelt

Sara Dunn

All events have been described in this book as Ross and I have remembered them. Most names have been changed, and some characters and events merged to give anonymity.

Matador
9 Priory Business Park,
Wistow Road, Kibworth Beauchamp,
Leicestershire. LE8 0RX
Tel: 0116 279 2299
Email: books@troubador.co.uk
Web: www.troubador.co.uk/matador
Twitter: @matadorbooks

ISBN 978 1785890 918

British Library Cataloguing in Publication Data.
A catalogue record for this book is available from the British Library.

Printed and bound in the UK by TJ International, Padstow, Cornwall
Typeset in 12pt Adobe Garamond Pro by Troubador Publishing Ltd, Leicester, UK

Matador is an imprint of Troubador Publishing Ltd

MIX
Paper from responsible sources
FSC® C013056

For our three daughters Sheelagh, Kirsty, and Ailish,
all born in Zambia

Contents

Malachite

Malachite is a green secondary copper mineral. Typically it is found as crystalline aggregates or crusts, often banded in appearance, like agates. It is also found as botryoidal clusters of radiating crystals.

Mindat.org

Malachite is believed to be a strong protector of children. It is said to protect the wearer from accidents and protects travellers. It is a stone of balance in relationships.

Cystal-cure.com

Mangoes

The mango is a juicy stone fruit belonging to the genus Mangifera. It is a nutritionally rich tropical fruit with unique flavour, fragrance, and taste. Contact with oils in mango leaves, stems, sap and skin can cause dermatitis in susceptible individuals.

Wikipedia

Copperbelt

The Copperbelt is a region of Central Africa running through northern Zambia and the southern Democratic Republic of Congo known for copper mining.

Wikipedia

PART ONE

CHAPTER ONE

Mud Rush

"All men are caught in an inescapable network of mutuality."

MARTIN LUTHER KING

25th September 1970

'Did you hear something?'

A sensation rather than a sound alerted them. They looked around for an answer. It came down the cross-cuts. They felt it under their feet. Their ears searched the darkness beyond their working area to eliminate a plethora of possibilities. They knew the throb of drills and the rattle of trains, and the whoosh and clank of the cage or the thrum of wheels on tracks, but it was none of those. Two men stopped their drills.

'Could that have been a blast?' asked a new man in the gang furthest away.

'No way! Only a major blast would shake the ground like that, and they're never done at night,' a low voice answered from the dimly lit tunnel.

Straining to hear now, the whole night-shift crew silenced their drills and stopped the shovels. A distant liquid sound travelled up the haulage. The thickness of the air felt different in some way, and a fetid smell came with it. The men stood silent and watchful in the narrow tunnel, every nerve alert to new messages, something to explain this fear they all had but none dared to voice. The sensation got worse and the older men stretched out hands to feel the hot wall of Zambian rock as if it had a pulse. Should they go to the surface and run the risk of being disciplined just for a bad feeling? In the biggest underground copper mine in Africa the rewards were good, and employment worth keeping. Decisively, one man lay down his drill and turned in the direction of the lift shaft, and soon there was a procession of them, trudging through the twists and turns of a secondary haulage. In the main corridor they met other small groups coming from different sections of the mine, a convergence of bobbing lights fixed to hard hats working its way to the main lift shaft. It wasn't time for a change of shift, and in the early hours of the morning no one should have been in that area. The shaft was empty when they arrived at the cage entrance, and peering up into the void they saw a small box shrinking upwards telling them it was in use.

'You see anything?'

'Did you hear an explosion?'

'We didn't fancy the risk of staying down here. A few months ago there was a small mud rush in a section near our working area, but we needn't have worried as they sorted it out.'

'Yeah, I heard about that. And someone told me there'd been another one shortly before that.'

'Ah well, it's probably just the same thing.'

'Still, better to be sure.'

'How long does that bloody cage take? I want to get out of here.'

'The last one left a few minutes ago. It'll be another five minutes or so before it comes back down.'

'A cousin of mine who worked at the tailings told me that a couple of years ago some sink holes had opened up from the slimes dam. They don't want to cause panic, so they keep these things quiet,'

'That's above us you know.'

'Well there's only one place for all those slimes to go if the ground caves below the dam, and that's down, so let's hope it's nothing to do with that. Those tailings are about a mile wide you know, and an incredible heat comes off them!'

They looked up at the arched roof above them as if searching for seeping cracks. Silence fell. A faraway crash and the sensation of being close to a waterfall came to them. They drew close to the cage shaft to peer up into a black column of excavated rock. At last the trio of cages appeared; their operator unlocked the door of the first one with a clang echoing up into the darkness. He clung to the gate to stay upright as a rush of men pushed past him. One hundred and twenty-five miners filled it in seconds, squeezing into every space. Using all his strength the operator held his arm across the opening,

'That's enough. No more in this one now,' he shouted, 'you must wait for the next cage. I'll move it up now if you'll just stand back. Try to be patient and stop pushing!'

He pressed buttons to shift the cage of restless miners up twenty feet, allowing the remainder access to the second one. Only fifty filed into the next cage, but there would be no waiting for further arrivals. The operator pulled a wire to relay a message to the surface and upward like a rocket it went with the third cage rattling empty. For once, each man felt grateful for the sensation of his stomach draining into his feet, and they all turned their faces upwards with a combined will for the cage to go even faster.

A small crowd of mine captains and shift bosses had joined the group of section bosses gathered at the head of the lift shaft, and a volley of questions came at the men as they stepped out on to firm ground.

'Which section have you come from? Did you notice any rock-falls? Was there any water running down the walls? How deep were you working? Did anything unusual happen? Did any of you hear anything? Has all of your crew come up?'

They stumbled out into the late September night, where familiar stars twinkled innocently over Mufulira, which means 'The Place of Abundance' in Bemba. Copper was its 'abundance' and had drawn black and white from far and near to offer their skills. In less than fifty years Mufulira grew out of wild trackless land into the fourth biggest town in Zambia, one of eight Copperbelt towns in an area thirty miles wide and seventy miles long. Moir and Bell had planted its seed during an expedition in 1923 when they worked their way up the west bank of the Kafue River in Northern Rhodesia (as Zambia was called before independence) towards the Congo border. In this area copper ore workings dated back centuries, but 20th Century prospectors wanted to know if large-scale ore extraction would be viable using modern techniques and processes. Massive workable copper deposits had already been found in Ndola at Bwana Mkubwa mine, in Chingola at Nchanga mine, and in Luanshya at Roan Antelope mine, so the prospectors' chances were high.

On their way back down the opposite bank they set up camp beside a stream called the Mufulira. Some peat moss stained with malachite caught Moir's attention, and they sent it for analysis. Several years would pass before feasibility studies revealed their discovery marked a vast site of rich copper deposits and the spot where they'd pitched their tents would grow into a town of 150,000 inhabitants by 1970.

In the early hours after midnight the usual urge to sleep gnawing behind the miners' eyes was replaced with a wide-eyed and anxious energy. A mutual question-and-answer murmured from man to man and group to group, with everyone desperate for clarity and news of their work colleagues.

'Do they know where the problem is?'

'Not really, they're trying to narrow it down still,'

'D'you think it might have been a mud rush?'

'Sounds like it to me, but can't be sure yet,'

'Have you seen my brother, Simon Ndhlovu?'

'I think he's over there sitting with the rest of his section.'

'Thanks, I'll go and check it's him.'

An hour had passed since violent blasts thrusting air up the ventilation shafts had alerted everyone on the surface to a problem. Something big must have caused that air displacement, rushing into every nook and cranny amongst the maze of underground passageways as it searched for a way out. The cage door clanked open to release the next batch of workers. More news emerged, this time reporting signs of flooding, and the cage shot down for the next evacuees. Everyone knew what they suspected, but for hours they huddled in small groups and kicked at the dust with their mine-issue boots in frustrated ignorance, waiting. Tensions grew after a final cage brought only a handful of grey-faced men. When the crews for the next shift started to arrive and amber hues of daylight seeped over the dusty expanse of mine workings and huts they used for offices, many had still not been accounted for.

'It must be pretty bad. Look who's just arrived!' the message passed from man to man like a snake through dry grass.

The General Manager marched to the fore, his khaki shirt-collar awry from having dressed quickly. Next to him stood the Superintendent, his next in command, and they looked anxiously towards a third man in their group, the Underground Manager. In the cool morning air his shirt was sweat-stained, and he strained to decipher sounds coming from the walkie-talkie in his hand which was useless for any messages from underground. It emitted loud crackling sounds through which a thin voice struggled to be heard. He was shaking his head. The General Manager paced and scratched the back of his head under the plastic strap of his hard hat. Registers showed that out of more than three hundred workers who had been in the Peterson shaft area on the night shift, nearly a third were still missing, and the cage which had taken the first Proto team of emergency rescue workers down to search had not returned.

'Are all these men who were working in the Peterson shaft area mine employees?' asked the general manager.

'No sir, some of them were contracted in to deepen two of the shafts. They are still missing.'

The manager took up his pacing again, and found the rough patch at the back of his head to resume scratching.

Over days 'Proto' rescue teams, named for the 'rebreather' breathing apparatus they used, arrived from all the surrounding Copperbelt mines. They converged on Mufulira to work in fifty sorties searching first for survivors, and then for bodies. Four men who would otherwise have died were rescued and brought to the surface, giving desperate hope to the families of the 89 men still missing. One survivor reported 'a great noise like the sound of an approaching storm,' and another compared it to 'the blast of an earthquake.' It had taken less than fifteen minutes to fill the east end of the mine with watery sludge. Thousands of metres of cross-cuts, haulages, raises, winzes and other tunnels had been rapidly choked with mud from a million tonnes of tailings, and there was no chance of survival for any but those on the outer perimeter.

London, late September 1970

'Have you heard the news?' my father asked Ross

'About the mining disaster in the Zambian Copperbelt, you mean?' he replied.

'Yes. They call it a mud rush. Lots of fatalities,' he paused. 'You wonder about the safety procedures in these countries…' and he left that thought lingering in the air.

We were all staying with my grandmother in London. Our preparations for an overland journey to get us there were well underway, and this news about a town thirty four miles from our destination was not what any of us needed. Ross had signed a contract for his appointment in Zambia months ago. There was no going back.

Notes

www.nrzam.org.uk/Mining/MufMine/MufMine.html with reference to an article by Kenneth Henderson in The Mining Mirror May 1994

Cage – the term generally used for a lift.

Tailings are the by-products left over from mining and extracting resources. They may also be called *slimes, and are usually dumped not far from the mine workings.

A winze is an opening in an underground mine that is sunk downward (as opposed to a raise, which is mined upward) from inside to connect lower levels. Cross-cuts join two tunnels on the same level. Haulages are tunnels along which the minerals are taken to the surface.

CHAPTER TWO

A New Home

"When I was in the Peace Corps I never made a phone call. I was in Central Africa, I didn't make a phone call for two years."

PAUL THEROUX

Chingola, Zambia, December 1970

A fresh career, an adventure, an opportunity, and a new life we'd been looking forward to for months had begun. We saw no further than the next three years of this contract and the future shone as bright as the African sun.

'Don't take the first place they offer,' advised new friends and acquaintances, 'they'll try to palm you off with properties no one else wants.'

These advisers usually lived along with other discerning expatriates in Kabundi, a more modern development two miles out of town where a car was required, along with the ability to drive one, for access to the town's amenities. I wasn't a driver and neither of us pretended to be discerning, so eager were we to take ownership of a house to call home. Ross had signed a three-year contract with NCCM, Nchanga Consolidated Copper Mines, in the Copperbelt town of Chingola, and we'd just arrived. After merging with other mining organisations NCCM had become one of the largest companies of sub-Saharan Africa, was state-owned and the Chairman of the Board was none other than the president of Zambia, Kenneth Kaunda.

Our twelve thousand miles overland car journey to reach Zambia had left us willing to accept anything. We'd navigated the Sahara, Biafra recovering from war, and the horrors of storm-wrecked equatorial roads, and fully appreciated the least comfort of civilisation. So to us every house looked like a palace. We would have been grateful for a *kaya*, the name for the servants' accommodation built in the corner of every mine house's back garden, with its own tap, and hole-in-the-floor lavatory, after living and sleeping in the car for eight weeks, the back seat stuffed with luggage. Nor had we previously been accustomed to much space. Our first year of marriage before leaving Edinburgh had been spent in a Murdoch Terrace tenement close to the wafting aromas of Scottish and Newcastle brewery. The two rooms were just that, with no bathroom, only a toilet cubicle off a tiny hallway, and an all-purpose sink at the living room window. Ross had hauled our electric cooker up three flights of stairs on his back rather than pay a delivery fee. I'd bought it in a second-hand shop for a fiver, and we squeezed it into a corner cupboard next to the sink, with no venting to carry away cooking smells, but the door could be closed on it when we had visitors. We loved our living room's rich red walls, deep purple carpet, and long stripy red curtains, which could hide the sink after dark. The colour scheme was taken from a shaggy Rya rug, which had tied up many Edinburgh winter evenings for me to create from brightly coloured shanks of wool and a rug-hook. One busy week let us completely redecorate our first home. A purple roller blind obscured the sitting room window, but since it was a new cover on an old mechanism the catch had worn, and it could spring back up on a whim. Ross was sitting on the draining board doing his best, in the absence of a shower or bath, to have an all-over wash the first time this happened. With the light behind him the occupants of the opposite tenements had an interesting view. They repaid us with entertaining and often drunken behaviour every Friday night, and an occasional chase over the patchy grass of the enclosed 'gardens' three floors down, under washing lines, jumping off cars, and in and out of doorways to the sound of police sirens. Our housing standards weren't high. But we didn't have the benefit of the briefing in London before we came out, as everyone else from UK had. Talks and films about Copperbelt life, including health and housing, had given them a good idea of what to expect when they arrived. We only gleaned information from the basic print-outs we'd received in the post.

By the time we'd made friends and acquaintances in Chingola to be offered this advice we'd already accepted the first house allocated to us, number 14, 11th Street, and had wandered from room to room glorying in the space. A square fireplace painted the same dark red as the floors surprised me, and hinted at a cold winter to come in July and August. As we wondered how we could fill all the rooms with the meagre house contents packed into our Hillman Hunter, a welcome pack arrived full of bread, biscuits, margarine, instant potato mix, eggs, tea bags, milk, a can of Silver Leaf peaches, baked beans and corned beef, and fresh oranges. Then a van pulled up in the driveway in front of the carport, and a Portuguese foreman supervised our furniture delivery. He apologised that the three-piece-suite would not be delivered until the following day. I felt confused by the apology, as if he was Father Christmas excusing his elves for not bringing even bigger presents. We tried to look as if this was normal for us as Ross signed the form. I pretended to examine our new rented goods with a critical eye, but as soon as the van doors slammed and the crew departed we had a second glorying in the beginnings of our home in Zambia.

'We changed our drab beige suite for a green one,' said Rowena when I announced that our furniture had arrived. 'The Wilsons chose a bright pink one, but they're Australian and there's no accounting for taste!'

We kept our beige one, again being satisfied with our allocated lot and not inclined to complain or demand better. Whatever colour it was, it would still look lonely in a large room with so few possessions.

Our new family member Sassi the kitten rushed out from the confinement of a closed and empty spare bedroom and home-life in Africa began. A car full of personal belongings didn't go far to pad out the magnolia and maroon concrete spaces of our rooms, and for months our voices echoed off the hard surfaces of newly painted walls, polished red floors, and windows devoid of curtains. Like other new arrivals we bought oil paintings on canvas stretched over a wooden frame from traders who touted them from gate to gate. Splashes of brilliant sunsets and charming African village scenes made colourful interruptions to the bland walls, and our favoured artist became 'Kachiza'. Prospective thieves could see through the burglar bars that ours was not a house worth breaking into, even without a dog to contend with for the first couple of weeks.

Torrential rain and storms punctuated our first afternoons in Chingola. Traumatic bursts of light and sound accompanied by conversation-stopping percussion on corrugated iron roofs heralded vertical downpours. Those caught outdoors ran for cover, kicking sandals and flip-flops aside to lunge into houses with a bang of doors. Following dogs had their collars grabbed to prevent a trail of paw prints over newly polished floors, and pale British faces watched the spectacle through metal-framed windows overhung with ornate burglar bars. It arrived like a 'son et lumière' show, full of drama, noise and flashing lights and within an hour it ended. Hellish dark skies gave way to heavenly light, steaming earth exuded the rich dank smell of African soil, sunshine crept through dripping trees and the sound of swishing brooms over red porch floors and verandas ended the performance as houseboys cleared mud spatters. *Chongololos* the six-inch giant African millipedes crawled out of the damp soil and travelled like shiny black trains under tunnels of plants and over paths. Garden boys emerged from the shelter of mango trees and resumed their rhythmic sweeping, being careful to keep to gravelled or concreted surfaces where slimy russet clay would not ooze on to their broad bare feet. Darkness fell with little warning at six o'clock and the metal roofs creaked as they cooled from the day's heat. The houseboy had left long ago and we had an evening to spend without televisions or radio to interrupt the sound of frogs croaking in cavernous storm drains and the crickets' shrill chant.

Newly arrived in Chingola, we were blunderers in a country finding its way under a new title. Coming from a Britain teeming with protesters against apartheid and vaunting equality for all, we felt comfortable with our choice of country. Equality and freedom were the ideals of our generation and we'd arrived with Bob Dylan and Joan Baez songs sounding in our ears. We would be a part of the African revolution shaking off the mantle of colonialism. Not for us the injustices of the white regime still in power further to the south where Nelson Mandela and Jacob Zuma languished on Robben Island. We were the new generation of liberals, open to change and encouraging every sort of freedom.

But the reality was different. We had no real understanding of what equality would mean in a country still familiar with old colonial ways, a land of white bosses, British imports, guard dogs, house boys and garden boys. Where Ross would be called bwana and I'd be addressed as madam. A country where many South African 'old hands' still chose to work, and hold their influence over new arrivals like ourselves. It was our intention like most of the newly recruited graduates, who'd arrived before us since they took the civilised route up from the south, to fit into both black and white society, but without understanding the implications or how to set about this grand plan. Adapting to a new order and making sense of our new life in the mining community would not be simple. The men would mix with black Africans at work but all my information about Zambians and their culture would come from white people or direct contact with the houseboy.

The town planners had determined Chingola's layout long before Independence with a distinct area for whites, and a 'township' area of more basic housing for the black population. Roads were laid out in a grid system, in the American way, and streets numbered from the mine outwards with some 'avenues' being given proper names, like Consort, Protea, or Oppenheimer where top management lived. Why the system should be American always remained a mystery to me, since the country's biggest outside influence came from Britain. Only the higher echelons of mine staff had houses in our area, which included anyone with a university degree and every new recruit including fitters and electricians and others holding specialist skills. African managers started to arrive shortly before Independence, but until then other African workers lived in the 'township;' a large conglomeration of smaller houses built on smaller plots with few facilities and generally inferior. White faces would rarely be seen there unless transporting a servant back to their quarters. The smells of the leach plant belching out toxic fumes usually wafted towards this area north of the main town. Not for them the easy accessibility of a smart swimming pool, a cinema or bioscope as it was commonly known, clubs and shops of the south township of Chingola, with a reputation for being the cleanest town in the Copperbelt. Any mine employee who had the funds could use these facilities, but other than the cinema and the mine club few black faces would be seen other than behind the bar or pushing a broom.

We busied ourselves with getting to know the way of things and trying to make a home with the allowance given to us. The ten pounds we had in our pockets on arrival didn't go far even when converted into twenty kwacha and our house begged for things to buy and arrange. Neither of us had regained our strength after our journey, and unlike our neighbours who'd come into town fresh from a cruise and a pleasant adventure through South Africa and Rhodesia, we needed time to recuperate.

'Townships,' the supply centre, became familiar as the provider of all things free from the mine, such as light bulbs. I discovered this too late, having bought our supply from the supermarket, but soon found the mine supplies were of a poor quality and blinked out at inconvenient times so constantly needed replacements. But we hungered for other home comforts which could not be bought; our old haunts, chats with friends, the familiar life we had left behind. The main link with our families and what we still called 'home' was through the post office, where we rented a post-office box. Above the boxes was a sign 'No photography.'

'It's okay to take photos of the town, but whatever you do avoid any government buildings including police stations, law courts, airports! The last person to do that had the film ripped from his camera and destroyed,' warned Chrissie my new friend and advisor.

Any other business at the post office, like buying stamps, took patience. After a gamble on the shortest line of perspiring black and white bodies, we queued for long minutes on our first visit, then shuffled forward a few inches to wait some more. At the counter the clerks gave long-suffering sighs, and worked unsmiling and unhurried, with beads of sweat on their dark brows and upper lips. Midday got closer, the humidity rose, my head swam, and then I fainted. So we lost our place and the half-hour wait to buy a few stamps for letters home had been in vain. We sat on the pavement with my head between my knees and waited for recovery before heading home still clutching our unstamped envelopes.

'Don't worry, I'll come back later when it reopens after lunch,' said Ross giving me an anxious look.

On the day he started work he fell ill. It was my turn to be giving him the anxious looks. We had visited the local Society for the Prevention of Cruelty to Animals to get a guard dog as advised by all our new acquaintances and I had fallen in love with a tiny tabby kitten we named Sassi. But what we'd really come for was a guard dog. Sheba lay in a cage with two chubby puppies feeding from her.

'She's a lovely dog, and very well trained, but she has distemper,' explained the kennel maid, 'so she's not available until she recovers.'

'How long do you think that will be?' I asked.

'Well at least another week, and then there's her puppies to consider.'

'Would you release her if we come back next week and take the puppies too?'

'Hmm. Well okay then, but you'll have to let them sleep indoors at night, at least for the first couple of months.'

She placed a 'reserved' sign on the cage door, and we came home with Sassi. He did what all kittens do and climbed everything there was to climb, including Ross's leg. This resulted in a scratch that can only be described as tiny since Sassi could sit comfortably in the palm of my hand.

The scratch became infected and shortly afterwards poison lines were coursing up Ross's leg. The first course of antibiotics didn't work and blood samples had to be sent to South Africa in order to prescribe the right one. The doctor prescribed complete rest until the infection subsided. It turned out to be "cat-scratch fever" which is not normally dangerous in temperate climates but this was Zambia. Travelling three times the length of the River Nile on our overland journey had cost Ross two stones in weight and a compromised immune system, so septicaemia was life-threatening. To take time off in the first week of starting a new job is no way to impress management, but he mitigated it with a growing reputation for having completed such a journey.

Within weeks of our arrival Sheba recovered from distemper and performed admirable guarding duties without any input from either of us. Within months her two puppies grew big enough to find them new homes. Like a high proportion of the town's dogs the strong Rhodesian Ridgeback gene gave them distinctive ridges down their backs where the hairs grew towards their heads. Then Stanley, the mastiff mongrel who lived opposite, and Sheba fell in love. Given the opportunity they would run, and bark, and sniff together and when Barry and Barbara, Stanley's owners came over for a chat, he often came too. But Sassi nearly didn't grow into a cat. One morning Stanley got a whiff of kitten and gave chase. Shouts and screams didn't get through to a canine brain in hunting mode, and our tiny stripy pet flopped out limp and wet from Stanley's mouth. He was dragged home in disgrace. I looked at the little body lying in the dust among the rotting leaves of an oleander and thought our rescue cat had gone. Ross inspected him and saw no blood, but he lay lifeless from shock. Although cats hate water, a warm bath in the wash-hand basin cleaned and slowly revived him. Possibly his indignation at being doused brought him round. Our wise little moggy had just learnt from his brush with death never to run from a dog in pursuit. Thereafter he'd stand his ground with stoicism, a courageous act given his size compared to that of his pursuer. Then he'd rub against the assailant, usually right under the threatening mouthful of teeth, and give a flick of his tail before a slow swagger to safety. A little wash along the way completed his show of nonchalance. Such a strategy of confusion never failed to work and brought out my mawkish side.

After Ross went back to work I explored the shops on my own. A ten-minute walk on tree-lined pavements led me from 11th Street to a row of stores in Kwacha Street and CBC's supermarket provided most things. For variety I could window-shop at Bata's the shoe shop, stop off at Stubbs the chemist, browse in Kingston's bookshop, compare produce in Bivek's or tour the mysteries of Solankis. Astute rummaging between voluminous and heavily embroidered baby's bonnets, plastic ornaments, or ceramic ashtrays showing a map of Zambia, could reveal smart basketwork table mats, a plain picture frame amongst the ornate, or a hand-operated coffee mill.

I didn't discover the butcher's for several weeks because it hid behind the main drag of shops, and then it became a regular Thursday morning pilgrimage. This was the meat-delivery day, and an early start had been advised.

'My neighbour has just seen lamb being delivered at the butcher's. It'll go fast, so if you want some get up there quick! I'll see you there.'

I'd put down the phone after Janet's call, and picked up my purse to see if I had enough. Crown roasts would be gracing dinner party tables all over town, as expatriates happily paid high prices for the rarity of lamb, usually with the circular red stamp of New Zealand on the skin. Being the end of the month I would not be offering a luxury like lamb on our menu. The still unpaid loan for the car hung over our heads and we wanted to get rid of the debt.

The long slow queue over a sawdust-strewn floor became an opportunity for exchanges with a growing number of women like me, and a chance to eye up the mounds of raw flesh stacked behind scratched plastic counters. Supplies for a week could be crammed into our five-foot fridge with its rounded edges and tiny icebox, so I'd silently plan menus as we all inched closer to be served, swatting away the odd fly and breathing deeply to avoid an embarrassing fainting episode again. Beef, pork and chicken looked innocuous; liver and kidney made for variety with heart occasionally on the menu, but a grim fascination came with a mysterious heap labelled 'bybles casings.' Zambian women opted for this brown and yellow mass of tubes and blankety innards, but I rarely saw a white woman make a purchase. Few would tolerate the smell of it cooking, and only then for feeding their dogs and cats.

'It's unbleached tripe,' explained Chrissie, 'needs lots of soaking and boiling.'

My mother had presented a mound of white stuff in a sauce to us once, and one mouthful had been enough, but this tripe didn't look like anything I'd want to put in my mouth. The sausage meat was in my sights until a maggot wriggled to the surface of the pink mound and I mentally scored that off my list, deciding instead to source a mincer, like the one my mother used to have clamped to the kitchen table, to grind my own meat. Africans would also buy goat, and I watched a smart Zambian woman select a goat's head complete with eyes and tongue, turning it over in her hand for better assessment. She noticed my distaste, and pushed it towards my face with a grin to match the goat's one.

Later that morning I lifted my bag of groceries and left CBC's with its stretched repeating tape of Christmas songs echoing around the supermarket shelves. The sentimentality of carols made me homesick for cold weather and dark skies. On the opposite side of Kwacha Street beside a row of empty parking spaces I passed two broad-backed contractors wearing smartly pressed khaki shirts and shorts. Their stout stockings and leather boots would resist snakes and thorns, the dust and rock of mine workings, and always looked clean, at least in the mornings after houseboys had performed their first duties of boot-cleaning. They were sharing a joke at the expense of a *pommie* baring bluish-white legs and wearing short socks with sandals. They were South African, and called us British newcomers *fikizulu,* which meant 'Johnny come lately.' The new arrival had yet to discover his dress-code *faux pas* and hadn't got around to buying his 'colonial' stockings from the expensive men's outfitters. I headed for the market, where women farmers and traders using their surplus to raise some cash. In a country suited to vegetable and fruit production, the disappointing selection consisted of misshapen tomatoes, wilting greens, and small potatoes. Dried fish hanging from wires were outside my experience, and didn't appeal. The poorest traders, who never spoke English, sat behind sad little heaps on a cloth laid on the ground with no prices. A smarter woman had arranged small baskets of wrinkly brown tubes on a small trestle table. A torn-off piece of cardboard had 50 ngwee written on it. I peered into them.

'Excuse me, what is this?' I asked, pointing at it and imagining it to be some kind of fruit.

'They are *infinkubala*, or *Mopane* worms. Verry good!'

'Worms,' I repeated.

'But they are not really worms, they are caterpillars.' She replied.

'Caterpillars,' I repeated.

'These ones are best soaked and then boiled before you eat. They are very good with *nshima*!' Seeing my puzzled expression she added, 'you know, *mealie* porridge.'

I replaced the grub in the bowl saying, 'Not today thank you,' and she laughed, pushing one towards me in her fingers, and dangling it under my face.

'Why don't you try one, these are very good and verrry tender!'

'Mm,' I said and moved on.

I paused at the next table with small piles of unfamiliar mushrooms.

'Madam, buy my *kawasas*. Only eighty ngwee!'

'Are they fresh?' I asked.

She lifted her head in agreement, 'Yes, I picked them myself this morning!'

It was only eight o'clock, so she must have been up early. I took a one kwacha note out of my purse and selected one of the piles to be wrapped in newspaper. They wouldn't add much weight to my shopping bag, which was already cutting into my hands. She handed me a twenty ngwee coin and I left the market.

Three women stood beside a large sack of *mealie-meal* on the pavement beside a lorry loaded high with them. One of them bent at right angles in the process of tying her baby more tightly on to her back with a knitted blanket. She stood up and her two companions hefted the large stiff bag on to her head, and with a sideways movement she adjusted her neck to take the strain. I watched the women sailing slowly away with their market purchases towards the bus station, their heads always level, like black swans. Red gold had lured us all to this town which was only a little older than ourselves, but our lives were poles apart.

African music jangled in Bivek's, another Indian-owned store. I strolled around vivid enamel bowls and considered the possibilities of bright *chitenge* fabrics folded into neat piles ready to be made into wrap-skirts or full suits. Zambian ladies favoured these durable cotton dress-lengths printed with large patterns, and on them they looked good. Tempted as I was, their bright colours overwhelmed my European complexion so only ever got used as tablecloths. I lugged my purchases home to see how our new 'houseboy' was getting on.

CHAPTER THREE

Red Gold

"It is no shame at all to work for money."

AFRICAN PROVERB

We made friends with our neighbours opposite, who like us had been happy with the town house offered. Bill worked underground and Karen was a chemist in the mine assay labs, so it suited them to be closer to work than Kabundi. We'd pop round to each other's houses to chat about this or that, to borrow tools, to discuss gardens and fences, and to share a beer.

Nationalization to give the Zambian government a majority holding had started that year in 1970, but foreign expertise was needed. To maximise production while the price of copper was high, NCCM recruited graduates from mainly British universities. Chingola was full of young people like us, attracted by good salaries and the chance of an adventure into Central Africa to go with it. Mining engineers came from Cardiff in Wales; Camborne in Cornwall; the Heriot Watt in Edinburgh and the Royal School of Mines in London. South Africans cut their teeth in mines close to home before venturing north to Zambia, or further afield. Ross was a mechanical engineer, and others were electricians, metallurgists, geologists, civil engineers, and chemists. The mine hospital recruited doctors, nurses, and pharmacists, and later when a mine school was set up for junior pupils there were teachers. Older children would be sent to boarding schools in Britain, South Africa or Rhodesia. Added to this young bunch were 'old timers' who had drifted up from South Africa, or done the rounds of other mines around the world. These were the hard men of the fifties when the white man was king. Like everyone else who came to the mines before the early sixties, they had been through every aspect of mining, whatever their skills or experiences.

Beside extensive underground works Nchanga boasted the biggest open pit in Africa and the second biggest in the world. This was to be Ross's workplace for the duration of his contract and the news of his placement came as a relief to us both after the horrors of the recent underground disaster in Mufulira. It seemed to offer a sporting chance for escape in the event of a disaster. The recruiting company Anglo American had promised a 'conversion course' for mechanical and civil engineers to perform the mining role, and it started in the driving school.

Huge investment during the boom of the seventies also meant expenditure on giant machinery and trucks that trundled up and down wide ramps inside the massive scar of the open pit. Managing drill rigs, front-end loaders, trucks, shovels, scrapers and bucket wheel excavators required skill and responsibility for getting the best out of costly machines.

'You can't be let loose on this equipment just because you have a license to drive a car,' announced Mr. O'Shaughnessy to a fresh-faced bunch of new recruits in training at the driving school. 'Just because you have a piece of paper that says you understand how things work doesn't mean you have the skills to operate them. And it does take considerable skill to get the best out of these babies,' he looked fondly at the posters of shiny trucks, 'so don't kid yourselves! Much of this machinery cost the company millions of Kwacha, and it's incumbent on you to treat it with the utmost respect. You have to realise the size and weight of these machines. If they are not used correctly the damage they could do is unimaginable!' He glared meaningfully at his audience of mainly under 25s, 'and in money terms, the most basic spare parts alone cost more than a year's salary for most of us, so pay attention please, gentlemen!'

A handful of smaller machines and vehicles were available at the school for practice, but aside from the mechanics of machine operation O'Shaughnessy's task was to engender respect and understanding for their management. The biggest vehicle in the open pit was a Lectra Haul M200 giant truck with only two axles which from a distance looked like a chunky yellow toy, but when a tall man stood beside it, the height of its wheel was around four feet higher than the top of his helmet. Big lorries we were used to seeing on normal roads had six axles and could carry a mere 28 tons. The front tyres of this giant had a projected lifetime of six months as a result of such enormous loads, and cost $US16,000 apiece to replace, which at the time was three times Ross's yearly salary. A picture of the Lectra Haul was produced since the actual models were being put to good use in order to repay the investment made for their purchase.

In a land-locked African country a dependable supply of spare parts was at best time-consuming to source, and vehicle breakdowns resulted in considerable expense if machinery remained idle. A degree of resourcefulness and ingenuity would come in useful, but avoiding breakdowns in the first place was paramount. In his search for a teaching aid and testing device for trainee drivers, the school supervisor, O'Shaughnessy, had invented his 'paralax' machine. An illuminated twelve inch diameter tunnel ran the length of a large room, and along its length two grooves had been made. Two blocks of wood ran along these grooves and were placed at varying distances from each other along the tunnel. Using lengths of string attached to each block of wood, the trainee had to guide them smoothly through to the end of the tunnel in parallel. It was like a children's party game, but until this operation had been performed to Mr. O'Shaughnessy's satisfaction, he would withhold the certificate of competence required to pass through the driving school and on to awaiting gainful employment.

'The manual dexterity, coordination and concentration required for the successful operation of this manoeuvre will develop your driving skills in the open pit,' announced O'Shaughnessy to a group of disbelieving graduates. They had imagined a more hands-on experience than this.

They laughed at his homemade 'Heath Robinson' invention as they downed their dust-drenching Lion beers after work at the mine club, but simple as it appeared it did encourage a certain skill akin to that required for driving in difficult conditions. Later it would be a Zulu from South Africa who taught Ross the practicalities of operating the actual machines effectively.

Every afternoon brought blasting in the open pit, preceded by a siren, to uncover a fresh seam of ore. The tremors could be felt all around the townships, causing people to check their watches and say, 'Ah yes, it's the two o'clock blast.' Visitors who were invited to don a *kampompo*, a hard hat, and watch from the perimeter of the pit distanced themselves further from the edge or clung to the rail, as the ground on which they stood shook from the explosion. Then huge clouds of yellow and red dust would billow high into the air followed by a crash of falling rocks and more dust. Then the 'all clear' siren sounded, exactly like the ones in war films about London. At one time thousands of tons of material could be blasted away.

'I left Ebbw Vale to sail to South Africa before I was twenty, and eventually made my way up here in 1955 when you were still a lad in short trousers,' rambled Davy, the self-appointed advisor to new arrivals who worked at the mine offices. 'All new miners like yourself started as lashers back then, working afternoons at collecting the rock blasted on the day shift, and then taking it to the surface. This open pit mining is soft stuff compared to what we did back then. Yes they'd be thrown straight in at the deep end with hard work and no chance of a social life on that shift! Now that was a proper introduction to what mining's really about, and it made men out of boys, I can tell you!' He stopped to pick at his teeth with a dusty fingernail. 'After that they went to production, tabulating and measuring the amount of rock broken in a blast. Then there was pipe-fitting which involved installing pipes for water and air used for cooling machines and ventilation during drilling. And then they had to learn timbering, which is building platforms for the rock-breakers, making ladder-ways, and ensuring that the passages underground were safe. And only after they had all that experience under their belts were they allowed to progress to rock-breaking, which is laying explosives and blasting the rock. By that time they knew a thing or two about real mining and all the challenges of each operation, not learning it out of a book like you grammar school boys with your fancy degrees. And if they didn't manage to break over 550 cubic feet per month they'd be taken off and put back to timbering. Oh yes, they had to prove themselves, mind. A top rock-breaker could mine around 1,200 cubic feet of rock per month. Now I could do that in my day! It was worth the hard work for 'The Copper Bonus.'

'What's the Copper Bonus?' asked Ross, 'do they still have it?'

'No lad, they stopped it a couple of years ago, more's the pity. It was the reward for everyone on a highly productive section and came to many times their monthly salary. It made a huge difference to me when I was a ganger!'

Young white workers were known as 'gangers' or supervisors until Independence in 1964 and were put in charge of 'gangs' of African workers with their word being law. They soon learned to work the bonus system to their advantage, and manipulated their gangs to get the best workers. Under a 'ganger' was an African 'boss boy', selected from the labourers and given special training. These mainly British newcomers were the creators of Cecil Rhodes dream to develop and work mineral concessions north of the Zambezi River, during a time when the colonial government encouraged immigration of white settlers. Their tickets to Northern Rhodesia were one-way. When huge expansion of the mines evolved along with the upward price of copper, they couldn't believe their luck. They had spent a lifetime of evenings by the light of sputtering Tilley lamps with a bottle at their side after rough, tough days which often compromised their health.

'Yes Megan and I had some fantastic times with that Copper bonus,' Davy mused with a distant look.

'Megan?' said Ross

'Yes I was married once and had a couple of kids, but they've all gone now, back to Wales. She missed the boys so much when they had to be sent away to school, see, and one year when she went over there with them she just didn't come back. I suppose it's quite a tough life for women out here, far from their families and no way of making contact. Specially back in them early days when there weren't many women around.' Davy stopped to pick at the growths on his ears which had become cancerous due to sun-exposure, then stretched out his legs to plant his clay-encrusted boots on the table and leaned back with a pensive expression. 'Oh yes, it's not all good times. I've seen my share of trouble and disasters, boyo.' He reached into his pocket for his cigarettes, offered the packet to Ross, and shared the lighted match ready to resume talking.

'Aye, most of my friends have gone too, with the Copper Chopper.'

'The what?'

'The Copper Chopper. After Independence they transferred all the whites onto a work-permit status. A few of us survived the first waves of Africanisation, but it was tough on those who didn't. They'd brought their families out here on a one-way ticket, you know, expecting to spend the rest of their lives in the sunshine. They'd got used to a better life than they'd had back in the valleys, with servants and all. You know, locomotive drivers, crane operators and the like, replaced by Africans as soon as the new wave of trainees came through. I think that's why Megan went back, because most of her friends had left. She was lonely, see, and knew things wouldn't get any better for the likes of herself.'

Men like Davy had little room in their lives for niceties and polite society, but had big hearts and strong hands. The good times kept them going through the bad, and many suffered the penalties of negligent health and safety measures from those early days. Davy distinguished himself with a racking cough. An occupational hazard of mining came with its dust and all exposed workers during the seventies had regular check-ups for pneumoconiosis, a debilitating lung disease. Davy had the misfortune of having worked in an asbestos mine in Southern Rhodesia and as a result suffered from asbestosis, the most serious type of pneumoconiosis. Fine needle-like particles of the mineral burrowed easily and permanently into soft lung tissue so there was no cure. In spite of this grim sentence he remained cheerful and refused to give up smoking, but his morning coughing spasms became legendary among fresh new graduates who learned not to pass his doorway without due care. Between drags of his cigarette he would hack away until he ran out of breath, gasping 'die ya bastard' with his last spasm, and hurling a volley of spit into the outdoor corridor.

The perpetual dusty atmosphere of the mine made it a challenge for everyone to keep their lungs clear. Charlie was another seasoned 'miner' who had perfected the art of spitting his dust-filled sputum into the waste paper basket, a habit which brought complaints from the cleaners.

'Bloody cleaning boys!' moaned Charlie, 'who do they think they are? Think they run the place some of them! I caught that Festus the other day washing our coffee cups with a toilet brush! I suppose he found it a perfect fit, dirty bastard!' He dug a dusty crust of snot from his nose and flicked it on the freshly cleaned floor. 'Talking of coffee, I think it's time. Fancy a cup?'

'Not right now, thanks,' said Ross.

These two old-timers adopted a paternalistic attitude to young graduates and Zambians alike, and saw it their duty to teach them a thing or two about life and the world of mining. Tales of the trenches of the Second World War was another favourite theme, and much-mocked in private by their protégés. War veterans spent their leisure hours at the Buffs club behind CBC's, an ex-serviceman's club full of hard-drinking men who'd seen life. Young graduates only went there by invitation. They used language considered rough even for the mining world whose various *lingua-franca* was spoken in mines all over Africa. In mining terms a 'mistake' was called *lo fuck-up* and many other expressions had the same root. The survival of these men would not have been easy outside the wild-west atmosphere of a mining community, and some depended heavily on their underlings of any colour to keep their own position secure. Charlie had a Malawian section boss who worked wonders on machines that dug culverts and drains. Where others saw an uphill slope, Michael could see a downward path for water to pass safely. So with his expertise a damaging torrent of muddy rainwater rushing along and carrying bouncing stones could be guided safely downwards into the open pit without danger to roads, road users, machines or their operators. Charlie gave his Section Boss a free rein knowing there would be good results, but counted successes as his own.

Ross came home during the first weeks with a blue booklet. 'The Northern Rhodesia Chamber of Mines Glossary of Chikabanga,' was written on the cover.

'I have to learn Chikabanga,' he announced, 'it's a sort of *lingua-franca* so that the Brits, the Afrikaaners, the Portuguese, local tribes, and anyone else can all communicate with each other when they're working in the mines.'

In South Africa they had Fanagalo based on Zulu, in Rhodesia there was Chilapalapa based on Shona, and Zambia's Chikabanga was based on Bemba, the language of the local tribe around the Copperbelt. Although it had been designed for use as a second language only, it was spoken by several hundred thousand people during the seventies.

'It's similar to what the colonials called *kitchen kaffir* because they used it with their servants. But that's seen as a derogatory term now.'

'Why?' I asked.

'Oh, *kaffir* is a bad word. It's the African equivalent of *nigger*. It was originally an Arabic word meaning 'infidel' or 'unbeliever' and was picked up by the Portuguese to describe Africans during the slave trade. It was widely used, usually in a bad way, and grew to be very offensive to black Africans, particularly in the south.'

Ross opened the 30-page booklet and started to study it. Few engineers are adept at languages, and Ross was not keen on learning a new one, but he was smiling as he read, 'this is my kind of language. There's no grammar or tenses to complicate things, just simple words, listen to this, "green light" is translated "*light ka lo blue*" to allow for colour-blindness which is apparently quite common, and some words have multiple meanings like "*sterek*" which can mean "hard, or strong, or very." Also r and l are interchangeable. Sounds Chinese, doesn't it?'

An additional four pages listed nearly sixty useful working phrases like "Bring the socket plugs – *buyisa lo blokosticks,*" "Look out for old explosives *–pasopo madula jalatini,*" or "Watch out for trains – *posopo lo stima.*" Some more social phrases had been included like "How are you?" or "Where do you come from?" and some less friendly,

'It tells you how to say "You are a fool" "Shut up," and "You are loafing – *wena lofa,*"' he laughed, 'I'd have thought calling someone a fool was insulting and asking for trouble, but if it's written here…'

He applied himself to learning Chikabanga and in a short time with practice at work, could communicate well.

'Be careful not to use offensive language with Africans,' warned his boss. 'I don't mean swear words. That sort of language is generally okay amongst the men if you feel you have to use it, but never call them "stupid," or you'll be in trouble. Not only are they likely to down tools, but they could report you if you upset them enough. The same goes for the word "monkey." Just avoid it okay? In Zambia you never call anyone a "cheeky monkey" even in jest unless you're looking for trouble!'

In spite of this the booklet listed 'you are a fool' as apparently acceptable. Our friend Dave got into trouble with an employee because he'd called him a 'lazy bugger.' The office boy reported Dave for calling him a 'burglar' which was seen as a far worse insult than the one he'd intended. Unlike Britain where free speech is a given, criticising the government, and particularly President Kaunda was the most serious offence of all and likely to be reported to the authorities. Rumours suggested that falling out with a Zambian co-worker could result in false allegations being made along these lines with resulting disciplinary measures enforced either by the mine or the police.

'There's one thing you don't want to do, and that's to spend a night in jail here! I'll leave that to your own imaginations! It has happened to others and believe me, you don't want it to happen to you! This is not your country; you are here to do a job and not to get involved in politics.

So I'm warning you to have absolutely no discussions with Africans about the government or any hint of criticism about the President no matter how much you disagree with what's going on. Okay? Private conversations amongst yourselves are another matter, but make sure they *are* private.'

The gist of this advice came from several management sources, and was generally respected despite the irony of the 'one party democracy' of Zambia's politics at that time.

'You really need to think before you say anything, don't you!' said Graham the metallurgist, enjoying an evening drink with his bottle of Castle beer. 'I heard that a Scot in Lusaka called Kaunda 'the gaffer,' meaning the head man, and the Zambian who reported him thought he'd used the 'k' word! He ended up in prison for a week before it was all sorted out by the British High Commission.'

A three-week rota of shift work made for maximum production and economic use of equipment, but played havoc with sleep patterns and any social life. Underground it made little difference until they emerged into the light after their shift, and found the rest of their world operating to a different time scheme. A short changeover from nights to days gave little time for recovery, but was compensated by three consecutive days off at the end of a three-week stint, and marked carefully on expatriate calendars as an incentive to keep going. The pay was good and made up for other discomforts, so both skilled and less skilled men came long distances to work on the Copperbelt, from faraway villages and neighbouring countries. With the added bonus of free healthcare, housing, and for those in higher grades an education for their children, there was never a shortage of labour. When Ross had attended interviews back in UK, the best offer for a graduate working in Britain was slightly more than a third of what he'd earn in Zambia. 'Red Gold' represented the country's fortune, and Zambia's boom would last as long as the price on international trading markets remained high. But shifts disrupted lives. 'Days' with a six o'clock start were favoured with free afternoons and the possibility of social evenings. 'Afternoons' allowed for a long lie in the morning, lunch at home, and sport. 'Nights' starting at 10pm interfered with any social activity but allowed free afternoons. The man on night shift could be spotted at any Saturday evening gathering silently checking his watch and downing a coke, looking apart from the frivolity of the rest of his crowd. Friends would find each other on a different shift pattern, single men sought solace with lonely wives, and the initial euphoria gave way to homesickness and squabbling. Wives and families had to fit into the pattern, and if they also had a job hardly saw their partners when on afternoon shift.

'We're like ships in the night,' said Janet who taught in the Primary School, 'and hardly see each other for the whole of afternoon shift!'

Gaining experience in every area, Ross worked his way around each and every area of the huge expanse. So one week he might be at Mimbula and Fitula open pits, the next at River Lode, then drilling, blasting, overburden removal, ore removal, and lastly supervising the maintenance of roads and drains. Although the work was hard, he enjoyed the challenges, working outdoors with real situations. The time eventually came for him to apply for a blasting license, and he moved on to the next stage.

Working with Africans at that time brought some odd challenges. Many had travelled far to seek their fortunes in the mines, and had little experience of life outside their traditional village. A man had been run over on a wide stretch of road in the open pit, and Ross suspected the blame lay with the truck driver.

'That man's office chair, eet ees cursed, Boss!' exclaimed the driver in his defence. According to him the man had been running berserk in front of the fuel bowser he'd been operating and had thrown himself under the wheels. The victim didn't survive to tell his side of the story. Meanwhile a Zambian manager, who had graduated from a British university, described the deceased somewhat scornfully as a 'bush African,' but for all his superiority the same graduate found excuses not to sit in the suspect chair. Ross decided the only solution was to break up the offending piece of furniture and burn it. This solved the problem of the chair, but can't have offered much consolation for the victim's family.

'I want you all to line up in a row outside. The muti man will then walk behind you all, and will kick the man who is guilty of this theft,' one of the managers announced to his assembled group of suspects when there had been unexplained disappearances from the office. He gambled on the witch doctor scaring the culprit and his ploy worked. The guilty man leapt forward without being touched. Incidents like this one earned Africans their reputation for being child-like with a strong belief in magic, and resulted in a paternal attitude for which colonials have been much criticised.

A different solution came to the manager of a soft drinks company in Kitwe where our friend Sandra worked. The Zambian staff claimed that the office had been cursed with a bad spell, and staged a walkout. Their Scottish manager evacuated the building, and with the workforce standing in a crowd around him near the car park outside, he drew intricate signs in the ground with a stick while chanting something from a Latin school primer he'd found, and scattering garlic. With a wary eye on his audience he prolonged the performances long enough to convince his listeners, and then pronounced the bad spirits to be exorcised. Everyone returned to work relieved and happy in the knowledge that the curse had been lifted.

'If an African thinks he is cursed,' said Kurt, 'he will get thin and weak, and unless someone like a witch-doctor can convince him the curse has been removed he'll simply lie down and die. I've seen it happen. They call it 'slims disease.''

This simplistic explanation of the illness which would become known as AIDS was common amongst non-medical people. No one knew it would snowball into a worldwide curse.

'Well that's my initial stint in the Open Pit done now,' announced Ross one day, sighing with relief. 'I've taken my turn on drilling and blasting; dumps and drains and the watch tower. No more shifts for me for the next few weeks because I'm starting in the planning department on Monday.'

To him this meant normal hours for a while, and a half-day off on Saturdays where previously he'd had to work six full days. He had missed a social life, but wouldn't miss the pressures of meeting production targets without compromising safety.

CHAPTER FOUR

Staff

If a man is called to be a streetsweeper, he should sweep streets even as Michelangelo painted, or Beethoven composed music, or Shakespeare wrote poetry. He should sweep streets so well that all the hosts of heaven and earth will pause to say, here lived a great streetsweeper who did his job well.

MARTIN LUTHER KING

'You have to get a houseboy, it gives a Zambian a job,' said Chrissie when I said I intended to do my own housework. 'Oh, and you'll have to buy a couple of floor brushes for their feet unless you've brought a polisher with you.'

'Floor brushes for feet? And anyway, why aren't there housegirls?' I wanted to know. The prospect of having a strange man around all day while Ross was at work didn't appeal. Apparently there were a few women, but usually it was men looking for this work. I assumed the name 'boys' and 'girls' to have been started by paternalistic colonials and reminded me of 'in service' language used in British country houses of the last century, but for all I knew it could have been a part of African tradition. A modicum of English was needed for the job, and men liked the status of having a paid job in spite of doing 'women's work.'

Our sparsely furnished bungalow with only the two of us to mess it up required little upkeep and anyone applying for the job would have to take on the garden as well. Houseboys found us, so we didn't need to go looking. Every new arrival from UK had a trail of them knocking at the front door, clasping a reference, and looking respectfully at their often bare feet as they awaited judgement. This required some bravado as within minutes of their arrival they'd usually have at least one dog growling at their heels.

'*To whom it may concern*,' the letter always started. Carefully written by an educated friend or a paid scribe, and very wordy, it was obvious they didn't come from an employer. It was rare to find a reliable testimonial this way. Personal recommendation from an expatriate planning to leave in the near future was a much safer bet.

'How long is it since your last job?' I asked the applicant on the doorstep.

'Mrs Turner she very pleased with my work,' he replied, briefly meeting my eye before casting his look down again, well trained by the village elders.

'Yes but how long is it since you worked for Mrs. Turner?'

'She say I her best houseboy. I do good work.'

Perhaps it was the word 'since' but getting a direct answer to a question often posed difficulties, and not only due to cultural and language problems. Mulenga must have paid for his certificate of approbation. He folded it up along its well-market folds and tucked it into the side of his shoe when I asked him to report for work the next day. For lack of a personal recommendation I'd decided to take a risk and thought Mulenga had a pleasant face. He didn't do too badly in the house, applying a smear of wax to the dull red floors before skating over every inch with each foot secure under a brush strap to bring a brilliant shine throughout our two-bedroomed bungalow. He kept a duster hanging from his back pocket and set a standard far higher than I'd have given myself, although his rearrangement of things afterwards was a little strange. The rooms gleamed when he left them, but furniture would be dotted around the outside of the room at random, and our few items which passed as ornaments put back-to-front on the sideboard. Then Ross asked him to wash the car, which he did with the garden hose. The outside shone, but when Ross returned to see how he was getting on with the interior and found the hose splurting water all over the upholstery, we wondered what we'd taken on. At the end of his first week he came to receive his first wage packet. He looked smart out of his work clothes, in fact very smart. Ross's best tie looked good under Mulenga's threadbare shirt collar.

'What the…!' exclaimed Ross, pointing at it.

'Madam, she gave this tie to me,' said Mulenga in his defence.

Five uncomfortable minutes after this blatant untruth guilelessly uttered with his main witness, me, standing next to him, we paid him the handful of kwacha notes due to him, he returned the tie, and we bade each other farewell. He would have to rely on his original letter, which he'd stashed in his unlaced shoe a week ago, for a reference.

'Africans don't like working for the Brits,' said one of the *yarpie* wives at a rugby club *braai*, 'they are too vague and soft, and want to be friends. The *pommies* feel sorry for them for one reason or another. Then they get angry when things go wrong, and the houseboys are confused by this behaviour. They prefer to work for the South Africans or people who've lived in this country for a long time, because with them they know where they stand. They're strict but fair, I think because South Africans don't put up with any nonsense, so their 'boys' don't try it on. But I tell you they hate working for other Africans. They don't pay well, and don't think twice about giving their servants a beating if they do anything wrong or aren't working hard enough!'

Ten days later Henry started work. A friend of a friend of a friend had written a letter of recommendation, apparently genuine this time. On a Sunday he moved his few belongings into the *kaya* in the garden, ready to start work on Monday. Henry looked like Sydney Poitier, and also had a talent for making himself invisible, a valuable trait in a servant. I tried not to be 'soft' or try to be 'friends' as I'd been warned. We got along fine.

Every house on the mine estate had a *kaya* in its garden, a one-roomed concrete block with a small high window standing discreetly close to the rear boundary of every plot. Some houseboys chose to cultivate the little patch of land around it with vegetables for their own use, and made a rough fence to keep off the bwana's dogs.

Henry started work at 8 o'clock every morning, and managed washing, floors, dusting and dishes throughout the morning. I tried to keep out of his way, and we didn't have much conversation. 'Sorry,' he'd say softly if I hurt myself, or dropped something, as if it was his fault. After a lunch break he did some light gardening, including watering, but mainly outdoor sweeping. Some 'boys' cooked, and Chrissie employed a 'garden boy' as well as a 'houseboy.' Every time I went to her house for a coffee and a chat, he would either be sweeping, watering the plants with his thumb held over the end of the hose to make a spray, or appearing from behind the *kaya*, bleary-eyed with a guilty look on his face because he'd been napping. I rarely saw him weeding or tending plants.

'Cook boys' could be miracle workers. Noah was famed for his delicious cherry loaf, whose fruit never sank to the bottom of the cake like everyone else's and his skill became legendary. 'What's the secret?' every self-respecting wife wanted to know. A demonstration in Carol's kitchen was organised for six of her friends.

Noah stood proudly in a clean white pinny and nodded happily to his young white female audience. He had assembled the ingredients in advance, the flour was sifted, the eggs cracked ready in a bowl, and he expertly beat the margarine and caster sugar into a fluffy foam before dribbling in an egg mix. A light hum of approval buzzed around the group of women. Then he reached for the carton of glacé cherries. Delivering a wide grin to the assembled ladies he then popped a cherry into his mouth, sucked off all the syrup coating, and dropped it into the cake mix. Another cherry followed the first. Speechless young women opened their mouths in horror, and a red-faced Carol put an end to the show.

Anderson worked for our friends in Kitwe, and he also could perform wonders with food. We sat replete after an excellent beef casserole one Sunday afternoon, remarking on his ability with the dish he'd prepared the day before.

'That was really tasty,' said Dave

'Yes and the meat was really tender,' I agreed,

'Was it beef?' asked Ross, 'it's hard to get lamb isn't it?'

'Oh definitely beef,' said Sandra, 'but I don't remember having beef in the fridge or the freezer,' she added with a puzzled expression on her face.

She disappeared into the kitchen, and soon rummaging was heard from the dustbins. We turned to see her horrified expression as she held up an empty can of 'Beefy Dog Food' in her hand. Without specific instructions but a vague request to prepare a meal for six, he had used his resourcefulness.

Light pilfering from houseboys was tolerated, up to a point. One morning after his first night-shift when his wife had left for work Mike fancied a biscuit from the walk-in larder which was found alongside every kitchen and usually kept locked. Sonkwe jumped at the unexpected intrusion, his mouth full of sugar.

'Have you been eating the sugar?' demanded Mike

'No bwana!' he protested, with white crystals flying out of his mouth.

More care was taken to keep the cupboard locked afterwards, but the next infarction would be his last in that employment.

More than a year after he came to us, our houseboy Henry managed to secure himself a job at the mine. Nchanga Consolidated Copper Mines employed 100,000 Zambians in the underground mine alone. They paid well, compared to a houseboy's wage, and their employees also enjoyed valuable peripherals like housing, education, and access to a good hospital. Henry would work as a security guard. On his last Saturday lunchtime before leaving us he came for his pay. In the usual deferential manner he held out his right hand, with his left hand under his right elbow, and bowed slightly. Although pleased for his improved circumstances, I didn't like to see him go. We wished him well and set about finding a replacement.

Daud arrived in bare feet, ubiquitous khaki shorts, and a threadbare shirt looking young, but keen, and in an ambitious, benevolent mood I took him on to train. The alien concept of housework for him, added to the language barrier for us both, made this a challenge. He lasted a few weeks during which time I think I learnt more than him, and then he simply disappeared. A treasured watch given to me for a twenty-first present disappeared with him, along with several items of Ross's clothing and we reported it to the police for insurance purposes, not really expecting to recover our goods.

A few days later as Ross gave me a lift to work at Chikola High School, I noticed the slight-build of our ex-houseboy in a distinctive black and white checked shirt walking across a stretch of waste ground. I recognised the shirt as one I'd bought in Edinburgh, and its wearer was Daud. Ross stopped the car and called to him. I expected him to take flight and being far from the road it wouldn't have been hard for him to lose us, but he ambled over to the car. After fruitless questions Ross suggested we take him to the police station, to which he agreed, happily jumping into the back seat of the car. Three days later we had a phone call telling us our property had been recovered. We went down to the police station to make a statement. Poor guileless Daud. He didn't belong to the local Bemba tribe, and as a result the police had beaten him mercilessly. He would be tried a month later and would pass the time in prison while he waited. For someone down on their luck this would, at least, mean he could rely on meals every day. The rest of his six-week stay awaiting trial didn't look so rosy and inevitably he would be picked on. As far as we were concerned, the beating brought about finding the whereabouts of our property. But we were not allowed to reclaim anything until after the trial as it would be needed for evidence.

Meanwhile I opted to do my own housework, at least for a while. Laundry was the hardest job since it had to be done by hand, and work shirts stained with dust, sweat and engine oil came as my biggest challenge. It didn't take long for me to suggest we buy a second-hand twin-tub. A new one would have been better, but was simply not available to buy, so the one on offer, which had originally been imported from South Africa, would have to do. Sassi, our little striped kitten who'd turned into a cat, liked to keep an eye on my activities, and for a while sat on the lid of the spin-drier to watch until splashing water forced him to flee. It chugged and churned, I pulled dripping laundry from one section to the other and after its final spin, lugged a heavy washing basket down the kitchen steps to hang it out to dry. By the time the last khaki work-shirt was pegged, all of the underwear at the near-end of the line had dried, in fact over-dried for ironing. So the drying process was continuous from pegging the whole load on the line then walking to the other end to collect the dry clothes. Everything had to be ironed, even towels and socks, because of *putsi* flies, although I doubted they'd have the time to lay their eggs in such a short time. The thought of grubs burrowing under our skin before a boil swelled up and the mature insect squeezed out, meant smoothing every cloth surface with a hot iron to ensure the eggs' destruction. I soon learnt to hang things I preferred not to iron indoors, and to get most jobs done in the cool of early morning. Afterwards I rewarded myself with a coffee sipped outside under the shade of the mango tree. Our dog Sheba flicked her fly-tormented scabby ears as she lay beside my slightly wonky garden chair, which we'd bought as one of a pair from a man on the Kabundi Road. Sassi arrived to join us after a few minutes, rubbing himself against my legs and under Sheba's chin before settling down with his back turned to lick his paws. They kept me company, and I talked to them like children. Sheba warned strangers off in her role as guard dog, and Sassi indiscriminately made friends with everyone.

Our floors lost their swirling shine after a week so I had a go at skating on brushes over the floors. While doing this on a regular basis would have improved my fitness, I couldn't get into the rhythm of it and nearly fell over several times. Sassi, still behaving like a kitten, thought it was a game and pounced out from behind furniture to tap my heels, which didn't help. Sheba had an annoying habit of trailing in with dusty paws just after I'd finished. So our next purchase was an electric floor-polisher, again second-hand. It was fun for a short while playing housewife, but the novelty of 'doing' for myself soon wore off, and a few weeks later we employed our next houseboy.

The day of Daud's court case arrived, I was summoned as a witness and given the day off work. Ross was on 'afternoon shift' so drove me to the court room on the other side of town, and gave moral support. There were inevitable delays but we'd taken a newspaper and books to read. Other trials proceeded inside the building, of crimes mainly committed on the compounds and sometimes alarming in their violence. We read about them in the Times of Zambia, of axe attacks and family feuds. The stoic and patient Zambian women we saw mingling quietly in a crowd with babies strapped to their backs could metamorphose into devils of fury if wronged, apparently. Not much would be gained by sentencing them, particularly for their families, and mostly they were let off with a warning. All but one of the accused that morning were men. We sat on a bench in the shade to wait, and I chewed a pencil while trying to work out a crossword solution. The clerk of the court approached me, an educated man, intrigued by what I was doing. I explained the basics of crosswords, which he hadn't seen before, and we talked for a while about his family before being called in for the trial.

Daud cowered in the dock looking pathetic with his head bowed. His hair had grown woolly, his clothes were unkempt and he'd lost weight. He was still handcuffed, and didn't look as though he'd get far if he tried to run. The young man who'd arrived at our house every morning with a jaunty step was barely recognisable. Ross's shirt was now part of the evidence, so Daud's own tatty shirt and trousers did nothing to promote his credibility. Aggressive questions volleyed in his direction and convinced everyone present of his guilt.

'Madam, she invite me for tea. After we drink tea, she gave me presents,' pleaded Daud in a timid voice, his head still bowed.

The case droned on with legalese, and the day's heat rose. Fans above our heads whirred. Black-robed bewigged figures behind the bench sipped water.

The magistrate called me forward and I laid my hand on the Bible to be sworn in. The contrast in tone for my questions was comical.

'Did you invite the accused to have tea with you?' I was asked kindly with a tilt of the head.

'No,' I replied, trying not to giggle.

'Have you ever invited him to have tea with you?'

'No,'

'Did you give the accused any clothing?'

'No.'

The prosecution asked me more simple questions in the same vein and relieved, I was dismissed to listen to the rest of the proceedings.

The magistrate sentenced Daud to a few more months in jail, and we reclaimed our stolen goods. During the six weeks since we had identified my watch someone had tried to prise off the back and deep scratches marked the previously pristine stainless steel. The culprit must have been a bored policeman. Fortunately the watch face was untouched and the mechanism still worked. We said goodbye to the clerk of the court who we'd be seeing again, and took our bits and pieces home.

CHAPTER FIVE

Settling In

The forest provides food to the hunter after he is utterly exhausted.

ZIMBABWEAN PROVERB

We accepted Dave and Sandra's invitation to their family Christmas in Kitwe with gratitude, and drove thirty miles along the Kitwe Road to join them for our first tropical Christmas. Sandra and their two little girls had set up a Christmas tree with decorations and lights, and we prepared to dine on roast turkey and Christmas pudding outside on metal garden chairs. To me the warm reassurance of familiar ritual couldn't be replicated, and I'd have cheerfully swapped that balmy day under a cloudless cobalt sky for a cold grey one with my family around a fire. Homesickness amid the stresses and strains of foreign living struck hard at Christmas. Attempts to phone home had failed due to huge demand on a limited telephone system. We'd booked a call several days before, but there were no guarantees, and on the one occasion in all our time in Zambia when we managed to make contact the minutes were so precious and expensive, we could think of nothing to say but 'hello' and 'how are you?' All of a sudden self-conscious and remote from old familiarities, we'd stumble over words, trying and failing to condense everything there was to say in a few chosen phrases.

Ross had come home early the day before. 'They've refunded our expenses at last!' he'd announced showing me a bundle of banknotes. 'The trouble is it's in cash because they said setting up bank payments was slow, and they thought we should have it before Christmas. So I'll have to carry it around with me until the banks reopen after the holiday.'

We caught the shops before they closed and bought a few treats to take with us to Kitwe. Children work their own magic at Christmas, and the girls danced around, thrilled at the novelty of celebrating Christmas in the sun instead of Scotland's gloom. Soon my mood lifted and I was glad to be with them. A smell of turkey wafted from the kitchen.

'Madam, I must see my brother today,' said Anderson, their 'houseboy' as he closed the oven door. 'He is a policeman and I must go to the compound now because today is Chreesmas. The dinner it is all prepared.'

'That's fine, Anderson, but it's a long way. Let me ask the bwana if he can take you in the car.'

'I've already promised to go and see our neighbours this morning,' said Dave.

'Well, I can drive Anderson over there if he shows me the way,' suggested Ross, and pulled his keys out of his shorts' pocket.

'Look at the number of accidents, Anderson!' he said as they passed yet another dented Peugeot taxi in the storm drain beside an unmade road with a bent and twisted bicycle nearby. 'That car in front is swerving all over the place. Oh no, there's another one coming the other way!'

Anderson tutted to show his disapproval.

The inevitable happened, and they witnessed two more collisions before reaching the police compound. A man who had passed out at the wheel, must have abruptly ground to a halt beside a bruised mango tree. Any passengers had abandoned him to his dreams, except one who lay outside the car still clutching an empty bottle of Castle beer.

'Ah, *meningi* beers and too much *chibuku*!' said Anderson, 'but they are happy.'

'Well they won't be too happy when they wake up covered in bruises and their cars wrecked!' said Ross 'The *shebeens* must have been busy last night!'

They parked outside a low barn-like building.

'You can come in with me,' said Anderson, 'we can have a beer.'

They heard a hubbub of shouts and singing coming from inside the building.

'I'll just wait in the car for you, thanks, I don't have any money with me,' lied Ross thinking of his unusually stuffed wallet on display to a crowd in various stages of drunkenness. Few white people ventured into the compounds and just sitting in the car made him uneasy. A few minutes later a man came out to speak to him,

'Buy me a beer, bwana,'

'I'm sorry, I can't because I haven't brought my wallet with me,' he lied again.

The man looked at Ross curiously, and then disappeared into the building. A few minutes later he was back.

'Here, take this beer, it's Chreesmas you must drink and be happy!' he insisted and thrust a bottle of Lion beer through the open car window into Ross's hand. 'You don't want to drink with us?'

'Well thank you very much, *natatela mokwai*,' mumbled Ross feeling like Scrooge, and knowing further refusals would cause offence he got out of the car.

They all entered the low concrete building. A fug of bodies and beer hit him as he ventured into the shadows. Festivities appeared to have been in full swing since the night before and he squeezed though a warm throng to join Anderson's group. Adjusting his eyes to the darkness he looked around at laughing drinkers, impromptu dances, and large seated ladies clutching gallon containers of home brew, their thighs spilling over the edges of their chairs. *Chibuku*, a thick brown opaque beer, was brewed in backyards and unsuccessfully 'cleared' with fish for finings which lay floating on the top. The unwieldy size of the pot let copious overspill dribble down the drinkers' neck and clothes. Ross drained his beer and brought out a packet of Benson and Hedges cigarettes, handing them out one at a time. Experience told him if he'd proffered the packet the first person would have helped himself to the lot.

'Eee, that is bad when a bwana has no money! Let me buy you another drink. Eet ees Chreesmas and you must dreenk with us. Happy Chreesmas, happy Chreesmas!'

Several drinks later they came out into dazzling midday sunshine and fresh air. Hungry and drowsy, Ross frowned with concentration to avoid adding to the collisions count, which rose by another three before they got back to the safety of Kantanta Street.

'We couldn't get away,' muttered Ross when I pointedly mentioned his late return.

'Well don't complain if the meat has dried out!' replied Sandra with a good-natured grin. 'The girls have made a lovely job of laying out the table, so you can take your seats and we'll make a start. Just uncork this wine will you Dave, please?'

The road back to Chingola in the dark of late evening was nearly deserted. Christmas had passed for another year, and the world was in recovery. We turned into our drive and headed for the kitchen door. At our approach Sheba sat upright from her sleeping position on the top step. The door behind her stood wide open. We had forgotten to close it, let alone lock it. Nothing had been taken.

'Our packing case has arrived!' announced Ross at the beginning of July.

'Packing case?' I asked, having forgotten all about the non-breakables we'd wrapped a year previously in our Edinburgh flat. The sealed wooden box had travelled to Zambia by sea to Beira in Mozambique, and from there overland 1100 miles through Rhodesia to Chingola. It would be easy to blame Africa for this delay, but Britain probably had more to do with it as weeks of the dockers' strike had paralysed exports at the UK end. Off the Mozambique coast a Royal Navy fleet patrolled the waters. Harold Wilson's government had reacted with outrage to Rhodesia's Unilateral Declaration of Independence and was implementing sanctions with a blockade as part of the oil embargo. They intended to bring the self-appointed Rhodesians swiftly into line. Five years later the Beira Patrol was still there slowing down normal operations. The Southern Hemisphere 'winter' had arrived before we saw our things again, and it felt like Christmas. A rug could be placed here, a picture there, a few items borrowed from townships could be returned as our own familiar ones replaced them, and wedding presents could be rediscovered and enjoyed. Our echoing house felt a bit more like home.

Other opportunities to gather moss in the form of ornaments and pictures had been presented at the garden gate, where traders dared not come any further with Sheba barking and baring her teeth. At weekends Congolese in exotic robes and embroidered caps sometimes brought carved ivory heads and malachite ash-trays to the front fence. Katanga province in Zaire, just over the border, had even richer copper deposits than Zambia and high grade seams of malachite often became available. We'd lock the dogs in the house so the men could spread their wares on a cloth on the grass for us to admire, but their prices meant we'd have to save up to buy them. My first purchase was a cheap rubber plant in a pot. For a week I tended it and wiped the leaves, and hoped it would thrive better than the one we'd had in Edinburgh which dropped its leaves one after the other before we discarded it as a virtual stick.

'You know they just cut a branch off a tree and stick it in soil in a pot, don't you?' said Chrissie when I told her proudly of my purchase. I had been conned, which a check for roots verified. Nevertheless it looked good in our living room, and lasted longer than the Edinburgh one.

Domestic skills for expatriate women were vital even if funds could stretch to several staff, because servants still had to be trained. Convenience foods in the supermarket didn't amount to much so most women cooked and exchanged recipes, baked cakes and biscuits, discussed ingredients and cooking methods, knew when something new arrived in the shops, and many turned their hand to dressmaking. Using up a glut of garden fruit inspired a shelf full of marmalades, guava jelly, and banana chutney in our larders, and lemon or grenadine sorbets, grilled grapefruit, passion fruit ice cream and guacamole found their way on to dinner party menus. Some women managed to find jobs, but still had time on their hands for such homely activities with the burden of housework taken off them by 'houseboys.' The best meals were often to be had in houses with a Kenwood Chef, and those housewives would produce wonderful sliced, or shredded, or meringue-and-whipped cream creations. I struggled on with a hand-operated rotary whisk, and basic grater which sometimes left my knuckles bleeding from rubbing too close to the metal. 1970s dinner parties made sense in a town where only the Mine Club offered restaurant facilities, so we prepared and served our quiche Lorraine, corn-on-the-cob, coq-au-vin, beef bourgignon, lemon cheesecakes and Black Forest gateaux with dedication and pride. Sonny and Cher, Stealers Wheel, the Carpenters, Crosby Stills and Nash, and Dusty Springfield LPs sang out from our record decks and those with stereo sound systems showed off their technology, discussing the merits of different sound systems in lengthy detail. A variation was the progressive dinner party where a party of six began at one house for starters, progressed to the next for the main course, and ended at a third for dessert. It worked well if everyone lived close to one another, and for more than six extra courses were added. Every woman wanted to offer a good spread, and every man wanted to be hospitable with drinks. *Braais* were the norm for larger gatherings, with halved 50-gallon oil drums and a grille serving as a barbecue, and always attended by men.

'I think I'll make a traditional Christmas cake this year,' I told Ross two months before our second Christmas in Chingola. 'They have everything I need for sale in CBC, even marzipan, so it should be good!'

The ingredients added up to an extravagance, but a treat for Christmas. In October I mixed together butter and sugar, flour and spices, currants and raisins, mixed peel, almonds, cherries and eggs, beating it all together with a wooden spoon as I'd done many times before. The rich brown mixture filled a carefully lined and greased cake tin, and I set the basic dial on 'medium low' for our small electric oven to cook it slowly. Several hours later it came out perfectly, and after the oven heat had filtered slowly out, I covered the promising fruity concoction loosely to allow air to circulate and placed it on a shelf in our walk-in kitchen cupboard before locking the door. Every few days I pierced the cake's crust with a metal skewer and dribbled brandy to sink into the holes, covered it again to keep off flies, and re-locked the door. In early December I inhaled its brandied fruitiness as I tucked a blanket of marzipan around it, stuck down with apricot jam. A few days later snowdrifts of royal icing made the final flourish, and I almost felt we could have a proper Christmas with such a cake. Visitors arrived, and the time came for me to cut slices from the proudly displayed creation. I carried it into the kitchen and with my mouth watering in anticipation sectioned off a quarter to cut into smaller slices. The conversation in the living room sounded cheery as my heart sank. My beautiful extravagant cake in which I'd invested so much hope and care was shot through with bluish green threads, woven all around the expensive brandy-soaked fruit and butter and eggs. Tropical mould had invaded every inch.

On first sight our plot looked good. Two towering jacarandas on the pavement outside cast dappled shadows over the front garden and inside our boundary a row of low 'Christ thorn bushes had survived the removal and subsequent replacement of the front fence by heavy-footed workers. A frangipani bush looking like a candelabra offered fragrant cream and yellow blooms to be enjoyed at nose-height, and a huge tulip tree with its resident blue-headed lizards stood to the right of the gravel-covered drive. Our back garden boasted mature avocado and mango trees, and a *paw-paw* palm, which stretched on a skinny bare trunk to eight metres before branching out into a spray of leaves. When our attention moved from sorting out the inside of the house, we considered our inherited quarter-acre patch. The previous occupants had paid for fencing to be installed, a lawn to be sown, and had nurtured a few plants.

'What happened to it all, then?' I asked our Portuguese neighbour.

'Oh, they removed or dug up what they could and sold it. That's what everyone does unless they know the person coming in after them, and then they agree a price with them,' he replied.

'So the fencing and garden isn't owned by the mine, then?'

'Not really, no. It's up to the new occupant to make their own.'

This explained why only large trees and thorny bushes remained. Much of the growth we at first took to be lawn was a covering of weeds which would die at the end of the rains. So once a fence and gate had been installed, our vision of a garden started with some grass.

'Turf is really expensive,' said Ross, 'so I think we should try grass seed. But first we'll have to rake it, level it off, and get rid of the stones.'

We cleared and raked, collected a few buckets of stones, and gave up on levelling.

'Right let's get some twigs in to stop the birds from eating the seeds.'

'But we've never seen any birds here,' I pointed out.

'Okay, to keep the animals off,' he conceded. 'I think I'll buy a sprinkler from the Greek hardware store to keep it lush.'

The animals didn't understand his rules of the twigs and the futility of trying to grow grass in the shade of large trees produced a result far from lush. After two years of coaxing, weeding, feeding and trimming, our lawn never amounted to more than a patchy thin covering of green.

'Why do we never have cauliflower or green beans?' asked Ross one day.

'Because you can't get them in the supermarket unless it's frozen, or in the market,' I replied, 'when they do come in they cost a fortune.'

The shops stocked lettuce, tomatoes, cucumber, courgettes, aubergines, sweetcorn and potatoes, plus white cabbage. Fruit was plentiful with pineapples from a plantation on the Solwezi road, oranges, guavas, *naartjies* (tangerines) and occasionally grapefruit always on sale. Otherwise there was Silver Leaf tinned fruit imported from South Africa, and we relished the kidney-shaped mangoes from our tree when they were in season. The dogs enjoyed them too, chewing the windfalls which fell on the dust under the tree.

'The best ones are the peach mangoes which don't have the stringiness that gets caught in between your teeth,' said Chrissie who was born in South Africa.

Many of our British friends craved apples which could rarely be found, and wouldn't touch mangoes because they were so messy to eat and the sticky skin could cause a rash around children's mouths.

So the next project was a vegetable patch at the side of the single concrete garage to provide our own produce. Things grew well in Zambia, but not in our patch. The soil had been depleted without anything being put back, but proof of good growth lay in other people's gardens.

'Be very careful if you go near the banana trees,' warned Ross, 'they attract poisonous green spiders!'

We didn't understand the management of banana trees, so our scruffy old specimens in the back corner against the broken fence never bore fruit. At least they'd serve to keep out intruders.

'I'll keep my distance, but I'm looking forward to those *paw-paws*,' I said, watching Ross tend his rows of radish, the one crop which had grown well, 'they're finally starting to change colour so should be ready soon.'

Three small papaya specimens were ripening at the top of the slender palm, and one had turned quite yellow. The trunk was too spindly to rest a ladder against, so we decided to try shaking the fruit down. We looked up at a yellow rugby-ball-shape falling as if in slow motion, and Ross stretched out his hand to catch it. Splat! Instead his hand filled up with rubbery black seeds and a mush of orange *paw-paw* flesh spread all the way up his right arm.

'Ergh!' he exclaimed, 'I was looking forward to that! Stop laughing!'

'Ah', said Gareth who had been brought up in Zambia, 'all you need to do is chop the trunk off at, say, chest-height, cover the top with a tin, and branches will sprout from the bottom of the tree. Then it will be much easier to pick the fruit.'

Following his advice we found an empty coffee tin to do the job, and left the tree to its own devices. The two remaining fruit never ripened and the stump had a solitary, sad look next to the struggling vegetable patch but we were patient. By the time we left two years later there were still no sprouting shoots.

The avocado tree, by contrast, was laden with green fruit twice the size of those found in the shops. It was a tall and vigorous tree at over thirty feet high, but one of its branches over-hanging the roof of our bedroom had died and during stormy weather we worried about our safety. I telephoned 'townships' to come and remove it. Three workmen and a Portuguese foreman turned up a few days later, just as I was leaving for school. Ross had already driven off for his early day shift, so I quickly explained the problem after taking the dogs into the house for the workers' safety, and I set off. They had gone seven hours later when I returned tired and hot in the early afternoon and I went straight around the back of the house to examine their handiwork. My hand flew to my mouth in shock. All that remained of our lovely tree was a stump. The rest of the trunk had been taken away with the branches, leaving fruit, torn bark and leaves strewn all over the back garden. I could have wept, but instead gritted my teeth and went indoors to make myself a calming cup of tea.

Then, using buckets and the washing basket, I gathered every piece of fruit I could find from the garage wall to the back fence, under the trees, and some that had rolled under the hedge on the far side of the garden. After that I brought out the bathroom scales and found a flat surface. I could barely lift the washing basket, and along with the buckets and bowls it all added up to 135 pounds of produce. None of the avocados was ripe, but several days later they all were.

'There must be hundreds of them!' I wailed to Ross when he came home, 'can you think of anyone who would like some?' But we couldn't give them away because not many of our friends were willing to give their unfamiliar taste and texture a try, so we ate what we could before they rotted, left a cardboard box-full outside the gate for anyone who wanted to help themselves, and made a compost heap with the remainder. Our garden now had two stumps, and seemed to be deteriorating instead of improving.

'I've a good mind to ring those idiots and give them a piece of mind,' muttered Ross. 'Bloody Portuguese, you'd think they would understand we only wanted the dead branch removed and not the whole lot! The trouble is that complaining won't bring the tree back.'

'No it won't,' I added, 'but I'll never trust them again. I'll send them away rather than leaving them without supervision!'

Our lives were on a constant learning curve in every area. My one small success with gardening came from a packet of Cosmos seeds, and the narrow strip of earth outside our sitting room window sported an impressive show of 'sea shells' only a month after I had sown them. Ross had moderate success with a vegetable patch, in spite of poor soil, but lettuces outgrew their strength throwing up a tall seed stem before they amounted to anything worth eating. Much later he'd grow asparagus and quickly learn that tips emerging in the morning would have overshot their ideal length by the evening; that such speedy growth meant soil which depleted in goodness equally quickly; that weeds gave crops some protection from the elements; and that a tropical storm could flood and ruin weeks of crop growth in one downfall. He had planted a row of plants outside the kitchen door against the house, most of which remained shrivelled and sad, but one had spread a profusion of leaves out on to the path with fat orange flowers followed by the tiny beginnings of cucumbers. Next to the passion fruit, creeper *Susu* vines grew through the wire fence and surrendered a steady supply of knobbly marrow-like vegetables which tasted good in a cheese sauce.

'So that's why this has done so well,' said Ross scratching away the earth under the cucumber vine during our daily walk around our patch of ground. 'There's a leaking water pipe underneath it!'

'Have you heard about the break-ins?' asked Barry 'There's been one in 14th Street, and another two in 12th Street. It will be our street next!'

'What did they take?' I asked

'It's mainly money and jewellery they're after because they're easily transported, but sometimes televisions are taken.'

'Well they won't find much of those things in our house, we don't have a TV and Sheba's great at guarding!'

'Oh it wasn't because they didn't have dogs! They throw meat over the fence to distract them. Or they sometimes bring a bitch on heat, but of course that wouldn't work with your Sheba. We're wondering about getting another dog as added protection.'

More robberies were reported with anecdotes and gossip spreading dismay through the community.

'Someone down our street had every single thing in their house cleared out,' said Chrissie, 'the thieves came after dark when they were out and took the lot; furniture, curtains, food, clothes and even light bulbs.'

I became paranoid about burglars getting into the house when Ross was on night shift, and we decided to look for another dog. Friends had a Great Dane who'd just had puppies, and a big dog sounded like a good idea. We knew nothing of the temperament of different breeds, and went to choose one when they were ready. Only one of seven remained, he was most likely the 'runt' and we called him 'Blue' after the song line 'me and you and a dog named Blue,' although we'd heard the words wrong, as it was 'Boo' not 'Blue.' He snuggled up to Sheba and Sassi on my hand-made red and purple rug every evening, in front of the empty fireplace, but hated being turned out at night. Sheba was charged with training him and he trotted around after her but never really grasped the concept. Sassi found him a good subject for bullying, and the houseboy chased him with a broom because the dog kept creeping back to sleep in the house during the day, which interfered with his cleaning. Not long after his first birthday we found him dead in the back garden, and never discovered the reason.

Sheba's persistent barks woke us after midnight. Ross drew aside the Indian cotton bedspread that still served as a temporary curtain, and saw her teeth bared. She charged in the direction of the garage.

'See him off!' hissed Ross. He'd opened a window. 'Go on Sheba, see him off. No, I'm not telling you off! Good girl. Go on, see him off!'

'What is it?' I mumbled, struggling to wake.

'I think there's someone in the garage. You stay here, I'm going out.'

The garage was just out of sight of the window, and cloud covered any light from the moon. Holding aside the Indian bedspread, I saw Ross making his way past the stump of the avocado tree, with a rolling pin in one hand and a torch in the other. *This is what it feels like to be burgled* I thought. A rustling noise was followed by a shout and then Sheba barked some more. And then silence. I listened, and peeped through windows, then jumped in fright when the kitchen door opened, and Ross came back in.

'He's gone. I think I saw him climbing over the fence into the neighbour's, but it's hard to see anything out there. The quarter light on the car has been smashed with a brick and my mine boots are missing along with my hard hat.'

How desperate must someone be to steal a pair of muddy boots and a plastic hat? I wondered, not caring about mine-issue stuff, but concerned about the car window and how it would be fixed.

'We'd better phone the police,' I said.

They arrived half an hour later, by which time the felon had long gone through back gardens and over fences. The crime was noted, Sheba was patted and praised, and we went back to bed. We'd been let off lightly but enough to provoke the installation of security lighting and we paid more attention to locking doors when we went out.

Back to ponder the frustrations of gardening, we were accompanied by wagging dogs and sometimes a tail-up cat. No birds sang in Chingola; 'they trap them on limed wires' Chrissie had told me, although she never made it clear who 'they' were. So our after-work amblings were to the sound of distant dog barks, sweeping brooms, the song of a house boy, and the swish and rev from an occasional car. We'd pause to take in the scent of the neighbour's jasmine smothering the wire fence, then move on to check if the *paw-paw* had sprouted, passing on our way an aggressive *Bloukop* lizard on the tulip tree, nodding his big blue head. He'd be safe from our animals, and Zambians said they were poisonous. Occasionally a chameleon rolled rotating eyes in our direction, as he made every tentative step like a dancer and Ross brought him down off the tree to test for colour changes on different backgrounds. The heart-shaped face of a bright green praying mantis, a stick insect or a rhino beetle could be waiting under a leaf, and even the red-patterned aphids fascinated us. Then we'd stop and marvel, sometimes taking a photo to add to our African album. After the customary one hour afternoon rainfall during the season, steam hovered over damp earth which always smelt stronger in semidarkness. Later, beyond the night-time chanting of cicadas we could hear the faint throb of a drumbeat if the wind was favourable. It drifted over from the compound, and made us wonder what really went on. There couldn't be a pith-helmet-clad missionary sitting in a giant cauldron and surrounded by semi-naked gyrating Africans, but we often wondered what they were doing to a drumbeat in the dark, and never found out.

CHAPTER SIX

Teaching

By learning you will teach; by teaching you will learn.

LATIN PROVERB

'They're looking for supply teachers at the Helen Waller Infant School,' said Claire who worked at Chingola Secondary School along the road. 'You know the one? It's a small private school next to the junior school in town. I took a class there for a while before I started work at the High School, and earned good money. They paid me eight Kwacha a day.' At the time this was the equivalent of about five pounds, nearly enough to buy half a tank of petrol. Having only had holiday jobs until then, and only the basic 'teaching practice' of my training, I was keen to get started.

We'd been in Chingola for a couple of months by this time, and with the house and 'staff' reasonably sorted I was looking for a teaching post. The High School in town, where Claire worked, already had a teacher of home economics and needlework, so I was still looking.

'But I'm not trained for juniors, let alone infants,' I replied.

'That won't matter. They sometimes take on people with no training at all. At least you're a qualified teacher. Give it a go, it's a doddle!'

I made some enquiries, walked a couple of blocks and into a circular drive, and stepping between tall concrete pillars, entered the impressive 1950's building for an interview. The following Monday I turned up early to meet my new reception class of keen young students in brand new uniforms. Most of the boys 'shorts' came down below their knees, with crisp white shirts tucked neatly into waistbands. The girls wore gingham dresses with shirt collars. Every one of them had dark-chocolate skin, and not one of them spoke English. I'd been armed with a set curriculum and pre-set national lesson plans for the job, and for the first week it was a doddle as Claire had predicted, because of their docility. All of the white children, I discovered, made up most of one class along with English-speakers of varying skin shades.

There had been no black people in my life in Edinburgh. I'd seen them in London when we visited my grandmother, but from a distance. A sort of exotic sighting where I'd stared, like African children stared at us, working out the differences. In Chingola few Zambian women spoke English, and the remnants of the colonial regime ensured the absence of a black middle class so our circle of friends and neighbours was only white. Seven years after Independence this had started to change. The day after I started work I was chatting to Grace, our neighbour. Once I had silenced the dogs, who felt they had to make a display of disapproval because of her skin colour, we talked about schools. She was a Zulu from South Africa, and bemoaned the inferior state education in Zambia. She was not pleased with the progress her two boys had made at the Junior school, but she had heard better reports of the Helen Waller where her daughter Rachel had just started.

'Come and say hello, Rachel,' wide eyes under a coiffure of cornrows peeped out at me from behind her mother's skirt, and I gave her an encouraging smile before she darted back to safety.

'I can walk her to school, if you like,' I said. 'I shall be going anyway, and it will save you a journey,'

'That would be very helpful if you wouldn't mind. Our houseboy usually takes her, but he has plenty of other things to do.' She pulled Rachel to her side, 'that would be nice Rachel, wouldn't it? Say thank you to Mrs Dunn.'

A barely audible 'tank you' came out, and the plan was made. I held her delicate hand the following morning as we walked a few blocks to the school. She had been placed in a class of predominately European children since she spoke English, but any conversation I managed to get out of her was minimal. Most of my attempts to talk were met with a nod, a shake of the head, or a wide-eyed stare.

'Some *Yarpies* are calling you a *kaffir*-lover,' said Chrissie, 'because you've been seen walking to school with that little Zambian girl.'

I sighed and said nothing, but a small knot of outrage had lodged in my chest and I became wary of passing traffic as we walked by the roadside every morning. Racism had spread up from the south with many white workers drawn to a healthy growing economy based on rising copper prices. It would not be wise to aggravate the situation. I didn't want to become an outcast from the rough-and-ready mining community, but nor would I be bullied into behaving like them. Every car and pick-up passing us felt like a threat to me afterwards, and it was a relief to arrive at the haven of the school. This was not the free African country I had imagined, and every section of the community had its own rules, opinions and prejudices which had to be learned in order not to offend. But my pupils were so sweet, timid, and well-behaved; it was tempting to sweep each one on to my knee for a cuddle. Sometimes I would feel a tug behind me as small black fingers examined the unfamiliar texture and colour of my long pale hair, so different from their own tight black curls, and looked fearful if I turned around to see who it was. For them I was an education in myself, and they to me.

They sat at their desks ready for instruction, and I launched into the recommended lessons from my bound set of detailed lesson plans.

'Good morning, children,' I pronounced, expecting some sort of response. One small voice offered a mumbled reply and the others looked confused. 'Okay,' I stumbled, and pointed at myself. 'I say "Good morning, children, and you,' I said stretching out my hands to the class as if I was conducting an orchestra, 'say "Good morning Mrs Dunn." Ready?'

So I became an actress-come-conductor, and they chanted responses with their African sing-song voices and shrill cheerfulness. We worked our way through the recommended phrases of 'I am standing; I am sitting; I am jumping; I am clapping,' to all the associated actions, and I added a few of my own until we all got tired. Then their little fresh faces looked expectantly in my direction, I looked at my watch and saw that I was half an hour ahead of the lesson plan schedule and still had to fill that time before break. I distributed paper and boxes of crayons with mimed instructions to draw a house. Claire might have found this a 'doddle,' but I realised the extent of the work I had in front of me. At break I discovered the other infant-trained teachers had a treasure trove of visual teaching aids which must have taken months to create. I begged an illustrated story-book, and returned to my classroom with its bare walls. By the second week their confidence had grown and they had picked up a reasonable vocabulary. Some of the boys displayed an alarming liveliness, and I wondered how long I would feel in control, and then a few days later their permanent teacher appeared, a Zambian who looked as though he would keep them in line. At the end of the day I waved goodbye to a class of shiny-faced pupils in their still-new over-sized uniforms, and set about searching again for a job. The accumulated sum I had earned over those few weeks had been fun to spend in the few shops Chingola had to offer, and I wanted it to continue but with something more permanent. I also had to get my first probationary year of teaching launched to finalise my qualifications.

My next interview was equally brief and non-demanding at Chikola High School, in the township a few miles out of Chingola. Claire gave me a lift up the hill through the compound and waited in her car while I presented myself to the Head. A permanent teaching post for needlework was becoming available for the following term, and I appeared to be the only trained applicant for the job. It would be unlike any other teaching practice I'd experienced in and around Edinburgh.

'The last teacher in the post also took the girls for netball,' said the headmaster.

'Oh, I'm afraid that's not really my forte,' I replied, having no instinct for team games, no experience of netball since the age of twelve, and only vaguely remembering a rule about footwork when in possession of the ball. The thought of being responsible for a school team filled me with dismay.

'Well you are young and look fit enough,' he insisted, looking me over. 'There's really no one else suitable for the job. I'm sure you'll pick it up quickly and there's a rule-book around somewhere which you can take away with you.'

Feeling cornered and in danger of losing the job I came for, I capitulated, and agreed to coach the team every Wednesday afternoon. He then took me along a covered veranda past a staff room strewn with papers, books and unwashed coffee mugs, around the corner to the needlework room. A dozen hand-powered Singer sewing machines sat on long tables with chairs lined up either side.

'Most of the machines were in need of some attention until recently,' explained the head, 'but one of our teachers, Mr Tomlinson, has turned his hand to fixing them and now seven are in working order. The problem is finding the spare parts, so he's cannibalised some to repair the others.'

After Easter at the start of a new term, I started work, and entered the spacious staff room of mainly British teachers employed through the Overseas Aid Scheme. Many of them lived on the campus and had only a stroll to work. A few friendly Indians, a French lady and a handsome Ghanaian completed the staff headed by Mr Wilkinson, a South African of British descent.

'This is the store room where needlework supplies are kept,' he said, unlocking the door. A few small bales of fabric sat on the shelves along with boxes of threads, pins and needles, and scissors. It would be my job to order new supplies and to safeguard existing ones.

Fresh from college with only 'teaching practice' for experience, I muddled through as best I could. The girls were making aprons, started before my arrival and I was keen to plan something different for the following terms. Ross took me to school in the car when he wasn't working, but being on shift-work this wasn't always possible and Gwen, a teacher who lived in town, would collect me. After a few weeks I was happy to go on foot in the cool of the early morning once the rainy season had ended, although it was a few miles' walk and also meant crossing the township, a sole white woman gleamingly different to the inhabitants. With the help of Mr Jones, we got another three machines up and running to allow one between two in an average class of twenty.

Blue trees welcomed me into 11th Street. The Jacarandas were in bloom and their dreamy tones against a pale cerulean sky were spellbinding. The town was at its best in the early morning when I walked to work. Assembly started at 8.30 so I set off before seven after dawn glows had burnt off the horizon. The last rains had fallen weeks earlier and freshness in the Autumn air speeded my step. Each garden along the way offered its own suburban character. A squeaking sprinkler set up the night before turned four spouting arms over a flooding puddle in an area trying to be lawn. A garden-boy starting work scraped a besom of twigs over a leaf-littered drive. A teeth-baring Alsation barked his way along a six-foot fence and then jumped up at the lower gate as I passed, alarming me before I crossed the road, which droned with early-morning purpose. I wove my way up to 14th Street then left the towering and leafless Jacarandas with their mists of flowers up to the Solwezi Road and crossing the dual carriageway where there was a gap in the Hibiscus hedge before turning left up to Chikola Township. It was too early for the flower collector I sometimes saw gathering crimson Hibiscus blooms in her basket. Occasionally I passed another pedestrian, but no other whites. An eighteen-inch gauze of snakeskin lay rejected by its owner near a pile of rocks, so when I heard rustles in paper-dry foliage near my feet, I walked in the road, but knew it would probably be lizards. Soon the tarmac road covering disappeared onto a stony track flanked by modest houses each set in its own square plot. Some of these had been cultivated with rows of vegetables and a few flowers while others had a single tree overhanging swept earth. A slim young woman held a saucepan under a tap fixed to the front wall of the house. It had been polished to a bright brassy shine and I realised it would be the only one for that dwelling. At the top of the hill I passed four pencil-slim first-years giggling amongst themselves. Silence fell as I passed, interrupted by a chorus of 'Good morning meessus Dunni,' followed by a flutter of giggles. Ahead I passed two shapely third-years swaying up the dirt track. Neat corn-rows adorned their heads like their younger sisters' but shapely bottoms defied the lines of grey uniform skirts whose hems swung up oddly at the back, the side seams strained and the waistbands gaping loose. Teenage hormones gave their drawled greeting none of the chirpiness of the younger schoolgirls. I knew I wouldn't pass the striding older boys ahead, looking like men at odds with their uniform shorts and straining shirt buttons across broadening chests. Some of them were indeed men who had to shave before school, choosing to fill in gaps in their education alongside boys half their size and age. They glanced in my direction without recognition since my subject was purely for the girls. Mature women were never to be found seated in classes with younger girls, and considered themselves lucky to survive in education beyond the age of fifteen. More immaculately clad children with scrubbed faces emerged from tidy humble houses as I approached the school gates. The dribble became a pour of young bodies, the sky's blue deepened and I took off my cardigan.

A form class had not been allocated to me, so I could ignore the first bell and enjoy a brief chat with Madame the French teacher who told me a funny anecdote about the school goat escaping into the vegetable patch and having to be rescued by the secretary. Then we downed the remains of our weak powder coffee and I followed her to the daily assembly. Enthusiastic renderings of hymns filled the hall, unrivalled by any I'd heard in Britain, with teachers perched on the stage and pupils lined up in forms. Mature tenor voices mixed with the contralto of the younger pupils. A black-gowned headmaster read from the Bible, deplored bad behaviour, and gave an uplifting lesson like countless others around the world, and we all traipsed off to the first lessons of the day.

At the end of the month the headmaster apologised to me, 'I'm afraid your cheque has not come through yet. It normally takes a while for the administration to catch up and register your details. The form was sent off straight after your interview, so it is definitely in the system.'

I watched everyone else receive their slips of paper and eagerly check the figures as he handed out each one in turn. Those on the Overseas Aid Scheme would also receive a portion of their salary put into their banks in UK as well as a pension fund, with the Zambian portion being for subsistence. I didn't receive anything the following month, or the month after that. Between 1964 and 1972 the total number of children in Zambian primary schools doubled, but in secondary schools the numbers rose from 14,000 to 61,000, and the government was struggling to cope.

'It will come eventually, don't worry,' cajoled Mr Wilkinson, 'when it gets sorted out you'll have back-pay as a lump sum and then be paid every month, that's the way it works.'

Working as part of the 'Overseas Aid Scheme,' most of the staff had been recruited in London. They lived on campus and could rely on a regular salary paid by the British government and at a far better rate than mine, which was called 'the local rate' and the same as for any Zambian staff. I had no choice but to be patient although couldn't help being disappointed at the end of every month. Ross and I wanted to pay off the loan for our car which my father had given us before we left Edinburgh, so my salary had already been ear-marked with this in mind. A long nine months after I started work my reward came, including the promised back-payments. It was the day after the government devalued the Kwacha by a massive 30%, so my much-awaited salary paid off far less of the loan than we'd hoped, and I felt as though I'd given nearly three months of work for nothing. At least my husband had a secure income, unlike Zambian teachers in the same situation where their salary might be the only money coming into the household and they had nothing to live on while they waited. So I moaned and groaned about the injustice of it for a few days and then put it behind me.

My classes were practical with individual or "small-groups" teaching. Only girls did 'needlework' and they were easy to manage, and mostly interested in what they were making. First years whispered innocently amongst themselves, looked neat in their uniforms before curves took hold, and were a joy to teach. There are always less able pupils in classes, and in mine it was often the more academic pupils who found practical subjects difficult. Emelda did her best to manage her work on the sewing machine. She had graduated from guiding paper through the machine in a straight line without thread to make a trail of needle punctures, and had moved on to sewing fabric samples with a threaded machine. Her concentration wavered as she glanced at her right hand turning the handle instead of watching the needle, her left forefinger got in the way and before she could stop to think what she was doing the needle had gone right through her finger. She didn't cry but went very pale. As the school first-aider, Mr Jones had to interrupt his woodwork class to come and remove it with a pair of pliers.

Hormones raged from third years onwards, wreaking havoc with standard skirt shapes, and challenging shirt buttons. The sway of their hips, their throaty laughs, the fuzz over their corn-rows suggested experience beyond their years. Camaraderie with a handsome new teacher stirred my suspicions. Getting a skirt in the making to fit both at the beginning and end of a term's work could be a challenge and I learnt to design wider seam-allowances. Gladys was one such girl whose waistband refused to fit. Her classmates giggled and whispered so much I had to investigate further. She left school the following week to be delivered of a baby very soon after, and I'd never guessed. Thus the older classes held a diminishing number of female pupils. It was a part of Zambian tradition to educate their girls last, but marry them off first, sometimes as young as thirteen. So any money available for schooling was first spent on the boys, while girls might stay at home to help with chores and caring for younger siblings. Much later I discovered that it wasn't unusual for teenage girls to have a 'sugar daddy' who gave gifts which could be in the form of education and uniforms. The girls would repay this apparent bounty in private.

That same class was dominated by Christine, a big girl several inches taller than myself, and one sultry October late-morning when heat and humidity made it an effort even to think, my consciousness stirred to sharp words instead of the usual quiet buzz in the room. Heads were turned in Christine's direction and as I moved towards her six-foot frame she gave Dorcas a firm shove on the shoulder accompanied by a meaningful stare. Dorcas didn't take this sitting down, and in an instant they were shouting, pulling hair, and clawing each other's faces. By the time the deputy head arrived to break it up, they were on the floor and we had to physically pull them apart. Sobered by this intervention both girls spent the rest of the morning in disgrace, cooling their fury with a long solitary wait followed by a lecture on good conduct. An eerie silence followed their departure as heads bowed to sewing. It seemed to have flared up from nothing. Quiet talking is expected in a practical class, but in another language it is difficult to monitor trouble brewing, so from that moment I allowed only English to be spoken in my classes.

Rowena lived in the same street as us, so her father would have a good job in the mine. A conscientious, well-behaved girl, with neat tight braids, she approached me after a lesson to ask if I'd have a look at their sewing machine which wasn't working properly. After school she took me to her house, and I was briefly introduced to her mother who then disappeared. The house was spotless and silent, with no animals and three people who had moved to another room. The treadle sewing machine was covered over with a piece of cotton printed fabric, and after unlocking the wooden lid I sat down to have a look. Rowena brought me some cloth to test the stitch and I worked the treadle with my feet. A simple adjustment to the tension was all that was needed and I wondered if the main object of the exercise had been to demonstrate that the family had a sewing machine. It was rare to be invited into a Zambian's house, and when Ross was given a similar opportunity everyone in the house also fell silent on his arrival.

Netball practise was purgatory. Much as I studied the rules of the game my instincts and grasp of strategy, let alone ability to impart this knowledge to others, were unformed and basic. The girls were eager and willing enough, standing around barefoot ready for my wisdom. So much leaping around and whistle blowing took place on these Wednesday afternoons, and I managed to enforce the basic rules reasonably well but further than that my skills were lacking. My purgatory became hell when matches were arranged. I loved the journeys on the coach with the team and was entranced by their singing, harmonising and impromptu solos all in Bemba, but the match itself was torture, as we lost every one and ended the season bottom of the league. *You always learn more when you lose than when you win*, said the African proverb, but I'm not sure it was me who was learning.

On one of our away matches, I met a woman belonging to a breed completely new to me. Caroline was slim, educated, friendly and astute, and had a much better grasp of netball training than me. She took me to her house on the school compound where she lived with her Zambian husband, also a teacher, and their three coffee-coloured children, running around barefoot. It was hardly a bucolic idyll set as it was in dusty surroundings with no visible home comforts, and living off teachers' salaries on local rates. I wanted to know more about her life, her family, and what it felt like to be anchored to Zambia without the constant pull from a distant land. But the coach was waiting and I never saw her again.

I had to learn to drive. Depending on others for a lift to school often posed problems and the rainy season was fast-approaching, so Ross started to teach me the basics.

Having a second car in mind, he'd already bought a blue Karmann Ghia from a South African who worked at the training school. The South African's hobby was doing up old cars which sat beside a rickety shed full of oily parts in his back yard, like casualties awaiting surgery. I pitied his neighbours.

'I've had to replace the windows with plastic,' he explained to Ross who was looking into it and under it from every conceivable angle. 'It's hard to get hold of parts here so I make do and use what I can, which is why I sell cars on at a bargain price.'

The sporty little vintage coupé slumped at the side of our drive waiting for me to learn to drive, but its performance turned out to be unreliable so my lessons would have to be in the Hillman Hunter.

'You need to be able to reverse out of the drive,' Ross announced after the third lesson, 'now hold the steering wheel in both hands and look over your left shoulder.'

He stood behind the car to direct my efforts,

'Pull you right hand down a bit now,' he shouted waving me away from a collision course with the frangipani tree, 'no your RIGHT hand!'

The strain of turning the steering wheel in a direction which felt wrong had the back of my cotton dress damp before we'd even got to the road. He climbed back into the passenger seat and we progressed to the first junction. It was a painful means to an end. Our marriage had survived eight weeks of an overland journey, but having Ross teach me to drive was another matter. Adrian, the geography teacher from school, offered to help out.

'I have an Advanced Driver's License,' he said, 'and I have Saturday mornings free. Let me know if you'd like me to help. It would be good practice for when my girls need to learn a few years from now.'

So my weekends didn't really start until after I'd run the gauntlet of my weekly Saturday morning driving lessons with Adrian. He was calm and gave clear instructions, and the roads had very little traffic, but I still became tense and worried before and during every session. My friend Claire offered to help out with driving practice using the Karmann Ghia, and we set off to tour the residential area. Two hundred yards from our garden gate the car ground to a halt without the help of brakes. Claire hadn't had her license long, and together we examined dials and struggled out of the bucket seats to search under the bonnet for loose wires. Then we walked home.

'You've run out of petrol,' scoffed Ross after inspecting the car some hours later at the roadside, 'but there's a reserve tank you could have switched to, look here is how you do it under here.'

I peered under the steering column at a small switch, and wondered at the responsibilities of driving. Claire and I didn't venture out again, but my lessons with Adrian in the Hillman Hunter continued. Soon it came to reversing.

'Put the gear into neutral, and apply the handbrake,' he instructed, 'Now put your right foot on the clutch, engage reverse gear, making sure it's properly engaged, see. When you're ready, look over your right shoulder, release the brake, and very very slowly move the car backwards.'

'Should I ever look over my left shoulder?' I asked, remembering Ross's advice.

'You could do in certain circumstances, but you have far better control and vision using your right.'

Gradually I improved and gained some confidence until the morning when I was deemed sufficiently able to start the lesson by reversing the car out of our driveway, a process which hitherto Ross or Adrian had done for me before my lesson. Now I had a problem, because of conflicting advice on which shoulder to look over. Both had insisted their way was better when I had suggested there might be a preferable option. So with my two teachers conversing in a friendly manner in the drive, I proceeded to reverse the car through our narrow metal gate posts onto the leafy shade of 11th Street. Hoping they might be so absorbed by their conversation not to notice, I cast a look in their direction. Adrian was talking while Ross watched my manoeuvres, so I looked over my left shoulder and moved back a few feet, and then turned to look back at the men. Ross was now talking and Adrian watching, so I looked over my right shoulder and proceeded a further few feet. By this time the car had started to go askew, my tee shirt felt wet at my back, and I had the full attention of both men advising on how to correct my course. Not knowing which shoulder to use, I tried to alternate and consequently reversed into the gate post. Now in a panic I drove forward,

'Stoooop,' they chorused holding up halting hands.

The bumper had snagged on to the link-fencing next to the gate post, and in forward motion the car was dragging it off the post. I applied the brake, and waited as Ross disentangled the wire and informed me the bumper was now bent. He turned with an ominous silence back to the house, and Adrian reversed the car out of the drive ready for me to start my lesson.

One afternoon at the municipal swimming pool I was introduced to Emerald and her husband Jay, both teachers at Chingola High School. One of the advantages of teaching in Zambia was the hours which started early but, unless I was on prep duty, finished at lunchtime, and the swimming pool was a popular afternoon venue for teachers and children alike. We immediately fell into easy chat, and Jay went off for a dip. They belonged to a large 'coloured' community in the town, drawn to independent Zambia to escape South Africa's cruel apartheid regime, and sticking together for their own identity since they never quite fitted into white or black society. They were mostly talented, clever, and hard-working and some including Emerald, were strikingly beautiful, but they betrayed a longing to be grouped with whites. Experience had taught them privilege came with a lighter skin. Jay could have passed for white, and that's why Emerald chose him because in spite of her looks, the sort to make people stare, she was ashamed of her pigment.

'I always think black and coloured kids look dirty,' she said looking around the pool verges at mainly white children and their parents, many trying their best to get browner skin with a suntan. 'To me blacks and coloureds always look like they need a good wash.'

This puzzled me and I wondered if she was testing my racial tolerance, because her views had never occurred to me. Her insecurity opened a window to another world about which I could only imagine.

While white people tried to look darker with the help of a suntan, black and coloured people wanted to be more pale-skinned. Here was a marketing opportunity waiting to be exploited, and skin-lightening creams sold well.

'Are you well, Twalumba?' I asked one of my older pupils one day, when I noticed her usual flawless skin had become dull and rough.

'Yes, I am well thank you Meessus Dunn,' she replied. But her friends giggled, and not being good at keeping secrets told me she'd been using too much skin-lightening cream. She even had a pot in her bag, which they pointed out to me.

'Why are you using this, Twalumba? You have lovely skin, don't change it. You know that "black is beautiful!"' I'd got a little carried away with the sayings of civil rights songs and cultural movements of the sixties and early seventies. 'And did you know these creams can damage your kidneys? It's not a good idea to use them.'

The "black is beautiful" comment brought a waterfall of giggles, particularly among the more shapely members of the class, and made me wonder what they were getting up to after school.

CHAPTER SEVEN

A Trip into the Past

So geographers in Africa maps, With savage pictures fill their gaps, And o'er uninhabitable downs, Place elephants for want of towns.

JONATHAN SWIFT

We needed a holiday. Neither of us had fully recovered from our journey down through Africa by car, and starting new jobs on top of that had left us limp. A few days in Rhodesia south of the Zambian border promised to provide the pick-up we needed, and our faithful Hillman Hunter would take us further south than we'd been before. Rhodesia would be the twelfth African country we'd travelled, and mixed-up thinking had it in our heads that since Zambia used to be called Northern Rhodesia our border crossing would be plain sailing. We had temporarily forgotten the strained relations Zambia had with its southerly neighbour since November 1965 when they had made a Unilateral Declaration of Independence (UDI) to worldwide disapproval under the leadership of Ian Smith, a year after Zambia's Independence.

On the way I had a little business to attend to in Ndola in the form of ordering fabrics for the needlework department of Chikola Secondary School. I was searching through the printed cottons for suitable skirt materials.

'Hello Sara!' said a familiar voice.

'Good heavens, what are you doing here?' I asked my old friend Alison from college in Edinburgh.

'The same as you I imagine. I have a job here.'

We exchanged addresses and phone numbers, and promised to get back in touch in a few weeks' time.

From there we headed for the border at Chirundu to the north of Lake Kariba. In order to gain the maximum number of days' holiday we'd left after work on a Friday, so it was late when we drove up to the Zambian border patrol. With confident anticipation Ross approached the customs hut to present our passports.

'Where are your documents for the car?' asked the uniformed officer, rubbing his eyes from the interruption to his evening nap.

'Documents?' said Ross.

There was no getting round it, we didn't have them. It was too late to do anything about it at that hour, and the prospect of either turning back or spending the night at the border looked a grim alternative to our eagerly anticipated break. Ross sat down at the roadside and cursed, a sure sign he'd reached the end of his tether, and I knew I would have to take over. I left him banging his fist on the ground in frustration, and returned to talk to the official. Our only hope lay in phone calls the next morning so we resigned ourselves to spending a night in the car, reminiscent of our eight weeks of discomfort just a few months earlier.

Frustration evaporated with the dawn sunshine, and a fax from the mine to show good faith in our trip over the border allowed us to continue. In a lighter mood we looked across at another country as we paused to marvel at the majestic curves of the Kariba Dam.

In the early 1950's Northern Rhodesian authorities had planned a smaller dam on the Kafue River, a tributary of the Zambezi, mainly to serve the Copperbelt which was in need of more power. It would have been closer, cheaper, and less environmentally damaging than Kariba but with the formation of the Central African Federation of Rhodesia and Nyasaland (Zambia, Rhodesia and Malawi in 1971) they were outvoted. The federation saw joint benefits with this far more ambitious project. Kariba became the largest hydroelectric dam in the world, and had been completed over five years at the cost of millions plus the lives of eighty six men. After the Queen Mother opened it in 1960, a power supply to the south began, but unfortunately for Zambia there was still no power to the north when the federation broke up three years later. Zambia's independence, along with a degenerating political situation between the two countries who had once shared the same name, curtailed it for many more years.

We stopped at the northern corner to see a modest gush of water flowing towards the Indian Ocean from a vast curve of concrete hundreds of feet below us.

'What a construction!' said Ross, breaking our silence in the presence of grandeur.

There had been forced resettlement of 57,000 mainly Tonga people living in the proposed floodplain of the valley either side of the Zambezi River. Colonial authorities claimed to have given due compensation including land, but the fertile borders of a major river were unlikely to be replicated for these luckless displaced refugees removed from their motherland. More fortunate members of the Tonga tribe inhabited the lands further west alongside the great river as far as Victoria Falls, but the greater part of the Zambezi River between Kariba and Livingstone would be inundated and new land had to be found for the involuntary exiles.

As waters rose above drowned forests and abandoned villages to lap against the man-made barrier, other less articulate populations became at risk. "Operation Noah," led by a specially appointed head game ranger, was responsible for the rescue of thousands of creatures whose instincts could not prepare them for such a flood. Using two cruisers equipped with nets, traps, hypodermic syringes, drugs, darts, sacks, boxes, cages, ropes, and maps, plus five small boats, a team of fifty men patrolled over two thousand square miles of newly formed lake. Accompanying rafts would carry the larger animals. Once returned to the mainland, rescued pythons and porcupines, meerkats and monkeys, bush babies and bucks of every kind, as well as rhinos, elephant and lion would swell the animal numbers by over 60,000 in Matusadona National Park along the Rhodesian shores of the lake.

We got back into the car and drove over the border into Mashonaland West Province where birdsong welcomed us to Rhodesia.

'What's it like up there north of the border now?' asked the hotel manager with clipped tones and scathing undercurrents. His hotel trade had diminished along with cooling relationships between the two countries, as holiday-makers on both sides of the border avoided a potential trouble-zone. Rhodesians shared their leader Ian Smith's opinion that Africans were not yet ready for self-government. They were unwilling to hand over the country's considerable agricultural wealth for what they believed would be inevitable mismanagement in the hands of the masses. Since the Second World War immigrants, largely of British, Irish and South African origin had swelled the white population from 69,000 to over 220,000 so with this sizeable minority Southern Africa's bread basket would remain under white control, albeit under punishing sanctions, for the duration of our stay in Zambia and beyond. The black population had also increased dramatically from 1.4 to over 3.5 million. The government's intransigence was not without reason. Lucrative farms in independent African countries notoriously got plundered by the families of favoured politicians, and land painstakingly nurtured for years by pioneer immigrants would risk returning to bush within a few years. Abel Muzorewa, Smith's moderate colleague, and members of tribes not favoured by the revolutionary forces gave him their support.

Ross gave a non-committal reply and tactfully changed the subject to wildlife.

'Every evening two elephants come around the swimming pool for water,' said the manager his expression softening with a smile, 'will you be staying on to see them?'

Picturing a visitation of the huge mammals padding up to the poolside, I wondered if they were old enough to remember the old trails now sunk deep beneath Lake Kariba, or the trauma of capture and release by a rescue boat.

'No, we're heading for Salisbury tonight,' I replied regretting an opportunity lost. We'd stopped in a quest for morning coffee, and suspected this beautiful haven in the Zambezi Valley would be above our budget. I scanned the surrounding bush carefully for a sighting of the thirsty elephants, but to no avail. This would be their time for foraging amongst the trees and not drinking from a swimming pool. We tipped our cups empty and got back on the road.

'Why do you stay in that black-run country?' the friendly petrol pump attendant asked with a toothy grin as he filled up our tank, 'you should come to live heeya in Rhodesia, eet is much betta!'

He looked happy with his lot. Fair treatment, and schooling, medical facilities, salaries and lifestyle appeared to be high by African standards, albeit markedly inferior to those of whites.

'Hello Anne, its Sara here. Joan's daughter,' I shouted into the receiver in a Salisbury roadside phone box.

'Sorry, who did you say?'

'Joan's daughter, Sara!'

After a long pause she said, 'Well, hello! Joan's daughter, of course! I remember now your mother mentioning in her Christmas letter that you're living in Zambia now. Well isn't this a turn-up for the books! We've never had a visit from my side of the family.' Anne had moved away from England in the fifties, and married a Rhodesian.

Once we'd found her bungalow set in comfortable grounds amongst other similar houses, my mother's distant cousin gave us a heroes' welcome.

'You must stay here, we have a room specially built for guests. All we need to do is make up a bed!' She showed us into an outbuilding of one room built behind the kitchen of the main house. A white rabbit darted under the double bed, and a small boy dived after it. 'Don't worry about Thumper, he's the children's pet and stays in here at night but shouldn't bother you.' A girl and two boys looked up at us; the older two were not around. 'I'll leave the kitchen door unlocked so you can come in to use the bathroom if you want. It's quite safe.'

After an evening of catching up with family news, we retired to our room with the rabbit and returned to let ourselves into the kitchen the following morning. Gloria, dressed in a maid's uniform greeted us shyly, and disappeared into the house.

'Today we could go to a park just outside the city, if you like. I know the children would love that but we'd have to use your car because petrol is rationed thanks to the British oil embargo. The pipeline runs from Beira into Umtali, but they've stopped the supply. We're all very disappointed with the way Britain has dealt with this you know, Smith is a good man!'

We made sympathetic sounds.

'Anyway, Claire will be able to show you a bit of the town later,' promised Anne, 'she'll be home from work this afternoon since its Saturday. Before we go I'll make Gloria's lunch,' she added.

'You make lunch for your maid?' I asked

'Yes, it's a legal requirement. There's a minimum wage too, and they keep bringing in new rules. She has to have a uniform which is quite expensive on top of that. I'm not sure we can afford to keep her on much longer, as it is we've cut her hours down to three days a week. She's been with us for years and if we let her go she'll be without a job, but there's nothing we can do. I'm not sure how much more the country can withstand, things are really quite tough with these sanctions now compared to the old days, and John's business is struggling.' Then with British stoicism she said, 'Never mind, I'm sure we'll survive! Perhaps you could call in the boys to get ready for our trip?'

I went into the garden to call in two carefree little boys who were sublimely ignorant of international relations. They fell out of a tree, and one had grazed his bare leg on the tree trunk, but still laughing jammed his sun-hat back over tousled blonde hair and raced indoors to get his towel and swimming trunks. Six of us squeezed into the car and made an uncomfortable journey to a small paradise where boisterous children slid down smooth elephantine rocks into a natural pool, or swung across its surface Tarzan-like on a long rope dangling from a tree.

In the afternoon we were ready for something more adult and drove into Salisbury on a busy, fast road with Claire guiding in the front and me in the back. A motorcyclist was travelling close to our car, and when Ross changed lane to overtake nearly knocked him off his bike. None too pleased, as he waved us over.

'Oh no, it's the traffic police!' said Claire.

'You were speeding, sir,' he stated bringing a notebook and pencil out of his pocket. The radio attached to his belt crackled with a distant voice, 'and I'm charging you with changing lanes without indicating.'

'I couldn't see you,' said Ross, 'you must have been travelling in my blind spot!'

'He wasn't speeding,' pronounced Claire, all confidence and indignation in her mini-skirt, 'you are picking on him because he has Zambian number plates!'

Arguing was futile, and we followed him to the police station to be charged. The procedure was lengthy, with a fine of 25 Rhodesian dollars which was half of our spending money. Claire and Ross appealed to the officer's superior, who admitted that a speeding fine could only be imposed if at least two officers were present, hence the other charge. Since he was travelling in Ross's blind spot the officer could not have seen the indicator whether it had been used or not, so after much discussion the charge was dropped. We felt liberated and went straight to a café to celebrate with cool drinks.

Most of our afternoon had been wasted and Claire had to go her own way. Having resigned ourselves to losing $25 we decided to have a splurge and spend it anyway, and set out to explore shops offering a variety we hadn't seen for months. We settled on a soapstone jar and a chess set of African figures having each face individually carved. Back in Chingola we would lay it out permanently on a side table for a continuing game, until our houseboy came to dust it and rearrange the pieces. Another shop tempted us to buy a fondue set in stainless steel, with which we hoped to add a different dimension to dinner parties.

Salisbury was a vision of everything England could offer at its best. Rows of suburban gardens displayed neat lawns, trimmed hedges and tidy flower beds, but with exotic touches of banana palms, orange trees, and tumbling bougainvillea. Dahlias, begonias and species only seen as pot plants in Britain thrived in the sympathetic climate where harsh winters never took their toll. Everyone showed old-fashioned good manners, crocodiles of tidy, uniformed, blue-eyed schoolchildren in caps and Panama hats made their way along swept pavements, the birds sang and the sun shone. People called it 'God's own country,' but under Ian Smith's government it was living on borrowed time. The United Nations pronounced it to be 'an illegal racist minority regime.' Over five years of UDI the world, apart from a few sympathisers and notably South Africa, had withdrawn their trade.

Early on our last morning we set off for the other main border post with Zambia at Livingstone, arriving at 'Vic Falls' on the Rhodesian side at lunch-time. We were still on the lookout for ways to fill our house, and scanned endless rows of animal skins and hunting trophies, which were not only acceptable but fashionable in the 1970s. An elephant's foot for an ashtray, and heads of buffalo to fix to the wall were too much, but the tactile feel of buckskins seemed to offer a perfect African souvenir. We could afford an impala skin, and after rolling one up carefully in brown paper the shop assistant presented us with a certificate to verify it hadn't been poached. Having no time left we bemoaned having to postpone the Rhodesian side of the 'Falls' for another visit, and headed for the border posts.

'What have you bought in Rhodesia?' demanded the Zambian customs officer.

There was a small allowance for importing goods, and friends had forewarned us to understate prices and to pass as much as possible off as second-hand. He asked us to empty the boot, and groped under all of the seats.

'I think he's looking for firearms,' Ross muttered to me.

'Well we don't need to worry then,' I whispered back with confidence.

The official pulled out the fondue set. 'You have bought thees cooking pot in Rhodesia,' he proclaimed.

'Oh no, we have been using it while camping,' pronounced Ross. We had removed its giveaway packaging, but the stainless steel gleamed with newness. 'The houseboys in Rhodesia are very good at cleaning pots.'

The officer frowned at this barefaced lie, disputed it briefly, and then let it pass. He rummaged in our pile of belongings sitting in the road. An hour had passed since our arrival at the customs post.

'Show me the import licence for this skin,' he demanded, holding up our recent purchase with triumph.

It had never occurred to us that an import license might be required. Instead Ross presented the certificate we'd been given in the shop, which the officer studied with care.

'Thees ees not an import license. You must show a proper license before I can let you take eet into Zambia.'

We looked at his cold chameleon eyes and the double barrel of his flared nostrils and knew that arguing was futile. Time-wasting meant we already had the prospect of a late arrival with an early start for work in the morning, so we left him holding our recent purchase. Rhodesian customs had been happy enough for us to take it out of their country. All we had to show for it was the original certificate and another piece of paper from Zambian customs.

'Hi Ross, fancy meeting you here,' called Rick, a friend from Chingola approaching customs from the other direction.

'Rick! That's a stroke of luck! Are you going into Rhodesia?'

'Yes, Carol and I are going to spend a few days at Vic Falls.'

'Would you mind taking this impala skin back into Rhodesia for us? We can't get it through customs,' Ross handed him our receipt and explained our dilemma. 'Once you've got it over there perhaps you could post it to UK for us to bypass red tape, here's the address.'

Wishing them luck and a good holiday, we went on our way.

'We'd like to take this item back into Rhodesia, please,' said Rick handing over our recently completed receipt.

'Ah, let me see sah,' and he took the form to consult with a colleague, returning after a lengthy discussion.

'You cannot do that, sah, without an export license.'

'But if it hasn't been imported in the first place, how can it be exported?'

'I am very sorry, sah, those are the rules.'

Beaten by the system, they returned empty-handed. I wrote a letter to the address on the form, but heard nothing back, so we gave up the struggle with bureaucracy, and thought of it as another bewildering and frustrating experience of Africa.

CHAPTER EIGHT

Nchanga Clubs

We must learn to live together as brothers or perish together as fools.

MARTIN LUTHER KING

'*Everything is bee-yoo-tee-ful,*

In its own waa-ey,

Like the starry sun... er sky, in the night,

La laaa la, pum pum, puh pah,' we sang, and for a few messy moments after the record changed, blended slurrily into

'*Ceceeelia, you're breaking my heart,*

You're la la my confidence daileee..'

John and his wife Sue were having their first night out since they'd been cooped up together for weeks, yellow with jaundice, too ill to go out. The disease compromised their livers so alcohol had been banned and now recovered John meant to catch up.

'You won't be able to handle so much drink now after your illness John?' I suggested at the end of the evening.

'I don't know about that,' he replied, already tipsy and taking my remark for a challenge. He gathered several abandoned glasses of Drambuie, poured them all into one large glass and downed the lot in three gulps. As he turned green I regretted saying anything. Ubiquitous drinking to excess, at least in the evening, kept many sane. A few took to religion, and Jehovah's Witnesses made their presence felt around our doorways. Some threw themselves into sport, some had affairs, and a few used every prop they could find to bury their demons. Gossip flourished as if we lived in a soap opera, and fed off everyone's weaknesses and mistakes, and women were hardest on their own sex. Zambian television failed to distract us from everyday frustrations and at best it's one black and white channel offered repeats of 'Dad's Army' and 'On the Buses' for those prepared to pay the rental, which didn't include ourselves. Programmes in monochrome started late and finished early with unreliable reception.

'Did you hear about the cat fight down at the rugby club bar last night? Two girls were on the floor pulling each other's hair out apparently!'

'And that tart Fiona, you know she used to get drunk on Babycham a few years ago and flirt with all the men, dancing on the tables wearing a tiny skirt. Well she's just become a teetotal born-again Christian, and her poor husband has to go along with it!'

'Really! I heard that Glynis was seen all dolled-up driving into single quarters the other day. This time she's seeing Tim Grierson. The affair with Simon Bell has fizzled out.'

'I don't know where she finds the energy! Mind you Angela who works in townships said Gloria's cooker was so caked in dirt when they moved to another house that they had to clean it with stones!

'I saw Jenny Patterson the other day coming out of Kingston's with some magazines. She's become really pale and thin. They say she's an addict and her husband, you know Doctor Patterson, keeps her supplied with drugs.'

'They say the convent offers the best education in town, but I heard the nuns beat the children…even the girls if they're naughty. And you have to pay to go there!'

To keep the expatriate population happy while far from home, NCCM provided an impressive variety of facilities. The cavernous 'Mine Club' could cater for large functions with waiters decked in tasselled red fez hats, and there were churches, schools, hospitals, a theatre, and a masonic lodge with arched windows. In the middle of Africa sports clubs existed in every Copperbelt town for mine workers, and in 1970 were largely run by and for the expatriate population with supporting Zambian staff. A few, like the badminton club, used the Mine Club premises, but most had their own building with changing facilities, showers and a bar. The Arts Theatre, the Flying Club, the Rifle Club, the Bowling Club and the Library, had their attractions, but mostly we frequented the Cricket Club, the Tennis (and squash) Club and the Rugby Club. Members organised competitions, tournaments and leagues. Nchanga gym also offered a weight-lifting room, where a group of body-builders helped and inspired each other. Aiming for Arnold Schwarzenegger physiques, they pounded out routines in an upbeat atmosphere which would spawn Douggie Edmunds who founded The World's Strongest Man competition, and Peter Fiore. Peter won numerous medals for Zambia, set several world records, instigated the CPF (the Commonwealth Powerlifting Federation) and was still competing at the age of 73, the year before he died. In a visit to the gym in 1971 Ross responded to Peter's enthusiasm.

'Okay, now try a squat with these weights,' said Peter, 'I'll stand behind you in case you get into difficulties.'

But Ross had overstretched himself and passed out mid-squat. He came to with Peter supporting him under his arms. Peter appeared to have no difficulty holding Ross's weight in addition to the weights which had caused him to pass out.

While their husbands occupied themselves with work and sport, many wives would organise activities at the clubs for children and suppers for families, with volunteers drawn up in rotas. At the tennis club's regular Saturday night event I found myself paired with Sheila to make moussaka for a few dozen diners. The tennis club boasted a large kitchen suitable for catering. Afterwards families danced to a disco, and when the children had been taken home we stayed on sipping Cinzano and lemonade or brandy and coke, while our wild-haired men with their sideburns leaned on the bar lining up Lion or Castle Beer. When the music blotted out conversation we danced: the men with luminous kipper ties and their thumbs inside hipster waistbands; the women with flared trousers and crochet tops stamping out the beat in their platform shoes to Spirit in the Sky, Maggie May and American Pie.

Two tournaments had been arranged for the public holiday on Independence Day, at the end of October. Ross intended to participate in both starting with squash in the morning and finishing with tennis in the afternoon.

'It's too hot to hang around the club all day,' I said to Ross, 'I'll walk down to join you later for the final. By that time it'll be a bit cooler. Make sure you have plenty to drink in this heat!'

The rainy season hadn't started yet, and I didn't share his enthusiasm for running around after a ball in the stultifying humidity typical of 'suicide month.'

'Let's meet for lunch at the swimming pool,' he suggested, 'we can cool off in the pool and get something to eat.'

So I made some sandwiches with the disappointing bread I'd just bought. Usually it tasted good, but during flour shortages the baker added mealie-meal to the dough-mix to extend his flour supply, resulting in small hard unpalatable loaves.

After his energetic day, Ross showered but didn't join the others in the bar afterwards because we'd been invited to his boss's house for dinner. His friends were planning their return home overland, and he wanted them to meet us to talk about our experiences. But Ross was behaving oddly. Our hosts' conversation was just beginning to break ice when he started talking about frogs with bulging eyes jumping into a river. As he broke into silly laughter, I looked at him, perplexed and concerned, nervous of what he might say next. He was acting as he might at the end of a boozy evening, and this in front of his boss. In a complete reversal, by the end of his first beer he became sober again and stopped talking nonsense. I relaxed, but the following day I spoke to Sylvia about it,

'Ah, that sounds like salt deficiency to me. He will have lost salts in sweat during his day at the tennis club, and needed to replace them. That's why a beer sorted it out, because it provided the minerals he needed.'

'Salt deficiency? But they keep telling us to eat less salt, don't they?'

'Yes, but doing strenuous exercise in a hot climate is different. It's not enough to drink water. The first time I came across it was with John, and he's never let me forget it because of what I did to him,' she chortled, 'he was working on the Kariba Project during the late fifties when we hadn't been married long. Every evening after work they'd all go to a 'watering hole' for beer, and sometimes he didn't get back until late, sometimes really late. 'A Farewell to Arms' starring Rock Hudson was on at the bioscope, so on this evening we'd agreed for him to come straight home and I had our supper waiting in the oven. Well he didn't come home, and it was getting to the point that we'd miss the start of the film. I was clock-watching, and trying to imagine what was keeping him, and jumping to the wrong conclusion.'

'Well yes,' I said, 'I'd do the same in the circumstances,'

'So anyway, I got myself ready, and ate my meal so that he could eat his and we'd go straight away. Then he drove into the drive, and I could see he was staggering as soon as he got out of the car. I was so angry with him! I marched straight into the kitchen in a fury, took his plated dinner out to meet him, and threw it at him.'

'I bet he didn't know what hit him,'

'Well he didn't!' She giggled, 'He had peas and gravy in his hair and it all ran down his neck on to his shirt, but he just stood there swearing he hadn't had a drink. I didn't believe him because he slurred his speech and was talking gibberish. So it wasn't until he'd had something to eat, and of course a beer, that he became sensible again. It was quite bizarre! Once he'd 'sobered up' I calmed down, but we never made it to see the film. Since then he learnt to take salt tablets while working in the heat of the Zambezi valley, which was even worse with all those machines around them.'

NCCM owned many hectares of land along with the mineral rights, and much of this awaited the attention of prospectors and geologists. Beyond that plenty of unclaimed 'bush' still existed for a small landing strip, and with it came opportunities for members of the Flying Club who could take flying and gliding lessons at a reasonable cost without the complication of busy airspace. Similarly the rifle club occupied a large area safely away from the town.

'There's a mediaeval supper at the rifle club at the end of the month,' Ross announced one evening, 'it sounds a laugh, and everyone is expected to go dressed for the part.'

I busied myself at the sewing machine to make Ross a jester's outfit which we'd designed together. He'd borrowed a Harlequin's Rugby shirt from someone as a basis for a plausible suit, and didn't mind looking daft with odd-coloured legs made from two sets of different coloured tights sewn together, short baggy pantaloons, and a fat hat. I lipsticked two rosy circles on his cheeks for a clown effect. Then a long demure dress over a blouse became a tunic for me with a fabric-covered cardboard wimple and a voile scarf floating from its point. We set off with directions after nightfall, Ross looking colourful and me with the tall wimple on my lap.

'Bugger it,' said Ross, 'we're going to need petrol. Should have got it earlier! Damn!'

'This should be interesting,' I smiled.

We drew up at the first petrol pump and Ross got out of the car, removing his jester's hat in an effort to look normal. The attendant came out of his hut, looked at Ross, grinned nervously while backing off, and ran away.

'It's okay. It's only fancy dress!' shouted Ross, but this man didn't know about 'fancy dress,' and rather had 'witchcraft' in mind. So Ross put his own petrol in the tank while the attendant hovered at a safe distance, still grinning nervously. 'I'll put the money here on your desk, okay?' Ross called out, and we drove off to our banquet.

We gathered in a barn-like structure, dozens of mainly twenty-something expatriates sitting on benches at trestle tables with a steak knife each to carve a small chicken set at each place on a wooden chopping board. The men supped their Lion or Castle ale from tankards, and the women sipped 'mead' made from cheap wine with some honey stirred in. Greasy bones and slopped drinks landed in the sawdust on the floor, and throwing food was encouraged. Those in the know had brought paper napkins for finger-wiping before attempting to eat a syllabub without a spoon.

Nchanga Golf Course was the best on the Copperbelt and owed its lushness to a good irrigation system, fed by pumped water from the sewage treatment plant. Non-players could enjoy a good walk and landscaping to rival any in the world, while players savoured the usual frustrations of the game. In 1979 after we had left, Nchanga Golf Club was rated number fourteen in the world outside the USA. Caddies were always on hand for a small fee, to carry clubs, spot where your ball had landed and give advice. A dozen or so would appear from behind a screen near to the first tee, each hoping to be hired for a round.

'Watch out for snakes in the long grass and under bushes,' said Ross when I played a few practice holes. We were far from watchful eyes around the clubhouse, so I would not be embarrassed if I played an 'air shot.' Golf required a dedication in time and effort, which I was not prepared to give, and the usual problem of not being able to drive curtailed such activities. I played my shot and it curved off to the right to land in a rough area.

'You sliced that one!' announced Ross unhelpfully, 'never mind, kick it away from that termite mound before attempting your next shot. Take these clubs and I'll meet you on the green.'

Off I trudged on my own with a pitching wedge and a seven iron to pursue the annoying little white ball, and found it in long dry grass. Preparing to return it to the fairway, I positioned myself and took a couple of practice swings, trying to remember all the rules and advice, as well as keeping my eye on the ball.

'Keep your head down,' I told myself firmly.

I leapt in the air. Something was biting me in a personal area. I looked down at my legs and saw an army of small red ants making their way upwards. The first one had waited until he nearly reached my pants before taking the first bite. Another bite penetrated with a vicious sting. I performed a dance, brushing my legs and trying to escape an army of insects intent on eating me. My ball had disturbed a platoon of 'driver' or 'army' ants on the move, revenge was swift and formic acid stung. Driver ants are entirely flesh eaters and nomadic, intent on demolishing all insect and animal life in their path. The *yarpies* called them Matabele ants, and I'd disturbed this battalion on its way to raid the termite colony in the five-foot mound nearby. What they lack in size they make up for in numbers. Something had to be done and there was only one solution. I took off my shorts. At this point Ross arrived on the scene with delight and amusement written all over his face. It didn't help, and I scowled at him as I jumped from leg to leg while trying to brush them off and pick them out of my shoes and socks. It was a losing battle, and I took off in the direction of the club house intending to reach the safety of the ladies' changing room. The sight of three approaching golfers brought me to my senses, and I ducked behind a tree to restore my decency with well-shaken shorts.

Other dangers lurked on the Konkola Golf Course in the small Copperbelt town of Chililabombwe, previously called Bancroft, to the north of Chingola and close to the Zaire border. The town's original Bemba name means 'place of the croaking frog,' and being on the Kafue River, it attracts grazing hippos with ten of its holes placed along a series of ponds.

'A ball coming to rest in a hippo footprint may be lifted and dropped in the nearest possible position to provide maximum relief,' states one of the club rules. With these bad-tempered creatures weighing up to 7,000 pounds their imprint is deep, and they are not the only visitors who frequent the ponds. Over the years several caddies have died in their attempt to rescue golf balls from the water when an unseen crocodile struck. Added to the risk of snakebites from a black or green mamba, a boomslang, or a spitting cobra lurking in tall grass, this is not a course to attempt with complacency particularly for those who find difficulty keeping to the fairway.

For rugby players and their families most Sunday afternoons in the season were devoted to a game. Rugby matches between the five main Copperbelt towns of Chingola, Ndola, Kitwe, Mufulira and Luanshya, and also with the capital Lusaka, were well supported. An occasional touring side also brought large crowds and everyone entered under the Rampant Lion sign for Nchanga Rugby Club. They were largely populated by the wives and young families of players and their supporters. After every match, fires were lit for the *braais* in halved oil drums, and soon the enticing smell of barbecuing steak pervaded the environs of the host town.

Children tumbled onto the pitch after the game to enjoy the wide space their fathers had recently vacated, and as the sun went down at six o'clock young men gathered round the bar. Women queued with paper plates at trestle tables piled with baked potatoes wrapped in foil, bread rolls, and mountains of coleslaw and mixed salad. Occasionally they yelled admonishments to errant offspring, or rushed off to catch a toddler, but older children were given plenty of freedom as half-light under reddening skies became dark. The firefly glow of cigarettes followed parents at the end of the evening when they went to fetch the children from the far side of the pitch. Hefty rugby players addressed a steak, a pork chop, and a sizeable piece of spicy *boerwors* sausage. Afterwards they'd stand in manly groups with legs firmly planted apart, clutching a bottle of beer at their chests. Then some went back for more meat, often eschewing the vegetables completely. These would usually be descendants of Dutch and Huguenot settlers, the Boer pioneers who had arrived in the Eastern Cape from the mid seventeenth century onwards. They'd carved out farms from the veldt and taught their Cape Dutch or Afrikaans to their workers. Conflict with British colonialism initiated the Great Trek in 1835 when they slogged northwards from the Cape with ox-drawn wagons in search of new lands. Tensions remained and culminated in the Boer War, so with this history behind them relations between Brits and Boers required an effort on both sides. We called them *yarpies*, and like the Australians they called us *pommies.* But most of us learned to rub along, and it turned out the *yarpies* were often kinder to Africans than us 'liberal' Brits, who didn't really understand the way of things in southern Africa and had a tendency to sentimentality. The South Africans treated 'blecks' with paternalism which could mean a clout around the ear for the slightest misdemeanour, or a generous gift of food, clothing, or bedding for their houseboy's family. Zambians knew where they stood with them, whereas they never really understood us Brits who were apt to be soft and then show surprise and get angry when things went wrong, like casual theft.

People born and raised in Zambia in the colonial regime of their parents found the earnest and critical attitude of newly arrived p*ommies* with no experience of African life more than a little galling. We became tolerant of their harsh words being used deliberately to provoke outrage, but no one knew where the edges of dark humour ended and the truth began. They chose to stay in this independent African country after all, and not just for economic reasons. One Friday evening when a large crowd gathered in the rugby club bar to celebrate pay day and the start of the weekend, Kurt decided to have some fun with a group of us.

'You know these people just aren't capable of doing the jobs we do,' he jerked his head at a waiter collecting empty glasses from the tables, 'Blecks have no common sense. It's trrroo!' He cast a mischievous look around the table waiting for protest. 'Just let me show you how stupid they are.' To demonstrate his theory he called the waiter to the table.

'Ey, Gideon, come 'ere man!'

Gideon duly approached the table clasping his tray.

'Yes, sah,' he barked, cheerily standing to attention in an oversized uniform, with mock seriousness. He clicked his heels.

Kurt reached into the pocket of his shorts and pulled out a handful of coins. 'Gideon, which would you prefer to have, all of this change in my hand, or the contents of my wallet? I will give you whichever you choose.'

Gideon grinned, and hesitated a little. Then he pointed to the coins. Kurt then drew out his wallet with theatrical effect, and showed everyone, including Gideon the wad of notes stuffed inside. He handed Gideon the change who accepted it in African style with both hands cupped, and made his way back to the bar.

'I ask him that every week and he always does the same. He never learns. I told you, they're all stupid!'

Ross leaned on the bar later. 'Why don't you ask for the wallet, Gideon? You must know that it always has more money.'

'Oh yes I know that, bwana,' said Gideon with a twinkle in his eye as he polished a wine glass, 'but if I take the wallet contents, he will stop playing the game and there will be no more money for me.'

A large crowd packed the open-backed wooden stands in Mufulira one Sunday. The previous rugby match had been in Kabwe which was never well supported, being a longer distance to travel and some players claiming 'Kabwe knee', the overused excuse not to go. So everyone was ready for a game, and the mood was upbeat. Wives neglected to keep an eye on their bags as they caught up with each other's news. A barefoot African boy suddenly ran past the stand with two burly *yarpies* thundering after his slim, barefoot form.

'Catch him, he's been stealing!' they yelled, and a purse flew into the air over their heads as the young thief gave up his bounty. A look of terror dulled his eyes, and a large wet patch spread over the front of his worn shorts. He darted through the stand supports underneath us.

'Poor lad, he's wet himself. I hope they're not too rough on him,' whispered Chrissie sitting next to me. All of us women wished the rascal enough guile and speed to escape his fate now that he'd surrendered his plunder. Ten minutes later the three reappeared, the thief with tear channels marking dusty cheeks, and being pulled along by his ear. There would be instant justice and the teenager would be taught a lesson. He was led out of sight.

'N-C-H-A-N-G-A' the crowd spelt out, cheering their team who were in the lead and had possession of the ball. They passed it to the winger, who raced towards the touch line leaving the other team too far behind to tackle. The crowd roared. Beside himself with frustration, the Mufulira line judge ran alongside the winger now ten yards from the line. Kurt was running too fast for the home team to catch him. The line judge could see another score about to be made, so in desperation he reached out with the flag and floored him with a single wallop.

After a match families never lingered around the stand. Still simmering with outrage, a handful of players often gathered in the shadows of the tiered wooden benches to settle with their fists any disputes unresolved on the field. A black eye was as likely to be suffered here as during the game

For the Lusaka away game the team decided to fly rather than driving a tedious 500 miles on the return trip by road. Players and supporters arrived at the huts that served as a terminal at Ndola airport. Their Saturday morning flight with Zambia Airways was waiting, but some of the seats had been double-booked. They muttered and moaned for a while, and then some supporters volunteered to catch the next flight later that day. Such was Zambian life. On the Sunday after an enjoyable match, and in the light of what had happened the day before, everyone pitched up early to claim their seats on the return plane. It proved to be a wise strategy and they all climbed aboard keen to return to their homes, wives and families having had a successful boys' weekend away.

'There is a problem with double-booking,' said the airport official who had boarded the plane, 'two of you will have to give your seats to these other passengers.'

The 'other passengers' stood behind him, looking expectant.

'Now wait a minute,' said the club's representative and former policeman from Southern Rhodesia. 'We've paid for these seats, and we were here in good time to claim them. We're not going to give them up to someone who has arrived after us, it doesn't matter who they are.'

It wasn't unusual for government ministers to demand airline seats without notice, with members of the public expected to give way to their demands. The 'other passengers' must have been important, as the official would not accept 'no' for an answer. After several attempts in the same vein to oust people from their seats, he went for back-up and returned a few minutes later with another, larger, official. The same argument ensued, and the same stalemate resulted. Voices got louder, the heat in the cabin rose, and more minutes ticked by. The men in uniform moved down the aisle looking to left and right and stopped at the smallest member of the group. Robbie was a slightly built linesman and respected member of the club.

'You must get off the plane, sir. This seat has been reserved by another passenger,' and they started to manhandle him out of his seat.

'Oh no you don't!' exclaimed the club rep.

'He's staying on the plane with the rest of us. You find another flight for your other passengers, because none of us is moving.'

'Yeah,' rumbled twenty other low voices in agreement.

Then they grabbed both officials and sent them stumbling down the stairs.

'I cannot leave with this plane until everyone is seated, and we need to leave soon,' stated the pilot firmly but peaceably, before turning around to sit it out in the cockpit.

Departure time had gone over by thirty minutes, and it didn't look likely that either side would climb down. Frustrated players shifted in their seats, indignation gathered momentum, and voices rose further. Zambian Airways staff stood firm. The pilot was called back, and more argument followed. The officials returned with more airport staff and two policemen, and headed straight for Robbie.

Enraged rugby players shouted, 'don't you touch him,' and turfed the officials off the plane.

'Guys, guys!' pleaded Colin. 'This isn't getting us anywhere. 'Can we have some calm please and we'll see if we can work things out? I suggest we all get off the plane, and see if we can talk things through with the authorities,'

'Okay, let's do that,' chorused a dozen voices.

He got to the door of the plane and started to descend the steps before looking around. No one was following. So he went back up and one by one persuaded the whole contingent of players and supporters to follow. They gathered in smouldering groups on the concourse, and started walking to the terminal building. But it looked like the last word would inevitably go with officialdom. Half a dozen Land Rovers had drawn up on the concourse, and out poured more officials and policemen. They intended to arrest Robbie, and pandemonium broke loose.

Ruan clenched his fists and looked wildly around him.

'They're not going to get away with this,' he repeated over and over again in a low voice, like a mantra, working himself up into a frenzy and deaf to reason.

His eyes got wilder, and his fists got paler, until with a primeval holler, he launched himself into the gathering of police and Zambian Airways officials with punches, kicks and expletives. A pack of players followed suit and there followed forty minutes of skirmishes with police truncheons, rugby tackles, punches and swearing.

Some were arrested, and the rest skulked off to the terminal building, sitting in small groups. Then the police made a surprise foray to arrest someone, apparently at random, and took him away to the cells. After a few more forays the small airport prison was full to overflowing, and when things looked calmer Colin came forward.

'Could I speak to the men who have been arrested please?'

Permission was granted, and he shouted, 'are you guys okay in there?'

'Tell those bleck besterds I'm going to kill all of his brothers,' shouted Kurt through the peep-hole in the door.

Most of the team and some of the supporters had been locked eight to a cell, destined to spend an uncomfortable night sharing a few stained mattresses.

Colin tried to smother the sound of Kurt's threat with his hands over the peep-hole.

'You're not helping your case, Kurt!' he pleaded. 'We all know you think it isn't fair, but James is doing his best to get you out of here, so try to keep quiet!'

Ross, James and Colin were three of a handful left outside the cells. Darkness fell, and the plane would not be leaving at all. As an international airport Lusaka had no limits to departures, but Ndola airport was little more than a landing strip and had no lights to operate at night, so the plane would be unable to land. There would be no return home until the following day.

CHAPTER NINE

Holidays

Patience is the key which solves all problems.

AFRICAN PROVERB

The mine personnel department organised a charter flight for visiting family in early March and a supply of haggis and whisky came with them complete with a piper and all his regalia for a very belated Burns night celebration. We hired extra furniture and bedding to furnish the empty spare bedroom from townships, made an extra effort to tidy the house, washed Sheba, swept messy mangoes from the garden, and headed off to Ndola to collect them.

After activities organised for everyone in Chingola, which were mostly of the jolly community variety, we took them on a tour of Rhodesia, starting with Umtali in the Eastern highlands where an old school friend of my father's had a tobacco farm. We found his house in the beautiful rolling hills of the Eastern Highlands, but he was not a happy man. Things had become tough on the farm since the declaration of U.D.I. in 1965 when Ian Smith had defied Harold Wilson's government and provoked sanctions over trade which they had previously enjoyed with the rest of the tobacco-smoking world. This area buzzed with the dissatisfaction and unrest which would soon morph into the centre of guerrilla war between white and black factions. The capital Salisbury felt less agitated but there lingered a disharmony of which I had been unaware on our last visit. My mother's cousin John managed the prestigious Meikles Hotel here. We donned our best clothes to dine with him and his wife there. John angled his head at some suited men sitting nearby.

'History's being made here,' he said.

A delegation of British government ministers at the adjacent table were charged with bringing Rhodesia's rebel white minority government into line and negotiations were in progress to come to some sort of agreement towards majority rule.

'The Rhodesian ministers are more British than the British!' remarked my mother

'That is so true,' said John, 'I'm afraid we're all trying to hang on to the past, but I do believe the changeover should be gradual. If it happens too quickly, which these people seem to be pushing for, it could be catastrophic, and not just for the whites.'

Miles of souvenir stalls fringed the road south to Bulawayo, and smooth-stoned *kopjes*, scattered villages, and *Mopane* trees punctuated our view out of the windows. Some rounded rocks could be mistaken for elephants or hippos at first glance with the same grey curves, but we saw no game on this part of our journey. Occasionally a giant baobab loomed up yards above the other trees from a swollen bulbous trunk, its branches reaching upwards. When African children hear the sinister cackle of hyenas, their parents tell them the fable of God giving this ugly animal the job of planting the baobab. Being cowardly, lazy and not too bright, he planted it upside down with its roots in the air.

We stopped near Masvingo to see the Zimbabwe ruins.

'Great Zimbabwe was the capital of the Kingdom of Zimbabwe during the country's late Iron Age,' I read aloud from a plaque, 'the monument first began to be constructed in the 11th century and continued to be built until the 14th century, spanning an area of 722 hectares, and was purported to house up to 18,000 people. Great Zimbabwe acted as a royal palace for the monarch and would have been used as the seat of their political power.'

'That's nearly three square miles, said my father. 'It must have been quite a place!'

Fed by the fertile Shashe flood plain, these people of Mapela Hill worked the nearby gold reef, and traded in ivory. While they were building with stone the rest of sub-Saharan Africa farmed smallholdings and herded their beasts as they'd done since the Iron Age. We passed through circular buildings and narrow passageways trying to envisage the lives led between these walls. An oasis of civilisation years ago appeared to be more advanced than the villages we could see all over the country centuries later, and certainly richer. The city's stone enclosures, towers and walls rose more than the height of two men, stretched for 110 yards and had been built without mortar, and a refinement in their structure which belied skilled craftsmanship.

Another old school friend lived in Bulawayo, and his South African wife cooked us all *bobotie*, a South-African dish of curried meat, dried fruit, and a creamy topping, followed by a memorable passion-fruit ice cream.

'We have a glut of fruit, and it freezes very well,' said his wife pointing at a rampant creeper covering their garden wall. Dimpled purple egg-shaped fruit dripped from twining cords. She picked up a few hours' windfalls from the ground.

'Here, take these ones with you. If you cut the top off, you can suck out the flesh and it won't make a mess of your car,' and she handed us a bag of fruit.

As we climbed back into the car for the long drive north, Ross peered under the bonnet to see how the engine was faring after all the miles we'd travelled. He shook his head.

'Water is leaking into the engine. It would be asking for trouble to keep going and the last thing we need is a breakdown in the middle of the *bundu* miles from any town.'

'This has had some punishment,' said the mechanic at the first garage on the outskirts of Bulawayo, 'how old did you say the car is?'

Ross explained our challenging journey across the Sahara and storm-wrecked equatorial roads before we reached East Africa.

'You must have been crazy to take on a trip like that in this car!' Said the mechanic, repeating what many had said before. 'But it explains a lot. I'm afraid this is going to cost a bit. If you'd like to wait we'll start on it straight away.'

We watched him grind down the cylinder head among the prosaic atmosphere of car engines with their accompanying smells, fumes and noises. Memories of our struggle to get to Zambia flooded back, along with the accompanying anxiety.

Ross was the only driver to take us the next few hundred miles. The temperature rose to midday heat, vegetation became sparser, and the road dustier. East of the Kalahari my parents dozed on the back seat, and I struggled to stay awake to ensure Ross didn't nod off at the wheel. Dust invaded our open windows and the heat became soporific. The excitement of spotting game as we entered Hwange Game Park, (at that time called 'Wankie') sparked us back to life.

'What elegance!' enthused my mother as a herd of impala sprang across the red dust in front of us. 'Oh and look at that little one, isn't it sweet!' She pointed at a tiny antelope not much taller than a ruler, which jerked its watchful eyes in our direction.

'That's a dik-dik,' I said.

Forever on guard, it darted back into the bush, a prime target for a host of predators. Bush buck, water buck, zebra, giraffe, wildebeest, baboons, families of vertical-tailed warthogs, a solitary eland, springbok, and lots more impala sprang, loitered, trotted, peered and darted past our windows. Cranes, hornbills and tiny bee-eaters flashed their wings. Of all the 'big five' pursued by hunters we only saw elephant but could hardly complain after the feast our eyes had enjoyed. Lion, leopard, rhino, and buffalo could wait for another time.

Upon our arrival at the Victoria Falls Hotel a troupe of vervet monkeys welcomed us with an acrobatic display on the telegraph wires. We eschewed an evening 'booze cruise' on the Zambezi above Victoria Falls and opted instead to sip cocktails on wicker chairs overlooking restful leafy gardens with neat lawns. A caged Congo Grey parrot paced his perch nearby and made noisy interruptions to the gentle footfall of uniformed waiters and the murmur of sprinklers. The peaceful days and evenings of such a life were numbered with an impending war on the horizon. The next seven years would bring snipers taking pot-shots across the border, and missiles landing on hotel roofs. All but the most determined tourists would be deterred and replaced with gun-toting men in camouflage.

The best came last at 'The Falls.' None of us was prepared although we knew it was listed as one of the seven natural wonders of the world. It was bigger, longer, louder, grander, wetter, wider, and more awe-inspiring than we could have imagined. Still on the Rhodesian side we passed David Livingstone's monument to walk in silence along the facing bank with raincoats and umbrellas, making stops to gaze and marvel some more. Early the next morning we stepped on to the bridge from the Zambian side and *Musi-o-Tunya*, the Smoke that Thunders, entranced us all over again until we had to tear ourselves away from the roar and towering spray for our long drive back to Lusaka, then on up the Great North Road to Chingola to total 560 miles in one day.

A month later my parents had returned, and on a long weekend we were ready to do a little exploring in Zambia. Others regularly went '*bundu* bashing' into the bush, to the 'game reserve' next to the Kafue River for boating, or further afield to camp. Our spirit of adventure had been exhausted by our overland trip, but it was creeping back into life.

Lake Bangweulu, the Bangweulu Swamps, and the Bangweulu flats or floodplain make up an enormous wetland system. Situated in the upper Congo River basin the Bangweulu system covers an almost completely flat area roughly the size of East Anglia. The shortest route of five hours driving over bush roads took us North-East from Zambia's Northern Province through the 'Congo Pedicle', or '*La Botte de Katanga*,' Katanga's Boot, a troubled area full of opportunist police and military. At the border we joined a queue as we approached a Stop sign, and the dour-faced gun-toting official waved us on.

'*Bonjour, monsieur,*' said Ross smiling with a brave effort to charm.

'*Bonjour.* You did not stop at the sign!' he stated bluntly in French, and I stirred my brain to take up simultaneous translation between them.

'But you waved us forward!' protested Ross.

'You must always stop at the sign. You must pay a fine,'

'This is ridiculous, I was obeying your instructions!'

'You did not stop at the sign so you must pay the fine. Give me one kwacha or you cannot go forward.'

This exchange continued along the same lines until Ross, tired after a long, dusty drive, shrugged and handed over the cash for his concocted aberration. The official pocketed the kwacha note.

'I'd like a receipt please?'

He shook his head, 'We do not give receipts. Drive on.'

The cash-strapped newly named Zairean government was famed for not paying their workers for months on end, if at all and the chance of their weapons being in working order and loaded with ammunition was unlikely. Police, customs officials, and the military therefore relied on their own methods of getting income and comparatively wealthy white workers were considered fair game. Like our friends who had travelled through the day before we rationalised the payment as a 'toll-charge' and, as there would be no way through otherwise, it was futile to worry about it.

King Leopold of Belgium had negotiated this finger of land for himself when boundaries were being drawn with British Northern Rhodesia, so that his colony would benefit from the rich wetlands around the lake. The Bangweulu surrounding area provides a good supply of game as well as thousands of tons of fish every year. Under his harsh regime of exploitation and violent oppression, he'd sought to gain lucrative revenue from the huge country's ivory, and then from rubber extraction by a means which became known as the 'rubber terror.' For twenty years around the beginning of the twentieth century the Congolese population was reduced to serfdom and often worked to death in the 'corvée' or forced labour system in which villages were burned and hands routinely cut off for punishment. Under the guise of trade agreements including the suppression of the slave trade, he'd ruled his private holding for two decades with greed and terror causing death and suffering on a scale the worst the world had ever known, and the population fell by millions. Belgian colonialism took over for the next fifty years before Independence in 1960, and then other violent struggles would follow for decades as though the land had been cursed.

During the 1970's the pedicle became a 'ransom strip' to provide another rich source of income, but from expatriate Zambian Copperbelt workers hungry for a beach-type holiday. It didn't seem a good idea to argue with soldiers coming from such a brutalised people. After we'd negotiated a second border post we drove back into Zambian land on the flat dirt road which continued to Mansa in Luapula province, and then we turned east to Samfya on the South-Western side of the lake. Dave and Sandra had arrived with their friends the day before and set up camp about twenty yards from the water's edge. We chose a reasonably flat area alongside for our tent and then waded into welcome water to wash off road dust and cool off.

'Don't swim too far out! There are crocodiles in this lake!' called Sandra. 'They're normally over the other side but they like to lurk in deeper water so I'd stay in the shallows if I were you,' she added, 'you can't be too careful!'

I squinted through reflected glare from the sun into the water around me, swirling with disturbed sand. The water became colder as it gained depth, and I'd swum a dozen yards from the edge of the lake, wallowing in its refreshing coolness. There could be no visible warning, and although a confident swimmer I wouldn't stand a chance against a hungry croc. I headed back with a tingling awareness in my legs, conscious of them being the first target for a grabbing jaw full of sharp teeth, and resigned myself to tepid waters by the shore, where the children splashed and shouted out to each other.

Late afternoon heat simmered down, our energies revived and Dave spotted some local women carrying bundles of firewood on their heads.

Having bartered with sign language he returned with enough to fuel a fire, and Ross hauled our crate of beer and soft drinks into the water for cooling. We pulled folding chairs around a smoky fire, prised tops off bottles, and settled down for a sundowner and *braai* of meat we'd double-wrapped in damp newspaper and ice to keep it fresh.

Saturday dawned with a brilliant sun rising over 'the place where the water meets the sky' and our day stretched ahead like the water on the lake, waiting to be crossed. With echoes of the previous evening's stories echoing in my head of a Chingola man taken by a crocodile and his body never found. His wife waited for six months and then took the children home with her, never knowing for sure what happened. I stepped into the water yearning for a long swim but unwilling to surrender myself to its alluring freshness. Later we decided to hire the services of a local fisherman with his dugout canoe, or *mokoro*. It would have to be a big one to carry six of us. Our ungainly clamberings rocked the solid craft, we settled, and he pushed on a long pole to steer us from the shore with the help of a wiry teenager, their tensing bodies nearly horizontal in the effort. They were Bemba, as in the Copperbelt, and Swahili traders sometimes referred to Lake Bangweulu as 'Lake Bemba' after the tribe, but these men had the long straight limbs of fish-eaters unlike their smaller cousins living in the mining areas. The sun gained strength in a sky devoid of mitigating clouds, and we donned cotton hats for protection. The fisherman poled his boat in a slow and steady rhythm, smiling at us with our questions and pink skin, bemused by our interest in his humble craft. He stopped far out on the lake near a dense growth of reeds, and busied nimble fingers with bait and lines while his canoe bobbed on sleek metallic water now stilled without the insistent push and pull of the poles. Silence wrapped around us, a spoonbill flew into the reeds with a flapping of wings and disappeared, a little egret rose up with an indignant 'gulla-gulla' and silence returned. I reached over the canoe's uneven side to trail my fingers in the water.

'Don't forget those crocodiles,' laughed Sandra.

The lake wasn't deep with an average of four metres overall, and I could imagine a cold-eyed reptile with crowded teeth creeping along the depths before springing up to grab my arm. The plentiful supply of catfish and bream should keep crocodiles satisfied, but I withdrew my hand just in case one had developed a taste for woman. Without the water's coolness and no shade, the sun burned from its reflection off the lake as well as from above. I gazed towards the reeds whose maze of shifting channels had baffled David Livingstone during his last expedition in the swamps to the north. He had been struggling to chart the seventeen rivers draining in and out of the lake, still hoping to find the source of the Nile. The complex masses of channels formed between these rivers quickly become choked by vegetation, forcing them to change their course. Like many things in Africa it defies order and befuddles navigators. The famous missionary-explorer had died nearly a hundred years ago in Chief Chitambo's village on the edge of the southern flood plain, about eighty miles from the lake. His loyal followers Susi and Chuma cut out his heart to bury it under an Mvula tree before carrying his body to the coast to be shipped to England.

Ross and I plunged into the lake back at camp and swam until the sun reddened as it approached the horizon. Ross ducked under the water.

'Dratted mosquitoes,' he said, spouting a mouthful of water back into the lake, 'did you hear that enormous cloud of them travelling over the water? There must have been millions of them!'

It was time to get dressed. The cooling swim had brought some relief to my hot skin, but it still burned as I zipped myself into the tent for the night, pleading a headache. We'd enjoyed a supper of the bream caught on our boat trip and I fell into bed early to an orchestra of frogs drowning out the hum of conversation around the fire.

The morning sun spilled molten gold over a silver lake, but I could hardly open my eyes to witness it. I staggered to the lakeside hoping for revival with an early swim.

'I don't understand it,' I moaned, miserable with a throbbing head and parched mouth, 'I never took my hat off, how could I burn so much?'

'It must have been the reflection off the lake,' said Sandra.

A combination of sunburn and insect bites conspired against me and our tent became the only refuge from the sun's glare. With both tent flaps open to encourage a light breeze I spent much of Sunday flat on my back longing for more cool swims but afraid of the consequences.

CHAPTER TEN

A Duiker in the Fireplace

Every morning in Africa a gazelle wakes up. It knows it must run faster than the fastest lion or it will be killed. Every morning in Africa a lion wakes up and knows it must outrun the slowest gazelle or it will starve to death. It doesn't matter whether you are a lion or a gazelle… when the sun comes up you'd better be running.

'What makes a good guard dog then?' asked June. 'Your Sheba is good, but Blue was hopeless, perhaps it's the breed?'

'Your Jasper's pretty scary for burglars too, so Alsatians must be among the best. The professionals use them, don't they?'

'Yes but our Monday is hopeless and she's part Alsatian, so it's not guaranteed!'

Monday would be more likely to lick unwelcome visitors rather than bite them, whereas Jasper looked vicious and commanded respect.

'Well how about mating our Sheba with your Jasper? Surely that combination would be guaranteed to produce reliable guard dogs!'

'Sounds good to me, and I'm sure Jasper would enjoy being a stud! Perhaps we could claim the pick of the litter in payment for his services?'

The following day Sheba went blind. She bumped into things, and kept rubbing her paws over her eyes. All thoughts of mating her were forgotten.

'It was probably a spitting Cobra,' pronounced the vet, 'they aim for the eyes and are pretty accurate. She may have disturbed one in your garden, but I don't think she got the full whack of venom. Chances are she'll recover in a few days.'

We bathed her eyes, and let her recover. The next time Sheba came into season she'd regained her fitness and Jasper was summoned. Every night noisy dog fights broke out in the garden because her scent attracted hordes of rampant canines we'd never seen before, jumping over our fences and leaping up with yowls at the windows of the stoep where we'd confined her. Sheba asked to join them, but we had other plans.

'I think we should watch just to make sure,' said June

'Pervert!' said her husband, 'leave them in peace. I'm sure they don't need an audience.'

So we put them both in a room together, and before the door closed we saw Jasper flop down on floor. Perhaps it was his arthritic hind legs. The 'stud' couldn't perform, and Sheba didn't look too keen either. After all she was in love with the mastiff mongrel from across the road. But Stanley's track record for guarding was unreliable, with items stolen from his owners' garden. Barry had taken to hiding up in a tree near the fence with his air pistol, on the lookout for a culprit who'd visited more than once.

Some persuasion and encouragement brought about a doggy union, and nine weeks later Sheba fussed around the *stoep*, scraping at the brick walls with her instinct to make a bed. The next morning two writhing, closed-eyed damp bodies lay beside her in a box Ross had hastily nailed together for her. We watched the next five being born. By the end of the afternoon another seven crowded beside her.

'Fourteen is too many for her to cope with,' said the vet. 'It's easier to find homes for the males, so bring in all the females and we'll deal with them.'

The following day we returned with five mewling female innocents. There was another one, but somehow she'd managed to elude us that morning. We delighted in watching the remaining nine grow, in handling their soft supple bodies and laughing at their stumbling antics. When weaning started with bowls of baby milk Sassi invited himself to dine with them, a dark feline amongst the blond roly-poly canines all radiating out from metal enamel bowls. Jasper's family had first pick of the litter, and one by one the others went to good homes and our spare room became spare again.

Everyone had a dog of some kind, and many had cats too. The Fiores also had a parrot, a Congo Grey gifted with mimicry. 'Shut the door,' he would yell in a perfect replica of Peter's voice, and four children would get up to do as they were told. He'd also perfected Peter's whistle, shouting 'here Rover!' followed by a whistle that brought the family dog running. One day the parrot escaped nowhere to be found. Peter asked his friends to keep a lookout for the bird, and Ross arrived at his house to see Peter, a volunteer fireman, with the fire engine at his gate. He was directing the hose twenty feet up into a jacaranda tree where his parrot perched. It was persuaded to be recaptured.

'Stupid bird,' scolded Peter

'Stupid bird,' said the parrot.

Sheila's parents had lived in Chingola for years, and for much of that time a Congo Grey lived with them. They left their daughter to house-sit while they went on three months end-of-contract long leave and Sheila's boyfriend Geoff joined her for the task. Frequent visitors from single quarters dropped by and usually found their way to the parrot's cage on the veranda. Silence fell every time Geoff or Sheila came out to talk to them.

'What's wrong?' Geoff would ask.

'Nothing,' they'd say.

By the time Sheila's parents returned the parrot had perfected a new phrase, 'You make the bed, Sheila, and I'll get the beers!'

One Sunday morning before the start of the rugby season, we sailed along the straight road to Kitwe to see our friends. The police had a road check, and we drew in.

'Good morning, sergeant' said Ross, 'nice day today.'

It was good to start these exchanges with a promotion, an upbeat greeting, and a disarming smile.

'Good morning, sah, I would like to see your driver's license.'

The constable examined Ross's green Zambian driving license and satisfied, returned it through the open window.

'Show me your wipers working, please.'

Under a cloudless sky in the dry season, Ross flicked the switch for the wipers to shift dust and a few dead flies back and forth. The policeman nodded.

'Now I want to see if your speedometer is working. Let me sit in the car with you.'

'I'm afraid that's a problem,' replied Ross cheekily, 'you see I'm not insured for you to sit in the car, and if we have an accident you would not be covered.'

'Oh, I see that is a problem.' He thought for a moment. 'Then you can drive and I shall run beside the car to see if it is working.'

Amazed at Ross's devilment, I had to stifle a giggle. He switched on the engine and started to drive with the policeman running alongside the car, hanging on to the upright between the open windows. Fifty yards on, he accelerated, leaving a puzzled policeman at the roadside.

'I hope he didn't have a note of your number,' I said, and we cruised along unhindered for twenty minutes.

'Slow down a bit, let's see what he's selling,' I said, pointing at a figure further along the road.

A man stood at the roadside holding an animal upside-down by its four legs. Ross drew the car up beside him. A tiny deer with a body the size of a cat's was struggling against the man's firm grip.

'Oh, isn't it sweet!' I cried. 'Poor little thing, he must be selling it for food.'

'*Mwapoleni mukwayi*,' said Ross to greet the man in Bemba, 'what is that animal you are holding?'

'*Mwapoleni*, sah. This animal, eet ees a duiker, a small deer. She is a baby and his mother is gone,' he explained, mixing up his pronouns. 'Do you want to buy eet? I will sell eet to you for ten kwacha. Very cheap, good price.'

'I'll give you two kwacha for it, replied Ross.

'That is not enough!' he laughed. 'This deer, he will grow fat after two maybe three months. Now she is just a baby. Give me six kwacha.'

'OK, four kwacha,' said Ross.

The man handed over the duiker to me while Ross fished in his pocket for money. The animal saw a chance of escape and struggled desperately, bruising my arm with sharp little hooves no wider than my little finger. I held it tight and lowered myself carefully into the car seat, using my thumb to close the car door without slackening my grip on the duiker. Ross put away his wallet and drove on.

Entering Kitwe my arms must have slackened because the little creature felt its chance and leapt out of my arms onto Ross, who then struggled to control the car with a swerve before stopping. It leapt frantically around the car, throwing itself at the windows in a bid for freedom, and finally settled on the floor behind my seat, panting from its exertions. Apparently worn out, and perhaps realising escape wasn't possible, it sat frozen until we drew into our friends' driveway. We crept cautiously out of the car to announce our arrival.

Four adults and two children peered in at the little creature looking up at us with doe eyes. A little tuft of hair stuck up on top of its head like a bad hair day. Ross managed to catch it mid-leap when he opened the door, and we all went into the sitting room. Dave put their dogs outside and closed all the doors. We all settled into chairs for a leisurely Sunday lunch, and the duiker folded its gangly legs under itself in a corner. Replete from our lunch we returned to the sitting room for a post-prandial Sunday afternoon.

'Lion or Castle?' asked Dave holding up a beer bottle in each hand.

We chose our drinks and settled down to while away a few hours.

'Do you think the duiker will survive without its mother?' I asked.

'We might have to bottle-feed it,' said Ross.

'But it's Sunday today, all the shops will be shut,' said Dave.

'I've got some rubber gloves,' said Sandra, 'we could put some milk into one finger, and make a hole in the bottom with a needle.'

We prepared the feeding glove, wondering if it should be sterilized. But the duiker wasn't interested in this arrangement, turning her head in disgust. Bits of lettuce, carrot, cucumber, leaves from the garden, and a variety of fruits were presented for delectation, and to each she turned up her shiny black nose. We had at least determined that 'it' was a female.

Finishing his beer Dave took out his next cigarette. He waved it in front of the duiker, who was sniffing around and exploring her new surroundings.

'Fancy a ciggy?' he joked.

The duiker sniffed, nibbled, then ate the entire cigarette. Next she found an ashtray lying on the coffee table, and demolished its contents, filter tips, ash, and all. Once over our amazement, we all roared with laughter.

'Well if you like that, how about a beer?' joked Dave.

A saucer was produced, Lion beer poured in, and the duiker duly lapped up every drop.

We returned to Chingola that evening to our usual welcome from our dogs Sheba and Blue. The journey proved better than the one to Kitwe without our new pet leaping at the driver again, as she'd tucked herself into the darkness behind my seat.

Having ensured that all escape routes were secure, we carried her into our sitting room and introduced her to the dogs and Sassi, the cat one at a time. After much mutual sniffing, they all settled down to a life together. Our house was not carpeted like the Rogers, so the poor duiker looked like Bambi on ice when I set her down on our red polished floor. Her little legs splayed this way and that as she desperately tried to get her footing. Taking pity on her we found an old blanket and after further sniffings, all four animals settled down on it together in a huddle.

We called her Dixie. It hadn't been long since Sheba's last puppy had been found a home, so she still had milk. Dixie sensed this and found a willing mother-substitute in our dog, so we could stop worrying about her initial diet of cigarettes and beer. A few days later a friend advised us that duikers need their mothers for another reason. To prevent predators from scenting their presence, duikers will only 'pooh' when it is safe to do so and predators wouldn't smell them. So duiker young will only 'perform' to their mother's command, and she does this by licking. Without her cue the poor babies can die of constipation. Advisors said we'd have to keep a soft paintbrush on hand to dip in warm water before administering to the duiker's bottom, but Sheba instinctively performed this service, so little piles of droppings soon appeared. We put up with the tiny messes for a short time until she could roam freely in the garden.

October brought dog days of heat and humidity. Bulbous grey clouds gathered, the air thickened, and murky skies dispersed into harmless cotton wool. The next day more clouds came, torpid air sucked away our energy, faraway flashes made threats and promises, and still the clouds wouldn't break.

'Everyone calls it suicide month,' said Chrissie when I complained of feeling homesick and sluggish. 'You've got the Chingola Blues, but it's only the weather. Things will improve when the first rains clear the air. Don't expect them until November though, and sometimes not until December, so you'll have to grin and bear it! It's such a relief when it finally rains that some people run out into their gardens and dance.' She was talking about Europeans, and the way I was feeling, I suspected I'd do the same.

Oppressive nights punctuated by the whine of mosquitoes thwarted refreshing sleep and at school I battled not to sink into lethargy. Fortunately my charges felt just like everyone else with no surplus energy for testing rules. I felt sorry for Ross working in the open pit where temperatures soared the deeper down he went, and dust brought its usual problems. The clubs did brisk business as Lions and Castles soothed parched throats and calmed fraught nerves.

Dixie got fatter, and looked less like Bambi now with sturdier legs. She joined the ritual greeting of animals when Ross drove the Hillman Hunter back through our front gate at the end of every day. Sassi held up his tail like a flag for Ross to follow with the car crawling regally down the drive and the dogs, who had been lounging in the shade, came alive with fierce barks at any unsuspecting African walking past. It was all noise and showing-off, but Dixie's performance was the best. Feeling drawn into the general festivity of welcome she did her bit with leaping circuits of the entire garden, before joining the rest of the menagerie to add her cold muzzle to the others as he opened the car door. Ross scratched each head in turn then walked round to the kitchen door followed by his animal escort.

Thunderous afternoons brought more sultriness and shorter tempers but the clouds refused to break. After a few false starts and rumbling skies without precipitation, the rains finally came. I resisted the urge to run outside and instead we stood side by side at the window mesmerised by a vertical downpour and full of silent wonder under the deafening timpani on our metal corrugated roof. A strong earthy smell pervaded the atmosphere and the world changed. New frustrations replaced outgrown ones. Every late afternoon would bring a fresh storm, but sometimes it happened later, after dark. Thunderclaps became gradually louder, like an approaching enemy assault, until one smack above us with a brilliant and terrifying lightning flash forced me to hunt for candles and matches, because the power had gone. Occasionally this meant a cold dinner.

Damp surroundings brought out insects. Flies not only pestered us, they bit the dogs' ears until they bled, fleas appeared crawling under fur, and ticks embedded themselves in flesh to gorge on blood until small red spidery shapes swelled into fat grey blobs. Mosquitoes were few and not malarial, because the mine employed an army of sprayers to regularly treat dustbins, storm drains, polluted water and houses. This last initiative involved an annual tying-up of curtains and taking down of pictures to allow a team to spray everywhere insects might hide. It was best to give the house a good airing afterwards to avoid damage to humans and animals from the strong-smelling chemicals. Citronella oil, a blander solution, helped to prevent ear-damage; fleas tended to rise to the surface if dogs were dunked in the bath; and ticks could be picked off if carefully rubbed with white spirit to loosen the insect's grip before pulling off.

'I knew someone who got 'Tick Fever' quite badly,' warned Chrissie. 'She didn't realise she'd been bitten, but suffered from headaches for months. Then her joints started aching and she was tired all the time. So she went to the doctor, who said it would be her heart and nervous system next. She had to go back home, and never fully recovered.'

It was now important to keep grass short, and to iron clothes more carefully to destroy any *putsi* fly eggs which could hatch from the clothes and burrow into adjacent skin as part of their cycle before maturing into a fly. Added to our efforts at avoiding muddy trails through the house, we had plenty of distractions.

Gastric flu struck and I lay in bed with a cold flannel on my head and a bowl at my side, too ill to take my classes. The pain suddenly worsened when Dixie leapt on top of me with four hard little hooves landing right where it already hurt. I think she was sympathising, but my reaction had her skittering on the polished floor as she ran for the door. Perhaps she'd planned to settle down with me like a cat.

When CBC's started to broadcast Christmas Carols again we returned from work one day to a lower count of our menagerie. Dixie had gone. With sinking hearts already missing her cold muzzle and circuits of welcome, we searched the garden for signs, but found nothing.

'I think she's destined for someone's Christmas dinner,' said Ross gloomily.

Her loss was the start of a downward turn in our lives.

CHAPTER ELEVEN

Opportunities and Changes

The sun will shine on those who stand before it shines on those who kneel under them.

AFRICAN PROVERB

In December on the anniversary of his starting work, Ross went for his personal assessment. At the end of it his boss asked,

'So what do you think about your last year here?'

'It's been really tough and a huge learning experience for me. To be honest I'd expected more than a book on Chikabanga and a stint at the driving school for training. When Anglo American recruited me they promised a 'conversion course' from mechanical engineering to mining engineering 'on the job,' and quite frankly I've had nothing. Things would have been a lot easier for me and better for the company as a result if I'd had some sort of instruction.'

As a result of this conversation NCCM made him an offer of sponsorship for Ross to attend the Royal School of Mines at Imperial College in London for the final two years of their mining degree. In return he would have to agree to sign another three-year contract. Ross accepted, and his contract was adjusted to send us back a year sooner than we'd expected. In preparation for his new degree he would spend six months before leaving in different sections of the underground mine.

Armed with a plan of the tunnel layout, Ross joined the queue to take his place in a vast open cage holding over three hundred men shoulder to shoulder. They all wore hard hats or *kampompo* of varying colours according to status, but his was the only white face. The metal gates clanged shut, a red light came on, and they shot downwards at double the speed of any lift he'd ever been in before, leaving his head light and his stomach churned. Mufulira still struggled to recover from its mud rush which had shocked the whole country shortly before our arrival in 1970, and the horror of it crept into every miner's mind before they could push it away to preserve sanity. At least most of them weren't bound for the really deep levels of the mine. Those poor souls who had died had been hundreds of feet deep, without a chance of survival under a million tons of slimes rushing down on them. The lowest levels would always carry the greatest risk from a breach in the tailings dam. It had taken weeks of the 'Proto' teams moving pumps from level to ever deeper level while clearing the slimes mud and searching for the eighty nine missing miners.

'A friend of mine in Mufulira told me that not everyone was accounted for after the disaster,' John had told us one evening at the rugby club, 'they said that some of the miners could have run for their lives, climbed the ladders from level to level until they reached the top, and kept running. They'd have been charged for not reporting back, if they'd been found out. The mines security is really strict on things like that, so they probably just disappeared rather than get into trouble.'

Scars on the rock-face looked like giant teeth marks as the vertical mine-shaft flashed past the men's peering faces and dim lights lit up trickles of water descending with them. The smell of sweat got stronger as the heat of Africa's earth swallowed them down, then a sudden jolt brought the cage to a halt, metal doors squealed open and they all trailed out into a cavernous, ventilated tunnel, stepping over train tracks and checking for *lo stima*, the train which could appear without warning round a bend. They dispersed to different sections and Ross found the next, smaller cage, which would take him deeper to narrower, lower passageways and some along which he'd have to double up, or even crawl. A few offices had been installed for 'shift bosses,' and were furnished with some files but also an electric stove, kettle and cups. They were much like the officers' rooms in the trenches. Grime around the teacup rims deterred Ross from accepting tea or coffee, but this was nothing compared to the filth of the communal toilets, whose stink sometimes contaminated the considerable length of a tunnel. The first day he took a packed lunch with him, but thereafter chose to go without food or drink until he returned home where he could enjoy his food in comfort and fresh air.

He progressed to shaft sinking, a deceptively simple title for one of the worst jobs underground. In previous days shaft sinkers earned the best pay for the risk and discomfort it brought. He joined Gordon's day shift team into the cages and they descended half a mile underground to an excavation the size of a house. Stepping over more train tracks they approached a simple wooden platform with a trap door. A large waist-high bucket four feet in diameter stood beside it attached by wire which was wound around a winch. Three of the Africans went straight to the bucket and climbed in and then to Ross's dismay Gordon joined them.

'Come on then,' said the shift boss when he saw his hesitation, and waving him in.

Ross had recently had news of a college friend who took a job in a South African gold mine. Malcolm became trapped in a deep tunnel by a collapsed wall which was dense enough to block off ventilation. He died before the rescue team managed to dig him out, and never saw his twenty-fifth birthday or his baby son his new wife delivered five months later. Ross took a deep breath, did his best to clear his mind and stepped into the bucket.

Two Africans heaved open the trap door to release a steady loud but distant roar emanating from the three-hundred foot dark and unlit hole they were about to enter. A damp metallic smell rose up. The shaft had been excavated into a large rectangle in preparation for future large cages which would be bringing future teams and equipment down to extract the 'red gold.' It was vital that its dimensions and angle of drop should be exact.

At a nod from Gordon the winch operator hoisted the bucket a few inches in the air and it started to swing despite the efforts of two assisting workers to hold it steady. Then they manoeuvred it over the void and slowly the bucket with its five passengers began to drop.

'Turn round!' shouted Gordon over the upcoming roar. 'You must keep an eye on the shaft walls for anything that looks loose. You don't want a rock to be falling a few hundred feet while you're down there.'

So in the blackness Ross trained the faint light from his cap-lamp onto the rock face with as much concentration as he could muster in this bleak foreign environment.

'Keep your hands and arms inside the bucket,' shouted Gordon, 'sometimes it sways so much it hits the side-wall especially as we get lower down.'

The bucket revolved and lurched its way down while the roar got louder and more distinct.

'How do the people below know we are coming?' asked Ross. 'And how does the winch driver know when we're reaching the bottom?'

Gordon couldn't hear him, so he never got an answer. He seized Ross's head, pressed his thumbs hard into the back of one of his ears and yelled, 'this is the only way to be heard down here!'

At the base of the shaft work had already commenced with a section-boss supervising eight men whose jack-hammer drills bounced in the drill holes. Ear defenders and goggles lay unclaimed in the store room at the surface, eschewed by men who thought they were for wimps. Boots and *kompompos* were accepted but even overalls were sometimes abandoned to work more comfortably naked under hot humid conditions. The walls of the shaft felt hot to touch having travelled so far down the thermal gradient closer to the magma inside the earth's crust. Ross half expected molten rock to spout out through one of the drill holes. He helped Gordon to monitor it all and they constantly took measurements to ensure the shaft kept the correct dimensions and angles. The safety of future miners depended on it. They charged the drill holes with explosives and returned in the bucket in relays through the trap door, with all machinery removed with them. Compressed air, ventilation and water pipes had to be raised out of the way of the fly-rock thrown by the blast at the end of their shift.

Before the following afternoon shift could go down to 'lash' or clear the broken rocks, the ventilation system had to extract all the poisonous nitrous fumes given off by the explosives. Then the same bucket went up loaded with blasted stone and came down empty until its last journey took the men back to the surface.

'You don't want to overfill the bucket,' explained Gordon later, 'or there's a danger of rocks falling down on top of you.'

By the time the last rail car had carried away the last of the rocks, night shift had arrived with their jack-hammers to make sure the shaft still conformed to the right dimensions and angle to the earth.

'So how did you enjoy your first day on shaft-sinking then?' asked Gordon slapping Ross on the back at the end of their shift. 'Let's get cleaned up and go for a beer to get some fluid back into our systems.'

At the Mine Club they'd started their second bottle of beer before starting to talk. Ross could hardly think for throbbing in his head and ringing in his ears. The first had been drunk in near silence, rinsing away the ordeal of heat and noise.

'How does the winch driver know when we're nearing the bottom?' Ross repeated the question which had been drowned out by noise earlier.

'Well he ties a rag around the hoist rope, and moves it each day as the shaft deepens. It's simple but effective.'

'And how do the people below know when to expect us being lowered on top of them?'

'They just do,' replied Gordon. He didn't want to talk about work any more. 'I don't suppose you knew Tom Blyth did you?' asked Gordon, 'Now he was a great shaft sinker. It must have been his Geordie roots.'

'Was he the one I heard about, who ended up in prison?'

'Aye, that's the one. Tom was the best man you could have on your team. Utterly dependable he was, but as rough as they come. He used to go into the compound for drinking sprees with one of his team. The trouble was he had a big mouth, and it got bigger with a skinful of drink inside him. Single of course, no woman would put up with him.' Gordon stopped to look thoughtfully into his beer, 'He'd been here since before Independence, so for years got away with it. He could bring in a fortune on the 'Copper Bonus' of the old days. His mate, Mwange I think he was called, dragged him away from more than a few difficult situations out there. It was just a matter of time really, and a year ago he got into a dispute with someone in a *shebeen*, and started mouthing off about the President. Big mistake! The police were called and there was no shortage of witnesses, some of whom remembered past grievances. The company got him good legal support, but he'd tied the noose around his own neck, so to speak.' He paused for his next drink, 'I went to visit him after they'd moved him down to Lusaka. Horrible place it was, and filthy. He was never big, but he'd been a strong man, you know, played a mean game of footie when he wasn't pissed. But he'd become stick-thin, and gaunt like an old man, it was pathetic to see that happen to a man in his thirties. He told me they'd formed a queue for him on his first night in prison to savour the thrill of power over a white man, and since then it hadn't got much better.'

'My God!' whispered Ross.

Underground Planning was an easier experience, being on the surface. Here he made a good friend of John, a South African who took him under his wing and entertained him with his dry sense of humour.

'Let me show you my collection of local newspaper cuttings,' he announced one day bringing out a scrap book from his office drawer. "Zambian Space Programme" announced one headline. In the mid-1960s a man called Nkoloso had planned to launch a rocket that would send twelve astronauts and some cats to Mars. He produced a passable design for a rocket, and confidently declared his intention to beat the United States and Soviet Union's respective space programs at the height of the Space Race. To train the astronauts, Nkoloso set up a makeshift facility in an abandoned farmhouse near Lusaka where the trainees, dressed in overalls and army helmets, took turns to climb into a 44 gallon oil drum which would be rolled down a hill bouncing over rough ground. It was also strung from a tree, and allowed to drop into water. These training exercises, according to Nkoloso, were designed to simulate weightlessness in space, spinning as the space craft re-entered the earth's orbit, and splashdown. Having requested a £7,000,000 grant from UNESCO for his space program, he had specifically instructed the missionary on board not to force Christianity onto the native Martian inhabitants if they didn't want it. He hoped that the rocket, an aluminium and copper vessel, would launch from the Independence Stadium on Independence Day, 1964. Nkoloso's space program never took off the ground, particularly because of the lack of grants and the fact that the 17-year-old 'spacegirl' who was to ride on the mission, had become pregnant. John gave a wry smile as Ross read 'the Zambian government has distanced itself from Nkoloso's endeavour.'

John's sense of humour would later get him into serious trouble.

CHAPTER TWELVE

Accused

Africa is a cruel country; it takes your heart and grinds it into powdered stone – and no one minds.

ELSPETH HUXLEY

One of the worst things you can do in an African country with a government of a different colour to your own is to end up in prison. Ross managed to do that a few months before our return to UK, albeit for the noblest of reasons.

It started when a newly arrived fitter moved into the house next door with his wife and two children. We'd got on well with chatty and charming Grace, our previous neighbour and were sorry to see them return to South Africa, her homeland.

'The education in South Africa is much better than here,' Grace said, 'not just for white people but for us too. My boys are not doing well here, and keep getting into trouble,' she added with a frown.

Although a Zambian, her husband must have managed to get a job there in one of the many mines, and their living conditions would not be the same. They certainly wouldn't have white neighbours, although we would come to see that as a distinct advantage. Like everyone else they sold up before leaving so their fence at the front and opposite side to our garden was detached from its fixings, rolled up, and removed to leave the property open.

We did the friendly neighbour thing when the Withenshawes arrived fresh from England, offering cups of tea and cold drinks and advice and playing with their children and generally trying to help. Pearl didn't seem to match her skinny mumbling husband, as she had a model's figure with long dark hair and exuded confidence.

'I've just lost three stone,' she confided, 'I had a medical problem so had to follow a strict diet, and here I am! I used to be quite shy.'

We invited them to come and share a coffee. I forgave her teenage reaction to a flying praying mantis, but struggled when her silly arm-flailing knocked over two of our wedding-present Suzy Cooper cups which broke on the floor, and muttered, 'they're harmless if you just leave them alone.'

We must have overdone the camaraderie because they started to take liberties. Enjoying a Sunday lie-in after Ross's late shift, when he hadn't come home until midnight the night before, their kids woke us at six the next morning, banging on our bedroom window and wanting to be entertained.

'Oh, we sent them round to yours so that we could enjoy a lie-in!' Pearl laughed when I mentioned it.

The next annoyance came in the shape of their pet monkey, a leaping, darting, unpredictable Vervet with malicious eyes. Sensing my dislike he would land on my head when we visited during our period of trying to be neighbourly. I felt sorry for their houseboy having to clear up the mess. Luckily the monkey wasn't allowed out and could be avoided when our initial 'friendship' cooled. Then they found the guard-dog of their dreams in a fully-grown Doberman before they'd got round to installing a fence. Dobermans are notorious for their short tempers and unpredictability, and this one's owners had rejected it as being impossible to train. As with the monkey they couldn't control it, but booted it out of the house to roam freely outside, unhindered by gates or fences. Our cheery milkman with his bell and cart of pyramid-shaped milk cartons soon learned to give a wide berth to our stretch of 11th Street, which added to my shopping burden.

Sheba and Satan's mutual hate was immediate, and they kicked up a dust-cloud along the dividing fence Ross had erected, jabbing their heads at each other with bared teeth while making an unholy row. Unable to bite through the wire, their barks and growls still filled me with alarm at what might happen should Satan get into our garden.

We tolerated their inadequacies as best we could and excused them as teething problems. Neighbours were neighbours and we tried to make allowances.

'Does anyone know of a family looking for a kitten?' Gwen had asked one day in the school staff room. So I became instrumental in getting their third pet. By this time the novelty of owning a monkey had worn off and they returned him to the SPCA to rehome. A kitten would have less objectionable habits, be more hygienic and a great deal less trouble, what with food theft, being forced to use nappies because of unsatisfactory toilet training and general disruption in the house. I offered to take Pearl and the children to see the litter and make their selection. The children ignored simple pleasantries offered by Gwen, wandered off to look in other rooms, and picked up her ornaments to inspect, without a word of control from Pearl. Gwen bristled, and encouraging a swift choice of kitten I got them out of the house before it became a bigger problem. My friendship with the Withenshawes cooled another few degrees.

Ross was working night shifts on the day it happened, so after a morning's sleep had free time at home in the afternoon. Eve, a frail-looking New Yorker who had delivered her son prematurely, parked her car on the road and carried her tiny charge newly released from an incubator towards the house opposite ours. She had been attending antenatal classes with Barbara, our neighbour opposite, and had come to visit. Barbara's very pregnant belly appeared at the back door first, and she walked down the drive to meet her friend. Stanley, their mastiff mongrel followed her. Within seconds Satan bounded up the road to attack Stanley. They collided with bared teeth and locked into hateful battle alongside Eve, pinning her to the fence. The racket alerted Ross who came out to see what was going on. By then both dogs had dug their teeth into each other's pelts, Barbara was screaming at Stanley and Eve cowered protectively over her new-born, unable to pass the growling, snarling scrimmage of dogs. Ross and Barbara tried to grab their collars without success since both dogs appeared intent on murder, and Barbara went back to her kitchen for a bucket of water. Now soaking wet they paused to have a good shake for a few seconds and then resumed hostilities. Barbara took her bucket back to the house and returned with Barry's air pistol which she handed to Ross. We all stood back. Pearl approached as the first shots were fired into the furious scramble of dog fur and teeth. Sheba patrolled our front fence adding her voice to the riotous racket, but it was Pearl's voice that rose above the whole hellish orchestra, screaming at Ross.

'What the hell are you doing shooting at my dog! How dare you attack him. I'll get the police on to you!' her face twisted with fury.

Both dogs seemed impervious to the few aluminium pellets fired at them, so Barbara returned to her kitchen and brought back a small drum of pepper. Ross took it off her, and with careful aim at a moving target, sprinkled the contents over the dogs' heads. Within seconds they'd released their grip on each other, and amidst convulsive sneezes allowed themselves to be separated. Eve crept away to safety with her baby, but Pearl kept up her rant, screaming at Ross and threatening him with the police. Stanley gave a last growl of hatred as Barbara dragged him back to the house, and relative peace was restored apart from our manic neighbour. Ashen-faced Eve followed Barbara with her wide-eyed infant. With Stanley off the scene Pearl let go of Satan's collar allowing him to roam in the road once more, free to attack at will while she gave all her energies to a foul-mouthed attack on Ross, deaf to any reason or explanation.

'It wasn't just *your* dog,' said Ross trying to be reasonable, 'the two of them were a danger to themselves and everyone around them. You saw it yourself, they would have killed each other. Anyway it's only an airgun!'

'You haven't heard the last of this!' echoed her departing words.

Ross shrugged and came indoors, 'It's an airgun. You don't need a license to use it, and anyway I was protecting a pregnant woman and another with a new-born baby. She's just an ignorant bitch!'

Due to return home for Ross to start at Imperial College, we busied ourselves with moving away from our house in 11th Street. It didn't take long to pack souvenirs and a few treasures into one small packing-case which would be shipped home to UK. The rest we sold or gave away, including all fencing, and gates which left the Withenshawes even less protection around the perimeter of their property. Preparations for our imminent departure helped to take my mind off the recent brush with our neighbours.

Rather than eking out our last weeks in an echoing empty house, we'd found a 'leave house.' Rick and Carol were returning to UK for their end of contract leave. Having completed three-years and signed up for another contract, they would enjoy three months paid leave, and we could move into their house while making our own preparations to leave. So with regret we handed Sheba over to Dave and Sandra in Kitwe, and found a new home for Sassi, since the house came complete with our friends' resident cat and three dogs. Everything else was put up for sale, including our Hillman Hunter, the golden car which had carried us 12,000 miles across the Sahara and much of Africa. Our temporary new home would come with the use of an MG soft-top sports car, and in London we'd have to rely on public transport.

We waved goodbye to Rick and Carol, and settled into our new surroundings in Kabundi.

'The police have been looking for you,' Barry our neighbour in 11th Street warned Ross one Saturday afternoon over a game of squash.

We put it out of our minds, but two weeks later as I was clearing the table of debris from a Sunday lunch with our friends Dave and Sandra and their daughters they found us. Someone was knocking on the front door, a rare event since most visitors came to the kitchen entrance. Two policemen stood on the doorstep with one of them brandishing a piece of paper. Pearl had reported the incident and they were looking for Ross who found himself accused of firing a revolver at her dog. A short discussion ensued with Ross protesting his innocence and explaining it was an air pistol and not a revolver. They looked sympathetic but had to carry out their orders to take him to the police station for a statement, hence the piece of paper. He could argue about the type of weapon at the police station. He set off with them and took Dave for moral support. Forms were completed and fingerprints taken. The minutes ticked by and Dave got bored as he waited outside the interview room, thinking about the glass of beer he could have been enjoying that Sunday afternoon. Two policemen were talking nearby, bemoaning the theft of one of their bicycles, which he called a *jinga*. One of them looked at Dave and asked

'Why is the bwana here?'

Full of mischief fuelled by boredom, Dave replied, 'I think he stole your *jinga*.'

The resulting outrage and confusion caused by this ruse kept him entertained until Ross reappeared.

'Are you willing to act as my bail bondsman,' Ross asked Dave after he'd emerged from the interview room.

'You must realise the importance of this,' said the policeman, 'you will have to pay money if Mr Dunn disappears.'

'That's okay,' said Dave, 'I've given you a false name and address.'

The policemen looked at him unsure of what to believe, in spite of Dave going back on his joke and admitting the truth to all concerned. His brand of Scottish humour confused most foreigners, and was risky with Zambians but somehow he always got away with it.

They both returned home fuelled by enough intrigue to keep conversations and conjecture going for weeks.

We rose early as colour seeped into the sky with streaks of pink and mauve. Within minutes the crepuscular spell vanished, replaced by harsh outlines against grey which gave foreboding for our day, but we didn't take notice. Soon brightness came shining through the jacaranda branches with a mango-coloured sunrise and the sky assumed a deepening blue to dispel that warning grey until dusk. Morning sounds heralded the day. Barking dogs let us know others were up to release their pets for fence patrol, a squalling cat fight played out in a distant garden, and our kitchen door banged to announce the houseboy's arrival. Soon his singing voice accompanied the squishing of the previous day's dirty clothes in soapy water. I held the gate open as Ross reversed out of the drive, and we set off for the High School.

True to her word, we hadn't heard the last of the dog-fight fracas, and Pearl had arranged for Ross to receive a court summons for that day. He'd retrieved his rarely-worn suit from the wardrobe for the occasion and selected a suitably sober tie. He pulled at the unfamiliar tightness around his neck.

'Do you want me to come with you?' I'd asked, prepared to ask for the morning off work.

'Reading out the charge won't take long. It'll probably be dismissed straight away,' Ross had replied. 'Most of the time will probably be taken hanging around waiting for other cases to be heard. You know the sort of thing, attempted murder and the like. Remember the other cases when we went to Daud's trial?'

He laughed at the triviality of shooting aluminium pellets at fighting dogs with an air-gun compared to a wronged wife attacking her errant husband and his mistress with an axe. She had been let off with a warning.

Half-way through the second lesson of my morning, the school secretary came into my classroom.

'There's a phone call for you, you can take it in the office.'

'Can it wait until break-time and I'll ring them back?' I asked, wondering who might be phoning me at school and not wanting to leave my class unattended.

'I think you should come now, it's the clerk of the court. A Mr Mwangu. He says he knows you. I'll stay with your class until you come back.'

Annoyed at the inconvenience rather than worried, I hurried to the office and lifted the heavy black receiver.

'Mrs Dunn? Good morning. This is Boniface Mwangu here. We met a few months ago at the court in Chingola when you had some items stolen. Do you remember me?'

'Oh yes, good morning,' I replied trying to work out the implications of such a phone call.

'Your husband was in court today. You must go to Chingola prison now with his passport and 100 kwachas to bail him out.'

Bail... Prison. These words could not be a part of our lives. And he'd need his passport for going back to UK. He kept talking and explaining but I heard nothing. My mind was trying to make sense of what I had to do. I had already asked him to repeat the message twice, and couldn't keep asking. He was telling me to get this large sum of money to the prison whose whereabouts was unknown to me. But classes would keep me busy until lunch-time, and then I was on duty for prep supervision. I wouldn't be free to walk home, get to the bank before it closed, and find the prison to hand over the bail until late afternoon at best. Nor could I remove myself from the responsibility to my class. A roomful of shiny faces looked up from their sewing as I returned to the room. Luckily there were no classroom crises because although I was bodily present my mind was elsewhere churning over my new dilemma.

The bell for break sounded, staff converged in the staff room for coffee and I found Gwen, blurting out my news.

'We'll have to get you down there straight away,' she took charge of the situation. 'I have a free period and can take you now. Which is your bank?'

'The Standard,' I replied, dazed and indecisive. 'What about my classes?'

'Someone else will deal with that, this is an emergency. Get your things together, I'll go and speak to the head. Oh, and we need to find out the whereabouts of the prison.'

Doing as she said, I fumbled around still agitated, but grateful for Gwen taking over. An hour later we parked in a dusty clearing beside a twelve foot concrete wall topped with rolls of razor wire.

Still depending on Gwen to steer my every action, I waited. The bail money was in my handbag.

'I'll stay here while you go in,' she said, her voice calm and steady.

I peeled the back of my dress from the car seat, and stepped on to the dust to approach a seven-foot high metal door. A lever at the side of the door seemed to be for a bell and I pulled it. A clang rang clear, but no one came. I could feel the back of my dress falling loose as the sun dried it. Eventually I heard a grating noise.

'You must wait here,' said the warder, taking my envelope of banknotes through the opened hatch and scraping it closed without further explanation, acknowledgement or a receipt for enough cash to pay all of our bills for a month.

'How long…?' I'd started to ask.

I felt as locked out as Ross must be feeling locked in. *Did he catch the name?* A turmoil of thoughts pursued me, and none of them logical. The chances of anyone else of our colour being the other side of the wall were slim and a name would be superfluous. Trees had been cleared from the area and Gwen and I found no shade as time moved up to the end of the school's morning session. We'd tried to be patient for over an hour. Gwen stayed in the driving seat writing lesson notes on a loose-leaf file propped up on the steering wheel. She'd flung open her door to encourage a flow of air, and I was grateful to her for giving up her free period. Dust clung to the sweat on my feet, my head felt hot and my mouth was dry as I alternated between pacing alongside the prison wall and sitting on the sticky car seat. Listening for encouraging noises coming from the other side of the wall kept me on full alert. We hadn't thought to bring water and had no idea of how much longer we'd have to wait.

The sound of a commanding voice and footsteps came from the other side of the door followed by a heavy lock being turned and the door creaked open. Inside I got an impression of an open quadrangle of swept earth surrounded by cells and offices around the internal walls of the jail. A heavy-set man with important stripes on his sleeve glowered at me, and gave my husband permission to leave. A suit and tie usually gave Ross a smart authoritative appearance, but this person in front of me was crumpled, drawn and grey in the midday heat.

'Thanks for coming,' he snarled through clenched teeth. 'I couldn't have taken much more of that without killing someone. How did you know I was here? They wouldn't let me make any phone calls.'

There was so much to discuss, to try to make some sense out of the situation, but we held back. Ross could hardly speak he trembled so much with fury and frustration, and hadn't had a drink since breakfast six hours previously.

Gwen drove us to the court where Ross had parked the car, and returned to Chikola leaving me with my angry husband. I still had no driving license, so Ross took the wheel and looking murderous, hurled us along the streets. A group of women ambled across our path and I feared for their safety as the car accelerated up to them before stopping abruptly and allowing them to pass with anxious sideways glances.

'Bloody *umfazis*!' he shouted, seething with rage.

He never behaved like this. I clutched the car seat and pushed out my feet on imaginary brakes. He revved the engine and propelled us towards our house on 11th Street. Ignoring the customary welcome from the dogs at the gate, he charged into the house to change into shorts and tee shirt. He'd always hated wearing a suit. Neither of us had the appetite for lunch, so we drank orange squash and then switched to coffee and cigarettes as he related the morning's events.

'I could have mown all those women down, you know,' he confessed, 'I could happily have murdered the lot of them, I was so angry!' He took a drag of his cigarette.

His was the third case to be heard by a 'Cape Coloured' magistrate called Badenhorst. The first case was straight-forward larceny and the second bodily assault where one man had knifed another in a *shebeen* after they had both drunk too much *chibuku*, the local brew. The victim lost an eye in the incident. Sentences were minimal and Ross felt confident. He entered the dock to be sworn in, and instantly the magistrate's humane tone changed to one of attack. After the charge was read out Badenhorst launched into a diatribe on how men like Ross were a scourge on the country; how cruelty to animals was a most serious offence; and how his crime could carry a six-month sentence. This would be decided at the next hearing. He sent Ross to prison pending his 100 kwacha bail, and on enquiring about a phone call they said, 'you can make one from the prison.' The clerk of the court watched him being handcuffed to the next prisoner, and without saying anything went into an office to telephone me. Then the string of prisoners were herded into the back of a van, and transported to Chingola prison. A motley bunch of Africans sat on benches either side of the van in a rag-bag of shirts and trousers in various states of disrepair and cleanliness, and among them Ross in his only suit and tie, the one he wore for interviews. Each was handcuffed to his neighbour and all their shoes removed to reduce the likelihood of them bolting en masse.

They stood in line, shoes in hand, in front of the governor, waiting for admission procedures. A truncheon-wielding warder kept the line straight. A clerk had made detailed records of each prisoner's possessions, including the condition of clothing which involved counting holes in shirts and trousers, and any fraying at necklines or cuffs was noted.

'Are you wearing underpants?' the official asked Ross after noting his suit, shirt, tie, socks, shoes and pocket-contents.

'Yes.'

'How many holes?'

'Only those that are meant to be there!'

He diligently noted the state of his underpants as part of the record along with everything else. 'Now you will go and stand over there.' He cuffed Ross's hands behind his back and pointed to a spot in the enclosed quadrangle with no shelter from the sun. Ross couldn't get the story of Tom Blyth out of his head.

'I'd like to make my phone call now,' said Ross, his mouth dry.

'No phone calls,' barked the warden.

The others had been allowed to wander on to benches in the shade, their hands now free, to enjoy long conversations with their friends, new and old.

His written record complete, the official paced the area making a full circuit every five or six minutes, and every time he passed Ross he shouted, 'STAND STRAIGHT WHITE MAN!' with a smack of his truncheon against my husband's stomach. Unaware of the phone call I'd received he thought he'd be spending the night in that place, feeling isolated, victimised and powerless in a hopeless situation. Several hours of this before my arrival had put him into an incandescent fury, which didn't subside until days after the event.

It was the talk of the town. The pros and cons, the possible outcomes, the ways it should or could be handled were discussed between us, with all our friends, and every trusted acquaintance. The weight we'd gained since our arrival began to fall off again and we found ourselves at the cigarette counter in CBC's more often than before. A satisfying diversion came with thinking up endless possibilities for revenge on our neighbours. One evening after rugby practice Kurt sidled up to Ross at the Rampant Lion bar, his favourite watering hole. He enjoyed nothing more than creating a stir, and was famed for putting a live crocodile he'd caught in the Kafue on the top of the bar. The poor creature was small, and terrified at the resulting pandemonium and screaming women, had done its best to escape. Kurt had revelled in the chaos.

'I've got a good suggestion for you,' he grinned.

'Oh yes?' asked Ross

'We sometimes use it in the bush. It's very effective, and doesn't involve poison as such…'

'What are you talking about Kurt?'

'Retaliation of course! You're not going to take all this shit without a bit of revenge are you?'

'Okay, tell me your suggestion then,'

'Right, well listen, all you need is a tin of sardines.'

'Sardines?' laughed Ross, 'you've got to be joking.

'No, listen man. You have to open the tin, it should be the one with oil in, and leave it out in the sun for at least three days where your own dogs can't get at it.'

'Oh yes, and then what?'

'You leave it somewhere your neighbour's dog can reach it, and just wait. Once the dog eats it he'll soon be in agony, and death won't be long after.'

'Is a properly fed dog seriously going to eat something that's been left out in the sun for three days?'

'Well that's the thing, man, he will!'

'Yeah, yeah, yeah…' said Ross, and walked away.

A surprise phone call told me Alison, my college friend, was in town. She came to the house when Ross was at work. Over cold drinks and biscuits which I'd checked and tapped carefully to knock out any weevils, I poured out our troubles.

Over our second drinks she confided in bursts, 'I'm worried too. It's about a situation at work. It involves the headmaster.'

I expected her to say he'd been making advances, but then she went on,

'At first he was sending boys to me for their trousers to be mended. I thought this was odd, but reasoned that this was Africa and they might not have sewing materials at home, so just did it for them. Then I discovered one locked in the needlework cupboard without his trousers. He was terrified, and muttered something about uniform and the headmaster. The cupboard is right next to the headmaster's office, and he has a key. The second time this happened I spoke to another member of staff, and she said, "Oh, not that business again! Leave it with me and I'll have a word." So it hasn't happened again, but it bothers me.'

'What is the headmaster like?' I asked

'Well that's the thing. I took him to be a family man because he's married with four children. They live next to the school. But there's something really camp about him. There was an evening 'do' for the staff last term, and he turned up with his shirt ends tied together at his midriff, and hipster trousers.'

I made a face, 'you said you left it with another teacher,'

'Yes, but I feel it ought to be reported to someone higher up.'

'I wouldn't know who that would be, do you?'

'Not a clue.'

We chewed the problem over and came to the conclusion that she could only keep an eye on things, because to date Alison had no proof of any wrong-doing. Zambia was a country of opportunity for people with the right qualifications, but some saw other opportunities which weren't always to do with money.

We still had to live with our nightmare after everyone else had tired of it, and Gordon's story about Tom Blyth rotting away in a Lusaka prison made it worse. We had been catapulted into an intractable situation and until the trial, which was likely to be with the same magistrate, we would have no peace. The rains were drawing to a close and increasingly clear blue skies mocked our misery. At night I lay awake picking at old mosquito bite scabs and mulling over the consequences of a simple dog fight. The next morning I'd wake up groggy to face a day's teaching.

'Why have you become thin, Meessus Dunn?' asked one of my older and bolder pupils. To have any claim on beauty, women in Africa should be fat.

It was true. Our waistbands hung loose, and our hair smelt of smoke. We didn't dare entertain the possibility of us not being able to leave, although Ross would not get his passport back until after the trial. Before all this could happen there seemed a mountain to climb. One of Ross's seniors took him aside at work to offer advice on the slowly advancing court case.

'Your only way out of this mess is to eat humble pie and apologise,' stated Mike. 'Justice is not the issue here you see. It's getting you off the hook that's important.'

'Never!' said Ross. 'Apologise to that stupid bitch? Over my dead body! I won't do it. Why should I apologise when I've done nothing wrong? It wasn't even my gun. I won't do it, it's not negotiable!'

'I know it's not palatable, and you feel unfairly treated, but it's a lot better than any alternative. You should also offer to buy her off. I reckon fifty kwacha should do it. Sometimes you just have to swallow your pride and do what needs to be done to reach a satisfactory conclusion,' insisted Mike, 'you've already had a taste of the local prison. Can you imagine how much worse it would be overnight, let alone for several months?'

'I can't say sorry to that cow! She's the one who should be begging for my forgiveness.'

A discussion continued in this vein for hours until eventually and reluctantly Ross came round and agreed to 'eat humble pie.' The alternative of risking a prison sentence was unthinkable. The tale of Tom Blyth still haunted his thoughts.

'Would you like me to come with you for moral support?' I suggested, but he wanted to do it alone. Seeing no other feasible way out of his problem, the following day Ross took a deep breath and prepared to proffer his apology, offering to 'buy her off.' He paced weary steps up their unkempt drive while I stayed in the car. Satan lurched out to sniff at our wheels and I scrutinised the windows for evidence of trouble, half expecting an explosion of conflict to burst through the burglar bars.

He trudged back up the drive as I waited, anxious for news,

'She accepted and asked for 100 kwacha donation to the SPCA,' he sighed, going into the house to slump into an armchair. 'She's going to drop all charges once the money has been handed over. I think the magistrate is the treasurer. I think I need a beer.'

Pearl and Badenhorst were both active members of the SPCA, and she'd obviously garnered his support with her version of the incident, starting with Ross's alleged use of a revolver. We were powerless to fight his obvious abuse of power.

The police station still held Ross's passport, and it would not be returned until after the court case, which still had to go ahead. He couldn't leave the country without it, and we lived in constant dread of Badenhorst turning on Ross again and things going badly in spite of charges being dropped. Weeks rolled on. A friend whose brother was a barrister in

Lusaka offered to help out, and we agreed to meet in Ndola, this being half way between Chingola and the capital.

'This is a joke, isn't it?' was Nigel's reaction.

'You don't understand, Nigel. This magistrate is coloured, a half-caste from South Africa and seems to have a big chip on his shoulder. He's already threatened me with a six months jail sentence!'

Ross gave him all the details, and explained about Badenhorst having a reputation for being anti-white. Nigel nodded and then shook his head in disbelief. He asked for details of points of law, what the actual charge had been and began to understand the problem.

'This should never have been brought to court in the first place. It's ridiculous! I'm afraid I can't guarantee a satisfactory outcome, after what you've told me, but I'll do what I can. The problem is that in spite of her dropping charges, the police could still uphold the charge.

The day of the court case finally dawned. The charge was read out, and after various legal statements were uttered, incomprehensible to our ears, Nigel whispered to Ross that it had been dropped, and he passed the message along to me. Like Chinese whispers I couldn't quite believe I'd received the true message. Out of the court room relief started to flood through us. Weeks of tension fell away. The following day Ross went to collect his passport and returned whistling, as I hadn't heard him do for months. At last we could start to look forward to a leisurely return home, and to what we saw as 'a cruise' on the SA Vaal from Cape Town to Southampton. Nearly two years previously I'd longed for this trip to prepare us for our new life in Africa, and now it would become reality but going in the opposite direction. Life without the threat of prison looming above us resumed, but we yearned to escape to a gentler land where blackbirds sang at dawn, a complete shopping list could be found in the supermarket, and justice was predictable. With a longing to swap the advantages of an idyllic climate and lifestyle for 'going home' I looked forward to cold dark mornings with stubborn contrariness and counted the days to our departure.

CHAPTER THIRTEEN

Heading Home

No man can know where he is going unless he knows exactly where he has been and exactly how he arrived at his present place.

MAYA ANGELOU

The court case over, we prepared to leave for London ready for Ross to start at the Royal School of Mines in October. Escape from trouble and responsibility couldn't have come at a better time, and unlike all previous study he looked forward to a mining degree along with the cushion of sponsorship. With a maternal grandfather who had mined Northumberland coal it must have been in his blood.

'You don't want to get yourself involved in mining, Ross,' his grandmother had warned. She remembered too well the toil, grime, disasters and associated heartbreak of a miner's life, 'and surrounded by all those darkies! I'm sure you could find a better job, a nice clean safe job in this country!'

'It's all right, Grandma, I'll be working in the open pit, not underground, and the pay's a lot better than it was in Grandad's day! And we have a great life out in Zambia.' Ross assured her, but she wasn't happy.

Already installed in our 'leave house' in Kabundi, the time had come to part with our Hillman Hunter. Like a trusty workhorse it slipped away with its new owner to live the rest of its days on Zambian roads. Feeling like Judas we swapped it for pieces of silver. Mr Bwalya bought it at a price reflecting its condition.

'We drove the car down from Europe across the Sahara,' Ross explained, 'so although it's only two years old, it's had a lot of repairs.'

Mr Bwalya's face lit up, and he asked for a list of all the countries the car had crossed. We'd never thought its traumatic history would be a selling point. We watched our 'golden dream' being driven away from our temporary drive like conspirators in an abduction. It had carried us through so much.

In compensation, Rick and Carol had left us the use of their MG Midget, a soft-topped, low-slung green sports car, and Ross had access some days to a work Land Rover. Enjoying the sensation of driving close to the ground, he had discovered a back road down towards the mine and he coursed along in the cool autumn air under an immaculate dry-season sky. Sitting in a bucket seat with the dusty bush flashing past changed the perspective of his usual view from a Land Rover windscreen, and his mind wandered to the next episode in his life in the UK, back to carefree days as a student. The prospect of imminent release from work accountability felt good.

'Homeward bound…' he hollered, and the Simon and Garfunkel song rang into scrubby bushes on either side of him as he cruised along. Sunshine warmed his head, 'Home where my thought's escaping…' He swung left downhill towards the compound, and stopped just in time to avoid hitting a policeman who appeared to step straight out of the bush. Another officer emerged, his khaki uniform a good camouflage, and they held their rifles menacingly over the little car. One circled the vehicle apparently searching for faults, while the other looked accusingly at the driver.

'Good afternoon, officer,' Ross put on his most engaging smile, trying to diffuse any trouble at the outset. He'd just reclaimed his passport and he didn't want to lose it again with more trouble.

'Sah, you did not stop at the stop sign!' Declared the policeman in a loud commanding voice. He took out his notebook.

Ross looked around the lonely dirt road and saw only bush. 'Oh, I'm sorry, officer. I didn't see it.'

'No sah, you would not see eet because the stop sign, eet was stolen three days ago.'

'Well that's why I didn't see it,' quipped Ross, trying to control the grin creeping over his face.

'But still you should have stopped because eet ees a junction.'

The 'junction' was with a narrow dirt passage little wider than a bicycle track which joined the main road at the bend he'd just passed.

'If I'd seen a stop sign I assure you I would have stopped,' Ross bristled, his expression morphing to serious.

The policeman hesitated over this logic but wanted to regain the upper hand, 'You should have known about the sign and stopped, sah.'

'But this is the first time I've used this road, officer,' he replied, trying to be reasonable.

'That does not matter. You should have stopped. Show me your license.'

Ross groped in his back pocket for his wallet, and handed over the green document. His patience was ebbing away and the memory of another man in uniform abusing his power with a truncheon rekindled in him the feeling of grievance he'd had when let out of prison. His blood simmered.

The policeman noted the details along with the car's registration number and returned the license.

'Thees ees an offence and you can be charged' he said replacing the notebook in his pocket. Ross studied them both standing over him. He got out of the car and stood as tall as he could. He'd often been stopped at police road blocks on the busy Kitwe Road or even the Kabundi Road, but never on a dirt track. Something about their arrogance made him suspicious.

'I can't be charged for not stopping at a sign that isn't there!' He insisted between clenched teeth.

Doubt showed in the policeman's face, but his colleague pushed himself forward, his brows lowered in anger at this challenge to their authority,

'We can charge you because eet ees an offence!' He shouted, 'we have your details and you will be hearing from us!'

Refusing to be intimidated Ross challenged the bully, 'This is ridiculous and a waste of everyone's time. I have an important job at Nchanga Open Pit, and you're delaying me unnecessarily. I have contacts with your superiors, and if you persist with this trumped-up charge I shall be reporting you both! You are trying to make trouble for me with a non-existent offence so you will be in big trouble. Your bosses will be very angry about you wasting their time. Oh yes, there will be *meningi indaba*! ' Ross stabbed his finger at them, and climbed back into the driver's seat. 'Good morning,' he barked with finality and turned the key in the ignition.

Taken aback by this retaliation the officer crumpled, but still wanted the last word, 'Okay, you can go thees time. But you have been warned.'

The Midget took off in a dust cloud.

At the leave house we lived other people's lives, with their possessions, pets, vegetable patch and houseboy around us. I soon learned to prefer Kabundi, in spite of its distance to town, as the air seemed fresher away from leach plant smells every time the wind changed direction and blew from the north. Our new neighbours were friendly, and we invited them one evening to share a meat fondue, using the set we'd bought the year before in Rhodesia. Tinned salmon went into a salmon mousse starter, and cheesecake or pineapple upside-down cake would provide a choice for dessert. I picked some frangipani flowers and floated them in water in a small crystal bowl found in Carol's cupboard. Two hours before our visitors' arrival, I chopped expensive best fillet steak into mouth-sized chunks ready for everyone to spear on to forks and plunge into the hot oil in the stainless steel pot. Each guest had a small bowl with two different meats, and more small bowls held a selection of sauces for dipping the pieces of cooked meat. Trays would hold all the bowls safely in the fridge until we were ready to eat. Three dogs and two cats pushed against my legs as I did the preparation. The houseboy had gone home, and Ross had not yet returned from work. I removed the tray of meat from the fridge to make room for the mousse I'd just garnished with parsley. A cat jumped on to the counter and I pushed it off impatiently, knocking the tray as I did it. The whole lot fell with a crash to the red kitchen floor, and five hungry animals couldn't believe their luck as a day's wages were gobbled up in seconds. 'Off! Off!' I shrieked. *Voetsek*! I tried in Afrikaans. There was no chance. One of the dogs cut his mouth on the sharp edge of broken crockery, and a small trail of blood mixed with the stains of raw meat smeared the floor. Screaming at them released my frustration, but could not reverse the accident, and after chasing the culprits out of the kitchen door with a broom and slamming the door the horrible detritus of our special dinner lay accusingly in front of the fridge door. The shops were shut and I had nothing to feed our guests.

Two hours later the inferior rump steaks found in a friend's freezer had not quite defrosted when our guests arrived. *If only I could find a way of warming up the middle,* I thought to myself dumping lumpy plastic bags of meat into a basin of warm water. But it would be ten years before we'd purchase our first microwave, and the melting process which in Zambia always happened too quickly at any other time refused to be hurried. I hacked into the first lump to redo the job I'd performed two hours earlier, and this time the kitchen was an animal-free zone.

A 'sundowner' was arranged at the rugby club to give us a send-off. Usually farewell gatherings were for those leaving permanently, and not just for a couple of years to improve their qualifications as Ross planned to do. Many doubted our return after the recent episode, but it was a clause of his sponsorship to complete at least one three year contract. Between drinks of beer, or Cinzano and lemonade we danced to Brown Sugar, Maggie May, and stomped on the floor to an inebriated chorus of *Knock three times on the ceiling if you want me…*' After speeches we ordered more drinks and danced some more to the Stones, Rod Stewart, the Carpenters and the Bee Gees. It felt good to let our hair down.

'Have a *chip*, these new beef and onion ones are good,' said my South African friend passing me a bowl of crisps.

'Thanks Jo,' I replied, 'will you still be here when we get back?'

'Probably not. Brian is looking at jobs back home. Now he has some good experience under his belt he thinks he'd be in for a good chance of a decent job. We have another year to decide, and then I think we'll be off.' She tapped her tummy, 'It would be good to be closer to my family too, since we're expecting our first baby in a few months.'

Our lives weren't the only ones moving on. Our own babies would have to wait for at least two years as I'd be the breadwinner.

The distance between the main deck and the inky water in the harbour below was huge, and we circled the deck stopping every few minutes to stop and look down to remind ourselves of where we were. Table Mountain loomed on the mainland, unusually visible with no cloud, and Robben Island festered to the South.

'This is the island, here you will die,' a warder had told Nelson Mandela when he arrived at the prison ten years earlier. South Africa simmered as it waited patiently for a great man to change things.

Our own brush with an African prison felt an age away. We'd left Chingola in a whirl of sundowners and farewells, knowing that by our return many of our friends would have decided not to renew contracts and we might not see them again. The flight to Cape Town took us South to mid-winter, and the shock of cold soon had me shopping for boots and warmer clothes. At last we boarded the S.A. Vaal, one of the liners we'd dreamed about since Ross had the Zambian job offer and we were still students. An enticing promise of twelve days of pure relaxation and spoiling in luxury was about to be realised. A penguin looking tiny down below us swam close to the hull near the kitchen's outlet, and reminded us of our proximity to the South Pole. We returned to the port side and searched the crowd for Claire and Jamie's faces amongst a sea of tiny bodies.

'I've always wanted to catch streamers,' Claire, my cousin from Salisbury, had said when they dropped us off, so we claimed a narrow gap to throw down pink and yellow trails to their outreaching hands.

The ship's horn blew, rattling chains raised the anchor, the hawsers were released and our stately parting to waves and kisses demolished the carnival of streamers. The abandoned quayside crowd dispersed leaving a tangle of broken paper threads.

'Well that's the last we'll see of Africa for two years,' said Ross with a sigh.

It could not be possible for us to change as much in the next two years as we had in the last. From our first alarming entry into Morocco, through eight weeks of that extraordinary journey, to living and working in a Copperbelt mining town far from home, and the threat of a jail sentence, we'd morphed into different people. I huddled into my scarf and turned my thoughts to another life in the place we still called home.

But first we devoted ourselves to having a good time, the good time others had raved about on their journey to Zambia. I relished the spoiling, the preparations for dinner and the luxury of gourmet dishes, the lounging around a pool and having waiter service for our every whim. Well-heeled passengers of many nationalities and ages had queued up for safety procedures, but all faces were white shading to Mediterranean, even among the crew. We stumbled on deck to find our sea legs, and for lack of much else to do watched Atlantic Ocean Penguins give way to flying fish, and pointed at our first distant sighting of leaping dolphins. We made some friends, tried our hands at bridge, and got to know the ship outside our tiny bunk-bed cabin. Every afternoon we headed to the bar to nibble peanuts and order one alcoholic drink because soft drinks were dearer than spirits.

On this journey we got fat. Our meals at the second sitting were at a table with a young South African doctor and his wife. Like Pavlov's dogs, our thoughts turned to food every time the tune for dinner played over the loudspeaker, and when it rang out for the second time we almost drooled. After every delectable dinner our waiter handed us the menu for the following evening to choose appropriate wines which could be 'aired' in time for us drinking them. We tasted our first cape gooseberries and many other culinary masterpieces. Anna and Johan were honeymooners and not short of funds. When she turned up for a meal, which was not every day and explained her slim figure, she wore a different fashionable evening dress each time. I had three, all home-made, and wore each one four times for twelve dinners, so I suspected our company was not quite on her level.

We spent our days at the poolside, deliberately indolent and eking out sunshine to store it up for our winter ahead. By the time we celebrated crossing the equator, our waistbands had tightened, lunches had to be abandoned, and instead we circumscribed the deck and sought the whereabouts of the gym. A crowd of us stayed up all night to welcome the hazy first dawn north of the equator, and then slept through two meals.

At Gran Canaria the ship docked for a few hours.

'This is our chance to buy a decent camera,' said Ross looking at our basic Brownie which had served us for several years. We raced off into town in search of a camera shop and found a large, heavy, complicated model free of tax, which we considered technically excellent, smart and compact. It weighed over three pounds without adding any zoom lenses. Back on board the S.A. Vaal Ross studied its workings for the remainder of the journey. Our holiday mood ended there, temperatures cooled, skies turned from gentian blue to mackerel, and our minds focused on our next life. A northern hemisphere purpose infused us ready to disembark in Southampton.

PART TWO

CHAPTER FOURTEEN

Starting again

The drums of Africa still beat in my heart...

MARY McLEOD BETHUNE

August 1974

Two years later we'd recovered from our misfortunes, and boarded a flight to Lusaka at Heathrow with optimism. The engine's roar zoomed us towards a fresh start for the same career, with new responsibilities and an altered perspective. In hours we'd be back in Zambia, a giant stride across the geographic and cultural divide, and it would all be waiting for us. The balmy warmth, ladies in tightly wound headscarves and colourful *chitenges* swaying along with a load on their heads and tiny faces peeping from the shawl at their backs, dazzling displays of bougainvillea, waxy frangipani flowers, the swish of *pangas* cutting grass, mango and avocado pear trees with pendant fruits, a full African smile. Underneath the wings of the plane stretched endless desert with a single track just visible on its surface. It could be the Hoggar Route we'd followed four years earlier, running north-south from Algiers to Kano in Nigeria. A cabin meal arrived, we ate, the stewardesses cleared them away, I dozed, and when I woke the bleak expanse of desert still filled the window of my vision. Two thousand miles of desert track finally plunged into steamy West African forests. I read my book, and then looked down at mile after mile of forests replacing the browns and golds of sand with shades of green, masking people, villages of thatch or more modern concrete, goatherds, wildlife and Africa's secrets. Like the desert it went on without a break for hours. The last time we'd arrived in Zambia after adjusting every day for eight weeks to changes, a long series of small shocks and surprises, perhaps travelling the same track just visible beneath the wings of our 'plane. This time it took the same number of hours.

I wore an ankle-length dress in unbleached cotton, bought from a bazaar-type shop at the Marble Arch end of Oxford Street. It wouldn't have looked out of place at a hippy festival and hid my small bump, which at the end of August was starting to show. The West End of London had become our local area when I'd found a job working as a housekeeper for a family in Wimpole Street. While Ross became a student again, I'd become a 'housegirl' for the family of a business couple who ran a market research company. The position came with accommodation, the spacious furnished basement of 57A, on the corner of the famous street with New Cavendish Street, and so proved a better alternative to teaching which would probably have meant an overpriced and cramped rented flat along with daily commutes. From our sitting room we watched who-knows-whose famous legs heading for their prestige dentist or plastic surgeon. I once spotted David Bowie in his Rolls Royce. It was our *kaya* equivalent and a few minutes' walk to Oxford and Regents Street, or to Regents Park where I sometimes walked the family's disobedient Chow Chow.

After the luxury of teaching polite girls eager to learn in Zambian schools, I'd been put off teaching jobs by fearsome reports of mouthy, arrogant teenagers making life a nightmare for teachers in British inner city schools so this alternative suited me well. Ross could easily travel from our posh new address on our less prestigious and newly acquired moped to The Royal School of Mines on the other side of Hyde Park.

A year later the family moved to Devon, and preferring to stay in London I found another job which still avoided teaching, this time at 'The Mineral Gallery' near Harrods. It was an enchanted cave of a workplace, being surrounded by sparkling crystals all lit up with bright spotlights. Every evening I walked past The Victoria and Albert Museum, up Exhibition Road to RSM and we straddled the moped to drive home. Our new accommodation was an Aberdonian whaler, which just fitted our needs and was moored on the River Wey at West Byfleet. The whole boat measured only 26feet and the cabin area less than half of that, so it amounted to something a little better than camping which was fun in the summer when we bought it. Travelling into London by moped became a daily torture, but it rarely rained. A few weeks after buying it we'd chugged down the River Thames to the sound of its diesel engine taken from a London taxi, and navigated past Canary Wharf and Limehouse Cut into the River Lee Navigation to a less salubrious but more convenient mooring at Tottenham Lock. The journey had taken three days with the help of two able-bodied university friends, Rupert and Mike, and was tougher than expected as we'd underestimated the Thames's strong current. We lived there alongside a gypsy encampment until the first frosts of winter made the deck icy and dangerous, condensation dripped icicles over our bed in the bows, and a family of mice invaded, running along the mooring ropes in search of food and warmth. They gnawed into packets of soup and made nests with my tights. Our youthful tolerance left us and we migrated to my grandmother's house in East Finchley until the weather improved.

During the holidays Ross went up to Edinburgh and found a flat to buy in Dewar Place near the Haymarket, and I stayed behind with my job. Britain's housing market was on the rise and we needed to get a foothold if we wanted to return at any time after the next contract. He filled the high-ceilinged rooms with furniture found at the 'lane sales' auctions behind Rose Street, put up his mother's old curtains, and left it with an agent to rent out. While others had taken expensive holidays we had been penny-wise in Zambia even after we'd paid off the car, and so had saved enough to buy it outright for £2,600.

Ross relished his time at university and made many friends. He joined the Chaps Club, a laddish group of drinkers who wore a signature blue and brown striped tie every Friday and shared ribald jokes and songs;

and the rugby club which apart from sport did much of the same. For a while he was captain. The demands of the course didn't seem to tax him the way they had at the Heriot Watt, perhaps because of his experience, and he'd thrown himself into the social life with abandon, a last grab at youthful freedom.

Returning to Zambia we were escaping strikes, bad weather and the IRA bombing campaign, but we both had new responsibilities ahead of us. We didn't expect the grey clouds of recession amid booming oil prices to follow us.

A woman more pregnant than me smiled as we queued under the 'engaged' sign.

'When is yours due?' she asked.

'January,' I replied, 'how about yours?'

'December. It's my third.' She looked down at the toddler clutching her hand. 'Darren, our five-year-old is back there with my husband. He's a fitter going out to a job in the Open Pit.'

A large proportion of passengers would take a connecting flight to the Copperbelt towns, and most were first-timers showing an anticipatory nervousness compared to seasoned businessmen rustling through papers. We shuffled up the queue.

'Which town are you going to?'

'Chingola. I expect you are too if you're husband's working in the Open Pit. They say it's the cleanest town in Zambia!'

'Is it? That's good. We've never been to Africa before. The furthest we've ever been is the Costa Brava in Spain on holiday. I'm a bit worried about tropical diseases though.'

'Well you don't need to worry about malaria on the Copperbelt at least, the mine sees to that with spraying.'

The green 'vacant' sign lit up and mother and child struggled into the small compartment.

At Lusaka we disembarked blinking into the brightness, and queued for another short flight followed by a chauffeured car to the Hotel

Edinburgh in Kitwe, the best in town. This was our first privilege in Ross's new position. A month earlier he'd returned to our boat on the River Lee with a big smile on his face.

'I've been promoted to mine captain'

'How did you manage that, you haven't even been in Zambia for two years?'

'Well I should have been starting as a shift boss underground, after the work experience I had before we left, but my old boss in the Open Pit wanted me back. So he upped the stakes and offered this promotion.'

'Trust you to land on your feet!' I laughed.

This news would make a difference to our lives in Chingola. As well as a salary increase, other benefits would make our lives more comfortable. An 'upset allowance' to spend on household items would be fun to spend, and the worsening of food shortages made a freezer almost a necessity. Closed borders with Rhodesia to the south of Zambia after UDI restricted imports, and when they did make their way into the shops you had to act fast, or they'd be gone in a few hours. Little came through any of the other seven bordering countries, which were either at war, too involved with their own difficulties, too poor, or too distant from suppliers. A freezer would allow us to store butter, margarine, cheese, and garden produce like mangoes during a glut, or mashed avocadoes. The cooker we'd had supplied in our last house had three burners and now we would be entitled to four, presumably to allow for easier entertaining and to impress visitors.

Once a week a small band of gardeners would turn up unannounced and cut our grass with noisy mowers, sending the dogs into a barking frenzy. Previously keeping in trim what passed for a lawn had been a job for our houseboy who swung a panga, a long sharpened blade not unlike a scythe. The rhythmic swing and swish had induced a restful calm to our afternoons unlike the intrusive revving roars we'd have to suffer in the name of privilege. We'd also get preferential treatment when it came to choosing a house. After our tiny houseboat moored alongside an encampment of gypsies in Tottenham I felt catapulted into a spacious world of entitlement, and never suspected there would be a price to pay later. So while my new pregnant acquaintance and her family headed for transit accommodation until their house was ready, we could stay at 'The Edinburgh' in Kitwe's Obote Avenue, with its swish 'Isle of Skye' restaurant and smart roof terrace, and I intended to wallow in it. A levelling justice came with a combination of hormones, excitement and a long journey which had me up half the night retching over the en-suite lavatory bowl. I rinsed my mouth and dried my face on a towel which looked and felt as if it had been washed in muddy river water. We were back in Africa.

The houses in Kabundi were built later than the original town development so felt more modern. A 'breezeway' or hallway sat between two outer doors and allowed a refreshing through-draught to cool the hot and humid months of October and November. Air-conditioning was not an option, and not really necessary in Zambia's enviable climate 4,000 feet above sea level and twelve degrees south of the equator. Someone with foresight had planted lemon, *naartje* (mandarin), grapefruit, and mango trees, which brought birds and their songs, which we'd missed in town. The suburb sat on a hill above town, with an airier ambience and distanced from Leach Plant smell, and the only downside was a two-mile hike to town. All I had was a provisional Zambian license, so I persuaded a fully licensed friend to accompany me every time I needed to shop, and used this weekly chance for a little practice driving.

My nesting instinct developed along with my pregnancy, and we'd arrived better prepared this time. When our packing case arrived there would be rugs, curtains and other comforts. This time there was no delay and it arrived a few weeks after us. Meanwhile with neither a fireplace nor a television we wanted a focal point for the living room and built a tall unit to fill the wall at one end, with planks of wood set on bricks for uprights. A box-full of books, LP's and cassette tapes would arrive in our packing case soon. The construction would house our new prized 'stereo system' chosen after much debate in a shop in London's Tottenham Court Road and consisting of a Garrard 'deck, Celestion speakers, and a Pioneer amplifier, all of which used a full shelf. Above it taped copies of E.L.O., Bob Dylan, Joni Mitchell, Leonard Cohen, and Don McClean had every song penned by hand on to the label, and their small plastic cases arranged in a satisfying block on the shelf. Beside them a pile of LP records included Sonny and Cher, the Beatles, Alan Price, Roberta Flack and some classical music.

An indoor trough built with matching red bricks divided the breezeway from the sitting room, and we filled it with earth dug from the garden to plant malachite green spears of 'mother-in-law's tongue' which grew perfectly well outdoors but we thought looked stylish in the house. Once the two rugs eventually arrived in our freighted luggage from London we were satisfied the whole effect was 'Scandinavian.'

I wanted to enjoy my pregnancy untroubled by work and in September when the weather warmed up joined Lorna and Sue for their regular afternoons down at the municipal pool in town. Still frugal with a well-entrenched savings habit, I'd been horrified at the cost of a maternity costume which would only be used for a few months. So I made myself a two-piece out of lighweight blue Crimplene. It looked fine until I stepped gingerly down the metal ladder into the water, when its weight made it lengthen and droop a bit like the knitted costume I'd had as a child, but still wearable. Women with schoolchildren who'd finished for the day, men on shift work, and mothers with under-fives made up most of the clientele at the pool. The non-mine population was not admitted, and a line of young and curious black faces often gathered on the other side of the low wall, until the pool attendant spotted them and marched up to the wall ushering impotent threats and shooing them away. By the time he got to the wall they'd scarpered. A few minutes later they'd be back, intrigued by minimally-clothed sun lizards and swimmers alike, but by then the pool attendant was too busy blowing his whistle at the dangerous antics of blond-headed boys near the pool edge.

'When are you going to drop it?' asked a single guy spending an afternoon at the pool after shift work. 'Er, sorry, I meant …'

'I know what you meant,' I laughed, 'our baby's due at the end January.'

Being September, I still had a few months to myself, to plan and prepare, to discuss and compare notes with other expectant mums doing it all for the first time. Prospective grandmothers had bought two dozen terry nappies and little cotton vests, I'd made hospital-stay nightdresses for myself and the baby, and my mother gave us some boys' clothes since Ross assured me that his family had only produced boys for several generations and we would inevitably do the same. He'd convinced me it would be a boy. A pram could be bought second-hand locally, I'd already sourced a Moses basket, which awaited a lining of quilted blue gingham, and the mine would supply a cot when the time came. Knowing what to expect from the local shops, I'd arrived with maternity dresses already made and as many clothes and essential household items which could be squeezed into suitcases without exceeding our allowance. After waiting months for our packing case last time we couldn't risk being without essential items.

'We'll dig dig dig dig dig dig dig in the mine the whole day through…' sang the dwarves. The Christmas pantomime that year was Snow White directed by Dave the pharmacist and Ross had the part of Elf the Huntsman, who doubled as narrator. With irony the producer sought out the tallest applicants for the seven dwarves, and the story had an apt link to mining for the local audience. Val and I continued our ante-natal conversations from the stalls as preparations rolled out over the weeks. Her services as prompt wouldn't be required until much later, and I awaited instructions for my contributions to wardrobe. Snow White bared more and more of her soul with every stage rehearsal, and lost more and more of her heart to someone else's husband, the tallest dwarf at six foot six. A mutual agreement between the two couples appeared to satisfy all concerned, and the spicy glow of their passion energized

the production with a sense of danger and possibility. By the end of October I was reaching the tape measure past my bulging belly to take the dwarves' inside leg measurements none of which came to less than 33 inches. Ross and Giles, Val's husband who played Happy, knew they were out of the stakes for trading partners if it had ever crossed their minds.

On 24th October Zambia celebrated its tenth year of independence, but our community had no involvement. More exciting was the prospect of Muhammad Ali challenging the title of boxing heavyweight champion against George Foreman on 30th October. President Mobutu, eager for publicity, asked for the event to take place in Kinshasa, so the 'Rumble in the Jungle' happened in neighbouring Zaire. Scheduled for four o'clock in the morning to accommodate viewing time in the States, it was reported as being 'arguably the greatest sporting event of the 20th Century.' Muhammad Ali won the title in the eighth round and became the talking point amongst the men of Chingola and the world for weeks afterwards.

Three months after our arrival we found ourselves back at Hotel Edinburgh. Danny and Lawrence had just arrived in transit accommodation before starting their contracts at Nchanga as metallurgists, and we'd arranged to meet them for their first evening in the roof-top bar. Ross first met them at RSM, and they promised to be valuable new members of the rugby team. Having no transport they had set off on foot without realizing the distance, so Ross set off to find them and a group of five graduates jumped into the back of the truck. Once over the surprise at the size of my bump, they settled down to a boozy evening as an initiation for the three years to come, and slowed only by the hotel's high prices.

They would be bound for single quarters once they came to Chingola, which for men consisted of smaller bungalows grouped together and much closer to the mine. Mostly their plots were uncultivated with only a washing line and possibly a barbecue in the handkerchief garden. One houseboy would "do" for two, three or even four, and a free masculine camaraderie existed between them all. More than a few marriages resulted from the proximity to the nurses' quarters, and more than a few marriages broke up as a result of the poaching activities of the 'single guys' preying on bored young wives left alone at home with not enough to do.

Lawrence had been in Chingola for a few weeks when we decided to drop in with a bag of mangoes from our garden. He enjoyed sampling local produce, and was picking tiny thorns out of his fingers when we arrived.

'Ive peeled these for us all to eat,' he said angling his head at a small bowl of wine-red fruits in a bowl set on a basket-work table which he must have bought from the roadside traders on the Kabundi Road. 'They're prickly pears, and really refreshing when you're thirsty, but the devil of a job to pick and peel without getting all these thorns in your fingers. Try some, but watch out for the pips, you could break a tooth if you're not careful!' He returned to work on his thumb bristling with miniscule spines. But in a few years his adventurous spirit would work against him.

A wild-west atmosphere prevailed around single quarters, with hard drinking and loose-living being rumoured. Jerry was famed for his heavy drinking, and shooting out his bedroom light with an air gun rather than getting out of bed to flick the switch. He soon had a reputation at Townships for high light bulb usage, and was one of a group who ventured up to the flesh pots and drinking dens of the Congo around Elizabethville. The country was by then Zaire and the town renamed Lubumbashi, but everyone still referred to the old colonial names. They were enjoying the drinks and camaraderie of a local bar when the police arrived and accused them of causing trouble. At the town jail the policeman in charge suggested they pay him a bribe for their release. The Zaire government had a habit of not paying their workforce, and the police lived off bribes which they found easy to extract with their official powers. Trumped-up charges against Europeans known to have fat wallets provided an opportunity. The single men asked to see his superior, who asked for a bigger bribe. Then they asked to see the top boss, who asked for even more. Their bravado crumbled as the policemen pushed and shouted with pointed rifles, took their wallets and lined up the adventurers against a blood-stained, bullet-holed wall. Then they blindfolded them. The soldiers watched the miners cry and beg, saw them grovel and sink to their knees in fear as they heard the click of an unloaded gun. Then with thigh-slapping laughter and hearty back-punches they released them; poorer, badly shaken and no longer hungry for adventures.

Less vicious practical jokes were played against each other. Mark decided he would build a swimming pool for himself, his neighbours and friends, although this would take up most of the space in his back yard. He'd left a space at the side for a grassy patch on which to sunbathe, and a narrow corridor for a washing line. For privacy he added a perimeter wall, and invited his friends round to show off his new construction. Tired of Mark's swaggering, the others decided to bring him down a peg or two. While he was at work they brought a crane up to his house and lifted his car over the wall next to the pool, where it would be impossible to drive out.

The 'single guys' quarters huddled close to the mine's office buildings in First and Second Streets. If problems arose they would be the first to be called as they had no family responsibilities to burden them. They were a mixed bunch of young men, and there existed a kind of honour amongst thieves about who had eased the loneliness of a solitary wife's evenings or nights. A few women with healthy appetites set tongues wagging about goings-on in cars, and behind club buildings. One such lady could be spotted at the wheel of her car heading down Independence Avenue during the day, in full makeup and her hair newly arranged after seeing her husband off to work, and leaving her children at nursery. Another found the energy for a long-term ex-marital liaison as well as excelling at the several sports. Other casualties of hitherto secure marriages mourned the day they signed up to the 'lovey' atmosphere of an amateur production at the Arts Theatre.

'Have you heard that Pearl Withenshawe has been P.I.'d?' Asked a friend at the rugby club.

We relished this piece of gossip about the ex-neighbour who'd given us so much trouble being made a 'prohibited immigrant,' or P.I.'d.

'Yes she really fancied herself that one, and got in with one of the *yarpies* from the rugby club. He's a confirmed bachelor, you know, doesn't want his freedom compromised with responsibilities, but not immune to offers if you get my drift! Anyway, she decided to move in with him, and her husband was so pissed off he packed up all their things and took their two kids back to UK. He didn't even complete his contract he was so fed up, so it must have cost him. And of course his work permit which had allowed them all to stay in the country went with him. It wasn't long before someone reported her as living in the country illegally, and as a result she was P.I.'d and thrown out of the country.'

I visualized her being frog-marched on to a plane by two uniformed men, possibly prison officers …

'Oh poor Pearl!' I said with derision and a broad grin. We both laughed.

Nursing staff, who were female and predominantly recruited from all over Britain, had their own quarters and might work in the North or South hospitals. The North was the preferred option for many who had come to Africa to meet third-world challenges. This hospital serving the townships and the larger, poorer portion of the Copperbelt population required more staff, and offered the opportunity to make a meaningful difference albeit under difficult conditions, particularly in the clinics situated in the township. A friend took me to see one of these.

'They treat 25,000 patients a month and deliver on average 12 babies a week,' she explained, 'the clinic never closes, because births can happen at any time, and it's funded by the mine for the workers and their extended families. There's a small ward with a few beds, some well-equipped treatment rooms, a kitchen, a bathroom, and an incubator although more difficult cases are usually referred to the hospital.'

'What does that sign say?' I asked her, pointing at a notice written in local languages near the bathroom.

'Oh,' she laughed, 'it says "mothers are asked not to give birth in the toilets." It was a recurring problem, perhaps because the mothers were seeking privacy, and not the most hygienic place to deliver a baby!'

We watched a British Sister and her Zambian assistants busy themselves with immunisations, examinations, first aid, suturing, and prescriptions. The white sister had an interpreter at her side. Apart from a clerk who registered each patient, and a doctor who visited twice a week, all of the staff and most of the patients were female. The queue stretched out of the door to the cleared bush outside, where they sat on the grass with their babies and children, fanning themselves.

'Like in the mine, these sisters are given huge responsibility considering their experience. But as far as I know mistakes are few, and these patients are getting treatment the rest of the population doesn't get. It's a highly valued service for the local community, and mothers are prepared to make long journeys to have their children immunised.'

'I've had a hard day,' said Catriona when I asked her in the cricket club bar why she wasn't her usual cheery self. 'A family brought their little boy into the hospital today as an emergency,' she explained, 'and try as we did, it was too late to save him. His parents had taken him to a witch doctor two weeks ago, and heaven knows what nonsense he gave them. The poor little mite might have had a chance if they'd brought him to us first. They call it '*muti*' which means medicine, but it must have been more like poison. They make it from all sorts of herbs and bits of dead animals, and to be fair many of the old remedies have been shown to work, but not always. The other sisters told me it's not an unusual occurrence and the '*muti man*' panics at the last minute and gets the parents to bring their dying child to us once he knows there's no more hope, so it's the hospital that gets blamed for the death. It's a month now since I started, it's my first job since I finished training and Sister says I'll get used to cases like this, but it's so frustrating!' She swigged a gulp of her Cinzano and lemonade, and gave a weak smile. 'I think Doctor McKinver was angry, but he couldn't show it. Then there was all that wailing from the women as they started to grieve, with me trying to control my own emotions. It's really hard to concentrate on your work with that going on!' Catriona was barely out of her teens and already homesick, but it would be at least two years before she'd see her family again. She was dating a metallurgist who worked in the leach plant.

In contrast to the echoing emptiness of the hospital for our use, the packed wards of the North were beset with streams of visiting extended family who sat on the floors getting in the way. Nonetheless hygiene was kept to a high 1970's standard, equipment was good, and staff well trained. At that time all British nurses finished their qualifications to be a sister with 'the midder' or midwifery training, which was vital for the young population of all sections of the Copperbelt. The South hospital would have offered Catriona a softer option except in the busy maternity wing where I would soon be going for our baby. But the general wards often lay nearly empty and there was little in the way of interesting cases to add to a young nurse's experience, so without challenges their days seemed longer.

CHAPTER FIFTEEN

Pundu

Make the best use of what is in your power, and take the rest as it happens.

EPICTETUS (55 AD – 135 AD)

'Next!' shouted the nurse above the excited chatter that hid the anxieties of young women waiting for their check-up at the ante-natal clinic in the mine's South Hospital. I'd got a lift down Independence Avenue, and we'd turned down 4th Street to draw up in front of a wide art deco style façade. Seen from the front it could easily be mistaken for a hotel were it not for the ambulance parked outside. The wards of the hospital were sparsely populated, but the ante-natal clinic and the maternity wing always buzzed with activity.

Most of us had married graduates from the latest recruitment drive, finding ourselves far from supporting families as we went through the joys, trials and uncertainties of a first pregnancy. The world of obstetrics was opening up to us, and we needed to explore all its mysteries. Three-year contracts and the only reliable communication with home being by letter forced us to depend on each other for support, often making life-long friendships in the process. Although the clinic started at 2pm we never waited for less than an hour, which gave everyone an opportunity to exchange information, compare dates and weights, source equipment and clothes and generally unburden ourselves.

A corpulent locum doctor checked my charts, and with a disapproving frown in spite of her own considerable girth, warned me of the dangers of gaining too much weight during pregnancy.

'Let's have a look at you now.' She said and I heaved my bulk on to the examination couch. 'Hmm,' she kneaded and prodded me with warm hands. 'I wonder,' she murmured.

I was on full alert. *What did she mean? What could be wrong?* I waited impatiently.

'We shall have to have a better look at you,' she informed me. 'See the nurse about an x-ray, we need to know how many you have in there, because you seem rather large but I can feel a small head.'

A large baby with a small head? And what are the dangers of x-rays on an unborn child, but I kept my thoughts to myself. I waddled out of the consulting room around the corner to reception, with a farewell wave to all my new expectant friends still awaiting their turn.

If we'd stayed in Britain the newly developed and less damaging scanning technique would reveal all, but in Zambia in 1974 the only option was an x-ray. I lay on a narrow hard bench, an uncomfortable position for me even on a soft bed, and winced with back pain while wide straps were pulled excruciatingly tightly across my belly.

'Now don't move,' instructed the radiographer as she slipped behind the protective screen. A week later I got a phone call, and having ascertained that I was safely sitting down and not in danger of fainting at the news, someone's secretary told me to expect twins. Twins! It wouldn't sink in. Twins! I could feel justified at my tiredness, and a now sympathetic doctor prescribed folic acid supplements along with eating plenty of protein to make 'big babies' over the next four weeks of my pregnancy. Apart from the obvious 'double trouble' I had no concept of the significance of this news for our lives in Zambia. After the birth we asked for the x-ray which clearly showed two babies perfectly fitted together head-to-toe, like yin and yang.

Christmas parties went by in a haze of heartburn and heaviness. One required fancy dress so we put on headbands over long hair, money-bead necklaces, and tie-dyed 'granddad' tee shirts to go as hippies. As a final touch I printed LOVE across the front of my distended top, PEACE on Ross's, and we found ourselves winners of the competition.

A few days before Christmas I went to the gate to see why the dogs were barking. They performed the equivalent of a doorbell. A dark-skinned Father Christmas, who I recognized as Lorna's houseboy William, handed me an envelope. She'd dressed him up to distribute Christmas presents to the children in her nursery then sent him out with a sack for her local card deliveries. He seemed to enjoy the role, and flashed a big smile before setting off for the next address on his list.

The x-ray started to fade, and on the morning of 17th January I felt strange when I woke up, stepped out of bed and flooded the red floor which our houseboy shined every day. My waters had broken a week early so we picked up the ready-packed suitcase full of nightdresses and nappies and headed for the South Hospital. Ross went in to work and I went into labour, pacing the maternity wards alongside four others. An Irish nurse kept a wary eye on us, and offered a cheery 'keep up the good work,' or 'aren't these gorgeous' to distract us as she bustled past with large vases of flowers to brighten the wards. We leaned against chipped metal bed frames for a breather and a chat between contractions.

'I think I'll do what my husband's family want, and stay at home for the first forty days,' said Nitsa, a Greek girl.

'That's a long time, aren't you afraid of getting bored?' I asked imagining myself with cabin fever.

'It's our tradition, but not everyone sticks to it now. My Mum says it will give me a chance to recover properly and to bond with the baby.'

Veronica paced alongside us, still having to go through it all.

'Her baby has died in the womb,' whispered Nitsa.

'Oh!' I gasped filled with a sudden sadness for Veronica, and my next contraction hardly hurt at all.

She had the privacy of a private ward, but she sought out company to distract her from her pain. She didn't want pity, but I felt guilty expecting two babies when she would go home alone. Maternity wards are generally cheery if apprehensive places, full of hope, but she put on a brave face and we all bore our pains together.

We never saw Jan who was wheeled straight in to the delivery room. She had the misfortune to be unable to last the full term, and felt the first twinges of labour while enjoying a drink with her husband in the rugby club bar. They raced down Fern Avenue, turned right down 4th Street, and she was taken straight into the delivery room. A few hours later they returned to the rugby club bar to announce their news.

'The baby is nine weeks premature so she has to stay in an incubator. She's really tiny, like a doll. They let me go because I had no stitches or anything, and although James is a contractor to the mine it costs us a fortune to stay in hospital you know. It's all right for you people on contracts from UK!'

The winds of change were blowing, and late that stormy January night with an audience of two doctors, three midwives and an attentive father, Sheelagh was born. Twenty minutes later Kirsty arrived, vociferously complaining at having just been manhandled by the doctor from a breach position to be born normally. I wasn't too keen on the procedure either.

'She has good lungs!' said the nurse.

Our daughters had disproved Ross's firm prediction of boys, and we had to find names. They kept me in hospital for a week in a private room so that Ross could visit any time he wanted. But he was so tied up with work that this turned out to be not very often. After a few days Nurse Beattie, a no-nonsense Scottish sister with an unfairly small waist for a maternity ward, took him by the ear and taught him how to fold and change a nappy. He took it in good grace, but smooth operations in the open pit remained his priority. Someone had to bring home the bacon for our newly doubled family. Nurse Beattie taught us first-timers the mechanics of baby-care knowing how few of us would learn the traditional way from our visiting mothers. Folding nappies turned out to be an art with many choices according to the sex of the baby and personal preference. The nurses helped us to establish a feeding routine, to bathe a slippery newborn with confidence, and showed us how to avoid piercing the baby when we inserted the nappy pin. A friend's husband had done just that to his son's tiny penis, but fortunately without lasting damage. They gave advice on anything from colic and nappy rash to cracked nipples and getting our figures back.

'I've tried to fit the Moses basket as well as the carrycot on the shelf behind our seats and they won't go,' announced Ross carrying them piled on top of one-another back to the spare bedroom which would become a nursery.

The shiny new red Toyota Hilux pickup Ross had chosen as our vehicle for this phase of our life had to go, and a few weeks after the birth he drove it reluctantly back to the show room in town. Sheelagh and Kirsty were so tiny they fitted easily into one cot back to back, then top to tail, but with space for only one carrycot behind the front bench seat he was forced to trade the fancy he'd enjoyed for less than five months for something more twin-friendly as they grew bigger. A Datsun 120Y two-seater white van became its unglamorous replacement, but allowed two carrycots to be stowed easily in the back. We'd address the problem of back seats later, and this became another one of many adjustments to our new family life.

Squeezed into my old pre-pregnancy clothes I adopted the new mantle of motherhood. Feeling engulfed in responsibility, changing hormones, new love twice over and sleepless nights, I lurched from day to day with a mixture of exhaustion, tearfulness and euphoria. After Nurse Beattie's insistence for him to help out, Ross felt he should somehow lend a hand with night feeds once we'd returned home. These were frequent with our babies being so small, and he offered to help with nappy changes while I attended to feeding.

A voice was pulling me up from deep sleep, and I forced open my eyes. Next to me, Ross was pushing a pillow at me,

'Have you fed this one yet?' He asked me in his sleep.

I could do without this sort of help, so opted to go it alone through the nights, sometimes getting only an hour's sleep at a stretch. They were my only responsibility as Stanley our houseboy attended to washing and housework, and I was grateful to be living in Africa as we wouldn't have home help in UK. He made up Bemba songs about his life as he worked and occasionally I'd hear our names and the word '*pundu*' while he polished a window, or swept under the mango tree.

We had bought a second-hand 'carrycot-transporter' locally, and two small babies could fit head-to-toe inside it for a few months. In Zambia's climate pram hoods were not a priority so long as we kept the babies in the shade, with an insect net stretched tightly over them. Twin prams were not available to buy in a country where most mothers carried their infants tied tightly on to their backs with a cloth. A sister or cousin would be assigned a second baby in the case of twins.

They filled my days, and much of my nights too, leaving no time to ponder my new life. Two weeks passed and after a reasonable night I decided to venture into town with Ross for food shopping. The rigmarole of getting us all safely into our small van, with everyone clean and recently fed, was our first hurdle and one I would have to learn to manage alone. In town some friends stopped to coo over the babies, and Ross went off to the Standard Bank while I pushed the pram to CBC's supermarket. There was an unusual throng of African women around the steps, and it took me a while to realize that the special attraction was me and the twins. Women were reaching out to me. Some had tiny slumping bundles on their backs, and nothing visible but a small knitted hat; some had a wide-eyed face watching sideways and strapped tight to her warm back; a few leaned back to counterbalance their rotund fronts but pushed through the crowd for contact with a mother of twins. They were mainly young and smiling and saying '*nampundu*' with wonderment. Soon several dozen had gathered around me, reaching out with the repeated words, '*nampundu, nampundu.*' I smiled back, confused, and not knowing how to react so I nodded, while trying to pull the pram up the steps into the store without tipping the carrycot part over. An older woman without a baby spoke English and grabbed my arm.

'Two babies, very lucky!' She grinned, still hanging on to my arm.

'Oh,' I replied dazed, 'why is that?'

'You have much power! These ladies want to touch you for good luck!'

I didn't speak Bemba and didn't really understand the fuss, so still smiling politely I felt all at once proud, elated, embarrassed, confused and panicky in the throng of warm bodies. I waited until she released me and pushed on through the crowd to the safety of the supermarket shelves to do what I came for. By the time we got home my head spun and the twins were stirring, waking up to the next round of feeding and changing. It had been too soon to leave the house, and I thought of Nitsa safely ensconced with her husband's family for forty days.

In some African societies twins are bad news. They are thought to be the result of the mother having a relationship with another man or evil spirit, and the second twin might have been killed or allowed to die. But here in Zambia we had hit on a lucky formula. The Bemba attach such importance to twins that they not only have a word for twin, *pundu*, but also for father of twins, *shimpundu,* and mother of twins, *nampundu*. In town one of the teachers at Chikola had lived in *Nampundu* Crescent. Bemba's society of extended family has no clear distinction between 'father' and 'uncle,' 'mother' and 'aunt,' or 'cousins' and 'brothers or sisters,' but twins merit a special word. At work Ross had often been questioned by African workers on the size of his family.

'How many children do you have, *bwana*?'

'None as yet,' Ross had always replied, and they'd shake their heads in disapproval. A powerful man would have many children. Word soon got round.

'You are a *shimpundu* now, *bwana*! Pleeeenty powa!'

As a man respect was given in direct proportion to the number of children he had. Rather like a game of poker, our double birth meant more than a large family of singletons. At work his recent paternity gave him added respect and credibility, so when the news travelled fast on the 'bush telegraph' about our new family it seemed that we had come up trumps by producing two at once. Twins and triplets are fairly common among Africans generally, but less common amongst Europeans,* and

* Twins and Supertwins by Amram Scheinfeld. Pelican/Penguin 1973

we had unwittingly found a passport to near-celebrity status. Stanley our houseboy, enjoyed some reflected glory too. As I prepared lunch ready for Ross coming home when he was on day-shift, I could pick out '*pundu*', '*nampundu*', and '*shimpundu*' now in Stanley's songs, and wonder what his ballad said that day.

Arthur and Betty, Ross's parents couldn't wait to meet their first grandchildren, and boarded their flight to Africa the following March. Arthur had sailed around Africa with the British Navy during the war but Betty hadn't ventured beyond Europe before.

We took them to Kitwe to watch a rugby match and during the game the girls started coughing. Clouds of white smoke coming from Nkana Mine nearby left a dusty residue on the ragged grass of the pitch. Health and safety standards were not a priority.

New babies curtailed our activities, but we managed the round trip to 'the Falls' as well as showing them the local sights in Chingola and further afield at the Kafue game reserve, and the hippo pool. Extra hands with child-care didn't go amiss, and when they left a month later I had to learn to cope single-handed again.

Men made up most domestic staff, but I preferred the idea of having a woman around to help with the twins and babysitting. Stanley had done a good job for us, so when we found Mary we owed it to him to find him alternative employment as well as providing a glowing reference for his future use.

Mary had a light touch with her unassuming presence, we no longer found rooms arranged strangely and ornaments facing the wrong way round, she doted on our babies and the twins loved her. Instead of skating over floors to polish them she got down on her hands and knees. Her big bottom wriggled with the rhythm of her arm strokes and I was thankful Ross wasn't around to make rude observations. The contours of her shapely head were outlined with fine braids, like the lines on an ordinance survey map, and her short sturdy frame bustled with energy.

I occasionally left Sheelagh and Kirsty with Mary when my loyal friend Dawn accompanied me to drive into town. Armed with a provisional driving license, this gave me a chance to practise without distractions from behind us. We often returned to find one of them tied firmly onto Mary's back with a length of cloth, while she sang softly in a high voice and continued with the housework, a strategy that always worked. Rarely did both babies cry at once, considerately acknowledging adult limitations to manage one child at a time. This would usually be Sheelagh, because Kirsty was a wriggler and a climber who used the firm platform of Mary's bottom to propel herself upwards and over her shoulder.

Mary didn't baby-sit very often, but when she did we had complete confidence in her. Ross always drove her back to her house in the compound, sometimes in the early hours. After dark we often heard sounds of drums from that direction, like a background beat to the hum of crickets, and in spite of all our travels he felt wary as if trespassing into foreign territory the first time he took her back.

Late one night as she was getting out of the car a chicken carcass and giblets fell out of her bag. '*Eeeh*,' she squeaked, gathering them up in her embarrassment. She must have retrieved them from the kitchen bin, so after this I stripped chicken less thoroughly and we kept any similar leftovers for her in the fridge. Her private life and struggles were invisible to us, busy as we were with our own concerns, and I wondered what else she might use of what we wasted so like most of our friends tried to offer what we could.

Most mornings Mary started her domestic duties with the washing, which mainly consisted of nappies left to soak in a bucket of Napisan. Her routines went unseen by us as everyone went about their own tasks, but on two occasions mysteries were solved when we watched her at work. The first was the growth of beans outside the back door. Ross had planted a line of plants stretching for ten feet along the wall of the house. At the far end the plants were tiny, but the closer they got to the back door, the bigger they got, culminating in an admirable specimen beside the steps.

'Perhaps there's a leak in the water pipe, like we had in the last house?' I suggested, 'besides, it gets more sun there too.'

But we were not convinced. One morning we happened to be in the garden training the tendrils of a new passion fruit vine growing on the fence when Mary appeared at the step with the nappy bucket, having removed the nappies to wash in hot soapy water. In one dexterous movement she sloshed the contents straight along the line of beans, a nitrogenous daily tonic for our beans.

The second mystery was a dent in the car's bonnet. As the main user of the car I found myself the main suspect, and protested my innocence denying all knowledge of its cause. It had just started raining one morning as Ross left for work in the company Land Rover. Mary had a full basket of wet washing at her hip and was swaying to the carport to peg it out under shelter. As Ross turned the key in the ignition, Mary stepped on an old chair, and from there on to the bonnet of the car in order to reach the washing lines suspended under the roof of the car port.

'Aha,' he said to himself, 'so that's the cause of the mystery dent!' He turned off the ignition, and addressed the problem of finding her an alternative mount which spared our car bonnet. She had put on her little-girl defenceless voice, reserved mainly for Ross, and which we knew was a sham because we'd heard her bellowing at the garden boy next door.

Around the Copperbelt police road blocks between major towns were a fact of life. Ostensibly they checked suspicious, unlicensed cars and unsafe or overloaded vehicles, but some days their work must have lacked interest. At the end of February Ross slowed the car in a queue of traffic and stopped beside armed, stern-faced police officers.

Our cheery '*mwapoleni mukwayi*,' was met with a grunt.

After examining our papers they paced slowly towards the back of our little white van, frowning and examining the state of our wheels or anything else that could be substandard. At the back of the car their faces metamorphosed. Severe, uncompromising, grim expressions broke into huge smiles. Bringing their hands together in a slow clap, all fierceness gone, one after another exclaimed,

'*Aiyee, Simpundu, Nampundu!*'

'I also have twins,' said one reaching out to shake our hands with both of his in the African way. There followed an animated tale of all the twins in their families and how happy this made them. The state of our vehicle was forgotten and after much friendly chat we continued our journey.

Officials enjoyed their power, and found a lucrative seam in speeding fines particularly along the Kabundi Road. Catriona, our nursing friend, had been in the middle of her driving test when she was pulled aside.

'No way was I speeding! I was in the middle of my driving test for heaven's sake! My driving examiner just shrugged, and said "what do you want me to do?" So now I have to pay for another test and book time off work again. Plus the fine of course! Bloody policemen! I'm sure my colour had something to do with it.'

Adjusting to celebrity status was a delight for us both, and we unashamedly took advantage of it. After failing my first driving test our new experiences offered a different strategy. Sheelagh and Kirsty at nine months accompanied us to the test centre, golden-haired, beautiful and identically dressed to leave no one in any doubt. Their eyes were now distinctly individual with Kirsty's being a startling blue, and Sheelagh's a deep brown and other differences were becoming more apparent but they were still unmistakably twins. Because of our entourage we were given a heroes' welcome as expected, my friend Dawn who'd accompanied us stayed behind to push them around in their twin buggy and I drove off with the examiner and the policeman in the back for my second attempt.

'Myself, I am *shimpundu,* and I also have girls. They are seven years old now,' the policeman told me proudly shaking my hand. Every time I caught sight of him in the rearview mirror he was still grinning.

Needless to say it worked. At last I could come and go in the car as I pleased.

'You should hire them out!' laughed my non-driver friends.

CHAPTER SIXTEEN

Problems and Projects

Sickness shows us what we are.

ANONYMOUS

It happened for the first time on a sunny Autumn morning in June. Sheelagh had woken from her morning nap, but Kirsty slept on in the pram on the front veranda. At first I was grateful to be able to attend to one five-month-old baby without the pressure of rushing to deal with the other one. But half an hour later it concerned me. Deliberate noises around her made no difference, and by lunch-time I was getting agitated. I pulled back the mosquito net and lifted her sleepy body to take her indoors. On the change mat she looked at me drowsily and her eyes rolled up. I watched helplessly as her little body convulsed and twitched for what seemed an hour but must have been less than a minute.

I had never phoned Ross at work, so he knew my call was an emergency and drove straight home. Luckily he worked in the planning offices at the time, and not in a distant part of the Open Pit. Sheelagh stayed with Mary, and we rushed Kirsty down to the South Hospital.

'It was probably a febrile convulsion,' said the young doctor, 'but since she doesn't have a high temperature we think we should perform a lumbar puncture to rule out meningitis which can be fatal. We've had tragic cases here before. As with any procedure on your child we would need your permission, of course.'

'What's a lumbar puncture?' I asked.

'It's a spinal tap where we collect some cerebrospinal fluid for diagnosis,' he explained. 'It's a standard procedure, and we'll give her a local anaesthetic.'

Worry filled my thoughts and clouded his words. I didn't like the sound of them. They were hospital words that shouldn't affect my family, only unfortunate people who got sick. Soon I would wake up and get my healthy baby back, the one who was always smiling and laughing. More words came out of the doctor's mouth,

'I'm afraid this is a painful operation in spite of the local anaesthetic, and not without risk, but here in Zambia it is important to rule out certain problems at an early stage to avoid long-term damage. We can't allow you to be present.'

I clung to Ross. He seemed to be taking in this horrible information. He was asking for clarification on those nasty words. I asked him to explain it all back to me hoping I'd got it all wrong, that I was fretting over nothing and it wouldn't be true, but it was true and we let them take her down an empty corridor. The nurse ushered us to some hard metal chairs and side by side we stared at a bare wall painted with sickly green emulsion. The sleepy little hospital grew silent. A harsh bare light bulb reflected a rusty glow in the polished concrete floor under our feet, and a caring voice from a passing nurse tried to distract us from the torment of worry. Then the baby scream from a distant room tore our hearts apart.

They gave her back to me asleep again. Tests done immediately had ruled out meningitis and offered some consolation for our tattered emotions, but she'd had another seizure while they took the lumbar puncture. Medication would be needed to keep the situation under control, and we left the hospital with a syrupy concoction of phenobarbital.

The day before this happened we had welcomed two visitors to stay with us. They were members of a visiting rugby team who would occupy our spare bedroom for a few nights, and being occupied with our crisis we'd completely forgotten about them. Fortunately they hadn't been neglected at Nchanga Rugby club whose members entertained them until late, particularly in the bar, so it was past midnight when they were dropped off outside our tall locked garden gates. They climbed over the spiky seven-foot barrier, found their way into the house, and fumbled in the dark to their bedroom. We heard the bathroom door opening and closing a few times.

Kirsty lay in her pram near our bed so that we'd wake to her slightest distress. A strange noise coming from her direction disturbed us, and Ross turned on the bedside lamp to illuminate a large rugby player in his underpants with one leg raised ready to climb into her pram. The baby slept on and twelve stone of disorientated and embarrassed intruder retreated to his own bed. We stifled our giggles under the covers.

Our families were five thousand miles away, and we needed them. Friends offered platitudes of consolation, but a phone call each to our parents stating the bald facts helped us more, were a 'trouble shared' and made us feel a little better. The crackly line and delayed sound put paid to any emotional outburst, but it was better and more immediate than a letter and helped us to continue almost as before. On low afternoons I played Roberta Flack,

When you smile, I can see, you were born, born for me,
And for me you will be do or die,
Oh baby let me hold you,
You make me want to hold you,
When you smile, smile, smile…

Kirsty smiled dazzling smiles as she progressed and developed reassuringly in parallel with her lively twin Sheelagh. Clear days of autumn freshened to winter, both girls started to move about, and we hoped her convulsions had been a 'one off.' Then it happened again. It seemed worse this time, perhaps because she was bigger and older, and as Ross rushed us all back to the hospital Kirsty was barely back from one seizure when she went into another. We left her sleeping in a cot in an adult ward awaiting tests.

A soaked sheet surrounded her screaming form when we returned later,

'She finished all the formula in the bottles you left us,' said the Zambian nurse in her defence, as if this would explain their abandoning our distressed infant.

'We left her here in your care because she's really sick, and you've ignored her!' I shouted, with my baby still sobbing in my arms.

After a big fuss they gave us a private ward. I'd be staying with her to provide proper care until tests were complete. A friend took Sheelagh on some days, but on others she came with us during the day along with toys and a baby-walker to keep her clear of the ground. She charmed all the staff, and the expanse of shiny hospital floors offered an irresistible opportunity for an eight-month-old on baby-walker wheels, scooting at an impressive speed and tailed by Ross or myself. Kirsty slept and slept, and we worried about the dosage of her sedation.

'She's become like a vegetable,' complained Ross, 'it's that phenobarbital, there has to be an alternative!'

The doctor changed her medication to Epanutin, a drug used to control epilepsy, and she became less groggy.

'This doesn't necessarily mean she has epilepsy,' said Doctor Geddes, the chief medical officer, 'and most children grow out of these seizures by their first year. We'll have to wait and see. Meanwhile keep her on the current dosage and when you return to UK have her properly assessed. I'll give you a letter referring you to The Sick Children's Hospital in Edinburgh, my wife did part of her training there.'

This dedicated Scottish couple were the mainstay of Chingola's hospital service. They steered us sensitively and wisely through our crisis, and offered huge reassurance. But times were changing, and those in power were pushing for more and more Zambianisation. The process had already started with nursing staff, some of whom couldn't grasp the basic principles of a caring profession which were fundamental to the British model. We'd had a brush with it over Kirsty's treatment, and again when I was admitted overnight with an acute attack of vomiting and diarrhoea. The nurse on duty had given me the distinct impression of disgust at allowing myself to get ill. Our confidence in the health system wavered.

'I think it would be best not to have the whooping cough immunisation for either of them,' cautioned the Scottish sister at the regular Wednesday morning baby clinic held in the South Hospital. 'The risk is tiny, but your twins are still small and I'd advise you to wait at least another month before having the diphtheria, tetanus and polio.'

Her counsel had been months earlier, and in view of Kirsty's history neither twin had the measles vaccination either. In Africa the disease could be a killer, and immunisation was normally given at eighteen months. Later Sheelagh developed a severe cough which lingered for months and I suspected was a mild form of whooping cough, but Kirsty was untouched. Measles, on the other hand, was to become someone else's nightmare the following year with repercussions for our own family.

Our friends Dave and Sandra in Kitwe had built a swimming pool in their garden, and Ross saw no reason why we couldn't do the same. This became his next project at the end of winter, which coincided with the end of Kirsty's convulsions, although we didn't know it at the time. The promise of the coming swimming season sharpened his concentration to design a completely enclosed area with a bar and *braai*. Days of pencil lines on squared paper brought the evolution of a workable plan showing a twelve foot square pool plus a six-foot square shallow-stepped area for access and somewhere for the twins to stand and splash. The remainder of our 'dip pool' would be only four feet deep for easy maintenance. A month of labour-intensive digging by workmen brought the dogs to a frenzy of barking every morning, and then the churn of a hired concrete mixer grumbled its way through our days. Most of the muddy part was over by the time the rains arrived, and Mary had silently tolerated the upheaval and mess of it all, stepping over mounds of earth to get to the washing line with a laundry basket that always seemed to be full. At ten months the twins crawled everywhere and into everything, so keeping Sheelagh and Kirsty out of trouble took up much of my time. They could be distracted for a peaceful twenty minutes to watch the building activities from their high chairs set inside the kitchen door, but the rest of the time had to be closely monitored otherwise they'd crawl outside for closer investigation, or scoot a baby-walker over the steps. Trying to source a baby gate had proved unproductive. The deep room-sized concrete-lined cavity threatened every venture outside as we waited for the plaster to set, and I was grateful the twins hadn't started to walk. Ross then spent evenings and day after day of his free time painting over the dried plaster. Coat after coat of thinly watered-down emulsion soaked into its surface and dried in the sunshine in minutes. Progressively stronger mixes followed, until the final coat had made a waterproof finish. Then we could attach a hose from our outside tap and another from our neighbour's, and watch our swimming water steadily rise. As hours ticked by the water eradicated the yawning hollow danger to replace it with another; the possibility of drowning.

'You can't be too careful with pools,' warned Catriona, our nursing friend, 'a little boy was brought into the South Hospital last year after they found him at the bottom of a pool. It happened at a party where there were loads of other kids in the pool, and plenty of adults around. No one had noticed him until it was too late. All the splashing probably hid him from view even if they had been looking. Someone really needed to keep counting their heads and watching the whole time. The family was devastated as you can imagine.'

So a six foot high wooden fence made from off-cuts surrounded our new pool area, which could only be accessed through a six-foot metal gate fitted with a spring closing device for safety. It wasn't worth taking any chances, and Catriona's words went through my head every time we were at a poolside with children so that I was forever doing head-counts, and missing conversations.

We enjoyed a brief trial swim which took only one or two strokes from side to side, and then waited several more days for clear water before allowing the twins to join us. After chucking in handfuls of granular chlorine with some acid and letting it settle for two or three days, Ross used his usual criteria for checking the chemical balance and safety of the water by tasting it. Presumably he based his judgment on childhood memories of Portobello open air pool outside Edinburgh, but aimed for a less chlorinated taste as ours wasn't a public pool. Then we could use it every day, and floated the twins in a boat made from an inner tyre with a rubber base glued underneath. But all they wanted to do was lean over the edge to smack the water before crawling in, and we had to catch one each.

Our new luxury brought unexpected extras. Creatures stumbled over the edge in the night and either drowned or became overcome with chlorine. Dead moths, flies, aphids, lizards, chameleons and the odd rhino beetle along with assorted wind-blown leaves and flowers had to be scooped out the next morning. Water scorpions hid in the leaf trap and looked threatening, but never actually bit us.

'I think I'll build an aviary,' Ross announced one afternoon on his return from the work.

'An aviary?' I asked wondering where this brainwave had come from. 'But why would you do that? We don't have any birds.'

'We do now,' he said, 'come and see what I have in the Land Rover.

As he'd been driving along the back road home he'd seen three boys dangling something colourful from the end of a string. Barefoot and gangly in their baggy khaki shorts and threadbare shirts, they were laughing and playful. Their plaything wasn't the usual elaborate wire skeleton of a car with mobile wheels, but something live. He drew closer and got out of the work vehicle. A beautiful bird with brilliant blue tail feathers and a lilac breast flapped one wing uselessly, as the other wing-tip had been removed. It was a Lilac-Breasted Roller.

'Good afternoon,' they'd chirped classroom-fashion.

'Hello. What has happened to the bird?' Ross asked, pointing at their victim.

'One wing,' replied one of them, having consulted amongst themselves how to say it in English.

'Yes, I can see. What happened to the other wing?'

'Wing … *muti*,' came the reply.

'Yes, *muti*,' and one of them pointed towards the compound.

Ross rummaged in the pockets of his shorts and brought out some change. 'Give me the bird,' he suggested, holding out the coins for exchange. After the briefest of consultations between the three boys, the string and attached dangling bird was duly handed over in exchange for the cash. *Muti* meant medicine, so Ross assumed a witch-doctor had found some way of making '*muti*' from the hapless bird's missing wing. It made for easy prey for the boys to claim as a plaything. Mostly *muti* would be roots or herbs, but animal parts would also find a use as magic portents to banish evil spirits, and in a poor society everything had a value. Ross tied the string to the steering wheel and drove home.

'So where can we keep it?' I asked.

'George has a huge birdcage in his back garden mainly for breeding doves. I'm sure he'll find a space for it while I get something put up in our garden. Now where do you think we should have it?' He marched off to survey our plot and choose a suitable site for the intended cage inside the perimeter of our pool's stockade fence. This would be the first of several new projects he'd undertake over the next year, and kept him busy most evenings with paper and pencil sketching plans. A week later Roly, our new pet, was installed in an aviary the size of a small garage. He had branches to clamber over since he couldn't fly up to a perch, and cat food for nourishment to replace his normal diet of insects and small lizards. His *rack-ack* cry became familiar as I opened the back door in the morning, and sometimes he managed to catch his own food in the form of a passing beetle or grasshopper. George gave us some 'doves' from his already overcrowded aviary, which were really pigeons, but Roly never managed to join them on their perch with his permanent disability. He seemed quite content in spite of everything, and hungrily gobbled captive offerings of live grasshoppers collected by visitors' children. We took long leave a few months later, and transferred all the birds back to George's aviary, but not long afterwards a rat got into the cage and he had no means of escape. I sometimes wondered if it had been a kindness to keep him, but we meant well.

The imminent arrival of my parents for a Christmas holiday focused minds on getting the whole project finished. Part of the plan was a high stone wall to give us privacy as well as shelter from the sun. Chisulo, a Malawian who worked on Ross's shifts, had invited him to see his own house on the compound which he'd built himself. A humble little dwelling boasted a different stone for each wall, painstakingly collected and assembled into a work of art. Standing indoors, Chisulo pointed out the different effects. Ross gazed at the first wall of dark slate neatly grouted between each thin layer. Opposite stood an equally impressive surface with large stones individually chosen to interlock a bit like a 'drystane dyke' but with a minimum of grouting. Large pebbles covered a third, and small stones speckled with tiny dots of gold-coloured chalcopyrite, a copper-bearing mineral, ornamented the fourth. Brimming with pride at his labour of love, Chisulo promised Ross a similar masterpiece if he would like to make a collection of suitable stones.

Rising to this new and pleasant challenge, Ross found himself in a perfect position to hand-pick his own choice of specimens as he drove from bench to bench of the Open Pit in his battered work vehicle. Every blast brought fresh material for selection, and a few of the most colourful rocks would take prominence in the wall, displaying shades of green and blue typical of copper-rich minerals he'd saved from the smelter. A touch of malachite here, of bornite there, some chalcocite, a little azurite, chrysocolla and cuprite could all be spotted by an expert eye if they looked hard enough. After a coat of varnish they shone out between the greys and browns of ordinary base rock, and with the attachment of a corrugated iron roof the wall made a good private and sheltered seating area next to the small square pool. On 17th January proud parents and grandparents assembled beside the new 'feature' wall to watch two babies in clean new dresses trying to blow out the single candle on their first birthday cake.

Mid-contract we were entitled to three months paid leave, and took the long flight via Rome and London to Edinburgh, with Kirsty's letter of referral tucked in a briefcase with the rest of our papers. As we waited in Rome the aircraft cleaners made an Italian fuss over the babies, whisking them out of our arms before we knew what was happening, and preparing them for the attentions of family later on. The flight exhausted everyone with Sheelagh screaming during take-off and landing from the pressure in her ears. At least this was the attentive air hostess's explanation. She pressed two green Alitalia blankets on us before we disembarked in London.

Both grandmothers had been knitting and sewing so our toddlers had plenty of hand-made garments to defy the chills of a gusty March in Edinburgh, and bought their first tiny shoes to cover feet accustomed to freedom since those first faltering steps before their first birthday.

'Can you remove her clothes leaving her vest and nappy, please, ready to see the specialist,' said the nurse at the hospital known locally as the 'Sick Kids.'

Our sturdy girls with sun-kissed skin played noisily around everyone's legs while pale puny patients watched cautiously from their mothers knees. Kirsty looked a fraud. Another nurse attached electrodes to her head in the treatment room, and gave her a toy to examine as the machine danced waves on a screen.

'There's not much wrong with her,' said the nurse nodding her head in Kirsty's direction. She was absorbed in playing with the toy they'd given her.

The specialist interviewed us all later, and watched her antics with the benefit of Sheelagh for comparison. He held the EEG print-out from the machine to show us. 'Her readings are within normal range,' he said.

That was all I wanted to hear. The rest of his detailed analysis and explanations of slight peaks and troughs on the graph washed over me in waves, while Ross concentrated properly and asked questions. She was to be taken off all medication with immediate effect unless there were signs of reoccurrence. We could get on with our lives. Reoccurrence would mean a return to the complete dosage for a year, and I refused to admit this possibility into my mindset.

'Well Kirsty's the only one in the family who's been certified sane,' joked Ross laughing with relief as we left the hospital building. The girls were reluctantly tucked into cosy wraps in their twin buggy, with hand-knitted hats buttoned under their chins to prevent removal, and wearing matching mitts tied with tape to their jackets. Their African start in life had never demanded such uncomfortable constraints. I held the crisp white envelope holding the specialist's report to take back to Dr Geddes in Chingola while Ross pushed the pram over the pedestrian crossing on Melville Drive. We strolled alongside well-tended beds of purple and yellow crocus, past tragically dying Elm trees and under the Whale's jawbone to release Sheelagh and Kirsty on to the grass for a muddy toddle in Edinburgh's 'Meadows' for our celebration of good health.

'My bum's burning,' wailed John, perched on the hottest seat.

Back in Chingola Ross had just completed his next project and we were trying it out for the first time. He bought a solid-fuel Raeburn cooker found in a derelict farmhouse, and decided it would provide the perfect heating mechanism for a sauna to stand alongside our new pool. Using off-cuts of wood he built a basic 'log cabin' over it then covered this inner shell with plastic sheeting for insulation and made an outer wall around it using more off-cuts and a corrugated iron roof. Entry was through a basic door and inside the hut he'd mounted slatted shelves around the Raeburn for seating. A large jug of water stood on the floor ready to pour directly over the hot plate for a steamy result. Our friends John and Carol arrived from Luanshya in the afternoon, and while I was putting the twins to bed the men stoked wood into the stove through its door in the outside wall of the cabin. It was dark when we ran outside clad only in towels, and John had chosen the seat directly above the hot plate.

'I'll swap you,' said Ross.

There wasn't much room for manoeuvre, and the lower seat barely got any warmth at all, so we shuffled around but finally even Ross gave up and we all jumped in the pool as a substitute for rolling in snow. It would have been traditional to beat one another with leafy bunches of twigs, but luckily Birch trees don't grow in Zambia, even in Birch Street.

CHAPTER SEVENTEEN

Friends

Friendship improves happiness, and abates misery, by doubling our joys and dividing our grief.

CICERO

A friend from the Royal School of Mines had announced his arrival in Chingola and we looked forward to his visit. Hoping to replicate our journey overland Mike had found borders which had recently been open now closed, new countries were at war, and fresh dangers and difficulties had developed. A possible route down the East of the continent through Ethiopia looked the most promising, so with a Land Rover and a friend he set off. Thwarted by the military and nightmarish, or absent, roads he had to resort to rail for a short section of the journey, but had at last made it. Ross gave him directions to our house in Birch Street, but a bit like ourselves having managed to negotiate some of Africa's most difficult regions, he was vague on detail and forgot our house number.

'Can you tell me which family around here have twins?' Mike asked a passing driver.

'Try that one on the corner with the tall hedge.'

'Bytheway' was written on the gate with the usual warning about dogs '*Pasopo lo Mbwa*' and a picture of a snarling Doberman. He was already familiar with this sign and knew the resident dog would commonly be a tail-wagging cross-bred mutt. He rang the bell. A genuine Doberman rushed around the corner of the house, stuck his head through the gate, and bit him on the leg with teeth identical to those in the illustration. Mrs Bytheway came to see what all the noise was about.

'Look at what your dog has just done!' he declared with indignation, showing her his bleeding shin. The dog growled, made a second lightning charge at the gate and bit him on the other leg.

'I'm really sorry,' she said heaving the hound back by his collar. 'You should have stood further back from the gate, let me get you some plasters. Oh, and you don't need to worry about rabies, his certificate is up to date,' She pointed at the metal tag on his thick leather collar, and then disappeared indoors dragging the dog with her. A few minutes later she returned alone, 'yes we do have twins, they're five now, but there's another couple who live a few doors up who have twin babies, perhaps that's the house you're looking for?'

So Mike arrived with a tale of woe and newly applied sticking plasters on his legs.

'Fancy a drink of something,' I asked trying to cheer him up. 'Perhaps you could keep an eye on the twins out here while I go and get it?' I'd taken him into the pool area where we could enjoy the beautiful September weather. At nine months Sheelagh and Kirsty were crawling, and it seemed an easy enough task for him to stop them from eating anything they shouldn't and keep them away from the pool.

I came out with a tray, and bachelor Mike was standing waist high in the pool, dripping wet and holding a bemused and equally dripping Kirsty aloft. His glasses had misted over. Sheelagh sat back on one heel and watched with interest. A sticking plaster floated to the surface of the water.

'She crawled into the pool, so I jumped in to save her!'

'Oh, they are always doing that,' I laughed. 'Sorry Mike, I should have warned you. We obviously try to prevent them from doing it, but things happen quickly with crawlers and they change direction without warning. It's impossible to watch both of them every second, so if they end up in the water they surface straight away, we fish them out, and point them in a different direction.'

Sheelagh wasn't crying, just gasping a little and looking surprised as she'd done the last time it happened. Poor Mike wasn't having a good morning. I changed Sheelagh's vest and nappy, lent Mike some of Ross's clothes, and we laid his wet ones out in the sun to dry. The contents of his pockets presented the biggest problem because rather than leaving all the foreign banknotes from his overland journey in his new accommodation with an unknown houseboy, he carried them with him. We peeled them out of his sodden pockets and spread them out on a table to dry, and settled down with our drinks.

Our glasses were nearly empty when a fickle gust of wind threw the nearly-dried notes up in the air and scattered them all over the garden and the plot behind ours, with a few returning to the swimming pool. He gave chase while I pinned the remainder down with our drinks glasses and kept an eye on the twins.

When he had been preparing his Land Rover for the overland trip, Mike had sourced three conjoined reclining aircraft seats, their mechanisms still intact, to make for a more comfortable journey in the back of his vehicle. He offered to sell them to us as he no longer needed spare seats. Once separated, two of them would be perfect to seat Sheelagh and Kirsty in our van now that they were growing too big for their carry-cots, and even had attached seat belts.

The first time I saw Gloria she was holding a Downs syndrome baby boy, and mounting the wide shallow steps into Solanki's with another woman. The other woman was the mother, but hated shopping in town with her handicapped son because of people staring. Gloria had a heart of gold.

Cecil, her husband, had taken the job of Assistant Open Pit Manager at Mimbula Fitula and had met Ross at work. They had recently arrived from Chililabombwe, "the place of the croaking frog" which colonials had called Bancroft. Now they lived a few streets away from us in Kabundi. Cool August winter nights gave way to pleasant Spring evenings at the end of September and they invited us to join them for a *braai* and 'plough share' one Saturday evening. We drew up at tall gates to the customary cacophony of barking. Gideon their barefoot but uniformed houseboy called off the dogs opened the gates and indicated where to park. The twins waited in the back of the van, bathed and fed, and we took one cot each to follow Gideon past the house into a large enclosed pool area with a covered *braai* and bar big enough to do justice to the demands of a small hotel. A Flamboyant tree spread flat-topped branches over the wooden stockade fence, its flaming orange flower clusters still startling in the fading light, and a vivid blue rectangle of swimming pool, five times the size of our own one and complete with a diving platform, slumbered between banks of cut grass. Aproned Cecil in shorts and tee shirt stretched over an impressive beer belly grinned as he welcomed us. He was about to light the *braai* and he passed on smudges of charcoal with his firm handshake. Gloria fussed over Sheelagh and Kirsty, who studied the unfamiliar tones of her West-Country voice then gazed up at dim lights in the thatched roof above the bar An untidy group of banana trees stood beyond the covered area, and sprouted a few red bulbous ends of new branches of maturing green fingers, the fruit still skinny and only a few inches long. When the twins fell asleep in their carry cots we stowed them into the changing hut, I relaxed to enjoy the evening and reached for my drink.

'Cecil get Sara a glass, she can't drink out of a bottle like you men!' instructed Gloria, dragging on a cigarette. They had met when South African Cecil had been studying mining at Camborne School of Mines in Cornwall. She stubbed out the cigarette and we walked back to the house and a long galley kitchen to prepare salads. Their two little girls Rachel and Claire floated round us followed by three dogs.

Cecil attended to the meat, which seemed to involve a little stirring and a lot of beer being added, while Gloria entertained us with stories of her family and the trivia of life. The 'plough share' had been converted into a conical cooking pot, big enough for ten servings, and chicken pieces bobbed in a bubbling sauce set over the *braai* alongside a coil of *boerwors* sausage. Without a lid the chicken kept drying out, so Cecil kept dousing it with beer. Another pot held *nshima*, a stiff porridge of *mealie-meal* traditionally eaten with the fingers and dipped into the chicken gravy. Their company was relaxing and fun, and after eating we played all the variations of dart games we could imagine, ending by throwing them backwards through our legs. Next came a music session. Cecil turned the tape recorder volume to high and smacked two spoons expertly on his thigh to the tune, while everyone else rattled a single one in their empty beer bottle.

'*Goin' up Camborne Hill comin' down…*' sang Gloria after a few more drinks.

'*…goin' up Camborne Hill comin' down…*' she went on…

'*With her knickers in the air…*' trilled Cecil followed by a gutsy chortle, his voice well-oiled with Lion beer.

'*The horses stood still; the wheels went around…*' sang Gloria…

'*Goin' up Camborne Hill comin down…*' they sang together.

Gloria collapsed into laughter, wheezed, and grabbed her inhaler for the asthma she'd suffered for years. Then she lit another cigarette.

Cecil boomed out Jeremy Taylor's song,

'*Ag pleez deddy won't you take us to the drive-in,*
All six seven of us, eight nine ten.
We wanna see a flick about Tarzan and the Ape-man,
And when the show is over you can bring us back again,' but Gloria's accent didn't run to Yarpie when she joined in the chorus of,

'P*opcorn, chewing gum, peanuts and bubblegum*
Ice cream, candy floss and Eskimo pie…'

This was the first of many similar evenings, and try as we did to reciprocate the invitation, the truth was their *braai* and pool area was the best place to be. Every time we ate the same food, watched the stars come out, played darts, and heard their silly song so many times we knew the words to join in. The men never left the pool area all evening, going behind the banana plants 'for watering,' and Gloria never tired of relating stories and offering advice.

Our twins eventually grew too big to take with us for evenings out, but rainy weather didn't curtail evening entertainment at the poolside.

While seeing the New Year in with them in1976 my parents came too. Alcohol flowed, dinner was long demolished, the 'decider' game of darts had been played, and everyone decided a midnight swim would be the thing to do. My father, in his seventh decade, could be seen at the far end of the pool and my mother became agitated.

'He can't swim you know!' she shouted, jumping in beside him.

Ross dived towards his floundering form and between them pulled him to the safety of the side. My father had tried to teach me to swim off the coast of Fife at Lundin Links, telling me to kick my legs as he cupped his hand under my chin. As soon as he took away his hand I sank and twenty years later I realised his skills shortfall. We all drank a sobering coffee and called it a night.

Lawrence was a keen rugby player, but his real love was sky-diving which he discovered in Zambia. The thrill of launching himself out of a plane to sail down over bush land satisfied something in his soul, and he never missed a chance to enjoy his sport. Free fall gave him an even bigger buzz, and after a night's revelry at the Arts Theatre his alcohol-befuddled brain told him to climb on to the roof and jump forty feet to the ground. His friends, of which he had many, would have stopped him but no one had suspected the intentions of unassuming Lawrence until they saw him teetering up there on the edge, and making a grand music-hall announcement to the 'Ladies and Gentlemen' present of his imminent leap. He then hobbled wincing to the bar, had a drink and drove home on his motorbike. The next day he couldn't walk, was admitted to hospital and an x-ray revealed that he'd broken both his ankles.

Months later he crashed his motorbike after a similar Friday evening. Lawrence gave the hospital nurse our phone number because he thought Ross the most likely of his friends to own a pair of pyjamas to borrow for his hospital stay. Ross found one pair, still unused, and drove down to town.

'We can't seem to loosen his grip on that tie he's holding,' said a bemused nurse. 'We had no problem cutting his trousers off his legs, but he's clinging to that tie as though his life depends on it.'

Ross laughed. He had the same tie, a brown one with blue stripes, worn every Friday by members of the Royal School of Mines Chaps Club. If any member of this drinking club was caught without it on a Friday, he'd have to pay for a round of drinks for all the other members present. It wasn't about money, because the others would then take it in turn to pay for their round, but a point of honour.

At the end of his contract and with all his bones mended Lawrence knew he belonged in Africa, and moved on to work in South Africa. Before leaving his parents who'd retired to the old family home in the Pyrenees, he posed for a photo carrying his own newly purchased parachute and wearing the latest sky-diving gear to go with it. They displayed it proudly on their mantelpiece, but never saw him in the flesh again. He'd joined a sky-diving club in South Africa and made many jumps, until that day. He jumped last of his group, but his parachute caught on a glider-hook at the back of the plane. The three remaining sky-divers went to the pilot to tell him what had happened. But no one could think of a way to reach the hook in order to release the parachute.

'You might as well go ahead and jump, I don't think there's anything you can do,' said the pilot.

So they did. Lawrence died on impact when the plane landed shortly afterwards. He was twenty-six.

'When he was about ten years old we were on holiday and went for a walk leaving him in the hotel. There was a crowd around the swimming pool when we returned, so we joined them to see what the fuss was about. Our son was standing on the railings of the second floor balcony of our room, and jumped into the swimming pool below. He'd been doing it over and over again,' confided Marie-Louise, his mother, many years after his death. 'He just loved the excitement and danger!'

Nchanga mines reached the apogee of their copper production at the end of Ross's last contract in 1973, but by then the price of copper had started to fall. Staff who'd worked in the mines for years decided not to renew their contracts and took their experience with them to harvest other minerals in South Africa, the Americas and Australia. Maintenance and manning allowances were trimmed to the bare bones; hiring skilled recruits on a budget became a problem, and those left behind trying to maintain the *status quo* found themselves in a downward spiral. Three electricians tried so hard to complete essential maintenance work around the Open Pit that they'd worked overtime every day without a break for months. Every evening they'd arrive home late, eat a meal with a wife who may have had no adult company all day, and fall into bed exhausted only to get up the next day and do it all again. In recognition of their efforts, management gave all of them three days off to spend with their families. But tensions at home had reached breaking point, and couldn't provide the refuge they needed to relax.

'What are you doing this afternoon, Chris?' asked one on the phone to another after the first strained morning at home.

'Nothing much,' replied Chris. 'Fancy a beer at the Mine Club?'

'I was just thinking along the same lines, I'll meet you down there in an hour.'

'Okay, I'll give John a call and see if he'll join us.'

So all three met up to unwind together, one beer followed another until they all fell asleep, still exhausted. On waking none of them could face going home to a scolding, so started again and spent their entire three days off together at the Mine Club, commiserating over their lot.

Cecil was promoted to Acting Open Pit manager for Nchanga, a much larger pit than Mimbula and Fitula combined, and Ross became his Assistant Manager. Both men were charged with new and far-reaching authority, but with little preparation or training. By then I was expecting our third child, and watched Ross become more and more weighed down by work, with machinery not working, parts being unavailable, and drastically reduced qualified or experienced staff to rely on. He rang me after work,

'I'm just letting you know I'll be back late. It's been a tough day and I'm going to spend some time with Cecil sorting things out.'

I heard the back door slam after I'd gone to bed; he staggered into the bedroom and collapsed on the bed. Within minutes he was snoring whisky drenched fumes. The next morning he overslept so I didn't find out what had happened until the afternoon.

'There was a fatality. We think he must have fallen asleep at the wheel. He probably woke up to see his forty-five ton truck hurtling down the ramp completely out of control, so he panicked and jumped out, bounced off the wall and fell under the wheels. He was in a terrible state and I had to stop the first aider from trying to resuscitate him.'

'Oh, I see,' I said, 'how much did you drink?'

'Well we started on beer, I don't know how many, and then we had a bottle of whisky between us. Anyway, to make things worse I am responsible because it happened on my shift, and the Mines Inspector arrived first thing this morning to look into it. It didn't look good that I turned up forty minutes late. I've never done that before and I had to choose the day a Mines Inspector comes to question me! Cecil was covering for me of course.'

A few days later he took the company Range Rover, a new expensive showy vehicle for top management only, to the funeral. Amid the wailing of the professional mourners and the large crowd of Africans, two of the men who'd been working on the fatal shift approached him,

'*Bwana*, the sand and cement has been left at the wrong grave. What shall we do?'

Grave robbers were a problem, so to prevent the theft of expensive coffins the mine supplied the materials to make a concrete lid over the grave and a night watchman to guard it while it set. The delivery truck had left it all piled in the wrong place and it was up to Ross to think of a quick solution. *JFDI* went through his head, the manager's mantra to anyone who turned up with an impossible dilemma at work which had to be fixed. *Just Fucking Do It.*

'Come with me,' he said, and all three of them jumped into the Range Rover which had just been valeted for the funeral. He parked it alongside the bags of cement and pile of sand, opened the back door of the vehicle, and they shoveled it all inside. When everyone had left the graveside they went ahead with making the concrete to cover the coffin before the gravediggers filled up the hole. The interior of the Range Rover never recovered.

If there was any major problem in the Open Pit Ross would be the first to be informed. His predecessor had been so involved in his work he kept a radio running beside his bed all night to relay all the communications in the pit. His wife complained bitterly, so he turned it down, but not off, and had trained himself to wake if a 'May Day' signal was given out. So when our phone rang at two o'clock one morning, Ross feared the worst and dreaded picking up the receiver.

'Hello *bwana*,' chirped the voice of Chileshe in the watch tower, 'I just want to let you know that everything is all right.'

'Thank you Chileshe, but you really don't need to ring me if that is the case!' He climbed back into bed muttering 'bloody African shift bosses,' pulled the pillow over his head and went back to sleep.

He became insomniac shortly after this, and would go to bed dog-tired, fall asleep for half an hour or an hour at best, then lay awake thinking of possible solutions for insurmountable problems at work. He had reached crisis point, and after days watching him descend in a downward spiral I finally persuaded him to see a doctor.

'I've not been sleeping,' he said to the newly qualified doctor, then burst into tears. Surprised and embarrassed at his own behaviour, he then started laughing. 'I don't know what came over me,' he said to me afterwards.

She signed him off work for an indeterminate length of time to recover. While I plodded around at home in the late stages of pregnancy he set off for the golf course most mornings, which caused some resentment among his peers, but didn't really become himself for months afterwards. Our friends helped us through this difficult time, and glorious September Sunday afternoons spent around their pool made him feel better, but without alcohol which was off-limits with his medication. Cecil and Gloria had taken two other casualties under their wing; Anita and Martin, a young couple who'd not been long in Chingola, and still didn't have a car. Their red-haired boy Jack was twenty months, the same age as Sheelagh and Kirsty, and sometimes they'd played alongside each other with Steven making up a fourth child. Measles vaccination was recommended at the clinic for their age group, although we were wary of all immunisation after Kirsty's illness.

'Steven's not well,' announced his mother, 'he kept me up all night and I found a rash behind his ears. I think it could be measles, so thought you should know!'

It was too late for Steven's jab, but Anita panicked, and took her sturdy little Jack to the hospital for advice. He had the injection. There was no way of knowing that he had already been incubating the virus caught from Steven. The African strain of measles is notoriously bad, and within two days of immunisation Jack became suddenly and seriously ill. Anita and Martin got a lift to the hospital where he was admitted as an emergency. The next day they watched helplessly as he lapsed into convulsions and died in his father's arms. It was debatable whether the injection had made the disease worse. Young, inexperienced and vulnerable they fell apart.

The young couple had flown in from UK, and opted for a cash allowance to buy a car on their arrival. They hadn't got around to choosing one yet, so depended on others to take Martin to work and Anita to shop. A week after their son's death Gloria invited them with us to an evening *braai*, and we left Mary in charge of the twins at home in Birch Street. They didn't need a reminder of healthy toddlers.

'We crawled into bed and cried for two days and nights,' confided Anita, 'we just wanted to die and nothing in life seem worth living for. I'm feeling a bit better now and have started eating, but Martin has no appetite, and I'm worried about him, he's so thin.' Marooned in Central Africa, they'd clung to each other for days without leaving the house. 'I wish my mum could be here, but none of our family can afford the airfare.'

Our problems shrank in perspective and I thought of our two healthy girls sleeping in their cots.

'There has to be a post-mortem, and then Jack will be taken to the crematorium in Ndola,' she explained later. 'We've already said goodbye to him, and have decided not to go but will have a small ceremony here in Chingola when we have his ashes. The problem is getting them back here. Do you know anyone who makes regular trips to Ndola? Someone who'd be willing to collect Jack's remains for us?'

Ross was still signed off work, and taking pity on them offered to do the five-hour round-trip for their child's ashes. It was the end of the month and our budget was tight so he hoped we'd have enough petrol which had become expensive. We'd decided to make a day of it and take the opportunity to have a little look at Ndola, so with Sheelagh and Kirsty strapped into Mike's airline seats behind us we set off. At the crematorium I stayed in the car with the girls while Ross mounted wide office steps clutching a piece of paper allowing him to claim Jack's ashes. The enormity of what he'd volunteered to do hit Ross as he received the anonymous brown paper package tied with string containing a box of the baby's remains. He cradled it back to the car.

'What on earth can I say to them when I deliver this?' he asked, placing the tragic package at my feet away from the girls. We drove back without much conversation. The petrol gauge swung closer to the red button and our supply only just held out. Once home we wouldn't be able to drive anywhere except to a petrol station until pay day, so Ross went straight to their house first to make the delivery, and with great dignity and gratitude they received the package. The relief we felt handing it over was pathetic compared to their solace at holding Jack's remains in their hands.

Months later I was visiting Anita at home, 'we're expecting another baby,' she announced. She'd just finished painting her nails, and seemed to have covered herself in a pain-resistant outer layer too. A year after Jack's death they had another boy who looked quite different. They left Zambia as soon as their three-year contract terminated. Steven, who had apparently recovered from his bout of measles, was found a few years later to be permanently damaged from the vicious virus. Africa had a way of doling out random brutality in this way, and we counted our blessings again that our twins were unvaccinated and unscathed.

'Cecil's drinking twice as much as he used to,' confided Gloria while the men were busy talking about the new *Kreepy Krauly* automatic pool cleaner now available in South Africa. She looked anxiously over at him, 'but he's not getting drunk. And he's smoking heavily too. It's this job! They take the men to breaking point. It can't go on. They give them huge responsibility without any training, and there's no back-up.'

Ross had slowly regained the gift of sleep and went back to work in October. We'd been so tied up with our own problems, and helping Anita and John, we hadn't noticed the strain on our friends. They had recently returned from an ostensible holiday in South Africa to visit his family. They returned with tales of shopping and fun in a country which ran like a sewing machine in comparison to Zambia. A few days after their return we learned of the job interview, and a new position down south, but Cecil didn't look happy with his new appointment. They'd have to leave behind all he'd struggled to achieve. Settling for a job which carried less responsibility along with a run-of-the-mill house, to gain them the stability they needed, held little appeal and felt like a backward step.

'Gloria's as happy as a pig in shit,' he used to say about his wife when they first arrived in Chingola. 'We've decided to make our dream home here.'

They had been allocated a manager's house on a corner plot in Datura Street, and poured enthusiasm, time and money into their project. They'd hardly had the chance to enjoy the fruits of their labour, when they'd have to leave it all behind. Cecil still had family in South Africa and they decided a move would be in the best interests of the whole family, although a backward step career-wise for him. We visited them in Coalville a year later, and didn't find the same carefree couple we had first met. His work made less demands, he slept better and drank less, they were secure, but he missed the challenges and adventure which

Zambia had offered and had lost his spark. They had done nothing to improve their house since they'd moved, as though it wasn't worth the effort and nothing could replace what they'd had before.

Because of his recent promotion, Ross was entitled to better accommodation, and before Cecil and Gloria left he made enquiries about availability. Many preferred not to have the upheaval of a move mid-contract but if there was a pool to be gained then it would be worth it. We'd already applied for one such house but someone further up the list took it. Better things were in store for us.

The imminent vacancy of their house interested us, but Cecil wanted to recoup the money he had spent. They agreed to a 1,000 Kwacha payment to cover their costs and we moved in the day after they moved out, also taking on two of their dogs as part of the deal. Ross had spent hours with Cecil discussing the foibles of the pool pump and other vagaries of the property.

Our new bungalow was arranged in a long series of rooms starting with a copious utility/laundry room at one end where Mary would start her day; this led into a huge galley kitchen fitted with Formica cupboards I'd struggle to fill; dining and living rooms were in the middle; then three bedrooms, a bathroom and shower room at the other end. Most of the rooms had the familiar red concrete floors, but the dining and living rooms had woodblock. The day we moved in, we wandered around the full acre of our new corner plot, double the size of our previous garden. On a wide lawn to the front sat a wooden support for two swings, which had seats cut from old car tyres suspended from chains; one each for our twins. Nearby a square sandpit had been dug with a wooden surround. The pool area had a six-foot fence made from rough wood off-cuts, like the one around our last pool, to provide privacy and safety with children around. A row of white Agapanthus sent out resplendent flower heads in front of the sitting room window, and around the back behind a tall hibiscus hedge stretched an L-shaped vegetable garden. Rows of tall browning *mealie* or corn stalks flanked towers of wilting green beans; lettuces sprouted seed heads from under straw screens; the vestiges of climbing pea twined up a mesh support; a leggy lemon tree spilled small fruit from overgrown branches at the far end, and weeds spread everywhere. I felt as though I was snooping in someone else's property, and could see work for an army of garden boys. Even the *kaya* was bigger and better, boasting two rooms instead of one.

'I never dreamed we'd live in a house like this!' I said to Ross that evening, having stashed our sparse belongings surprisingly easily into copious cupboards and wardrobes.

'Yeah, this is probably the biggest and best property we are likely to live in for the rest of our lives,' observed Ross downing a celebratory Lion beer, 'we must enjoy it while we can.'

In the small hours of the following night I tossed and turned with the discomfort of late pregnancy. In search of a glass of water I crept out of bed, felt my way along the corridor, and clicked on the kitchen light. The room was completely black and seething. I blinked. In seconds the room was clear. *Did I just dream that?* Then a creature on the work top caught my eye. *A cockroach*! I opened a drawer and more insects scuttled away into corners. *Everything in the kitchen which I'd so recently housed will have to be cleared out, the drawers and cupboards sprayed, and then everything washed and put back in place.*

Men in white overalls from pest control arrived a few days later with sprays and goggles and warnings about toxicity. Gloria had refused to have the house treated because of her asthma, and the cockroaches had enjoyed a free run for several years. We left doors and windows open and went out visiting for the day. We didn't let them spray the bedrooms.

Ross had a more threatening experience. He was giving the pool its regular clean and finding this took twice as long as our old pool when he heard a droning sound and looked up to see a black cloud of bees streaming over the hedge and heading in his direction. After considering a dive into the water while they flew over, he reconsidered and throwing down the skimming net raced to the house, not even stopping to ensure the gate was locked.

'What's the matter,' I asked, seeing panic written on his face.

'There's a swarm of bees out there, thousands of the blighters,' he panted, brushing bees off his clothes, 'are the girls indoors?'

'Yes, they've just had their supper,'

'Just as well. Let's make sure all the doors and windows are closed. African bees can be killers! These ones seem to be aggressive and I felt as if they were chasing me.'

The next morning he ventured out to have a look in the garden. The top of the swimming pool was sprinkled with drowned bees.

'I'm glad I decided against diving into the pool to escape them,' said Ross, 'if I'd tried to surface I'd probably have inhaled a few, and I don't like to think what that would have done to my mouth and lungs!'

The rest of the swarm had settled in a seething oval clump on the trunk of the Flamboyant tree next to the pool fence. We approached it with caution, but there seemed to be no danger. It stayed there for a couple of weeks gently humming before it disappeared.

Our next unwelcome visitor was a monkey the size of a six-year-old child. He had escaped from a leave house whose temporary resident couldn't control him. Shaking our kitchen burglar bars, he stared in at me and the girls with malevolent red eyes, and showed off his vicious yellow canines.

I ran to lock all the doors, and we cowered under his evil gaze.

'Oh thank heavens, you're back. What can be done about that monkey,' I said unlocking the back door for Ross and wasting no time in pointing out our new intruder.

Undaunted he took his oldest tie, coaxed the monkey to come to him, and attached the tie to a leather collar around his waist. Then he tied it to a small tree, but almost immediately the creature had ripped the cloth apart and escaped. So Ross disappeared into the Land Rover, and emerged with a long chain. This did the job, and they both set off down Datura Street to find the animal's owner. A group of village boys jumped up and down, their fists in their armpits as they called 'ooh ooh ooh, eeh eeh eeh.' The monkey strained angrily on the chain, and Ross let out ten feet of slack to release him in chase. They scarpered in fright, and laughing, Ross drew the chain shorter again.

'Oh no, you haven't brought it back have you?' said the man at his leave house door. 'I thought I'd seen the back of that monkey. I hate him, he's nothing but trouble!'

A few weeks later our new address in Datura Street had become more like home, a new place had been found for everything, and we became accustomed to the pulse of a bigger house. At last we could sit back and enjoy it in preparation for our next addition to the family.

CHAPTER EIGHTEEN

Spice

Do not try to fight a lion if you're not one yourself.

AFRICAN PROVERB

A spate of burglaries when we first returned to Zambia persuaded us to add to our canine defences. Sheba had been staying with friends while we were in London, and recognised us before we reached their gate to reclaim her with delirious tail wagging, and dancing in circles. Two years of absence had not altered her, and she became part of our new household again. A back-up for her excellent guarding skills would be useful, so Ross went to see about an available candidate. Spice had a sister, Sugar, and they were Bull Mastiff cross-breeds, but the fearful owner couldn't cope with hefty Spice and was trying to find him another home. Intimidated by the mastiff glower, his powerful neck, and bone-crushing jowls, he'd been too scared to care for him other than feeding, and the poor dog was covered with ticks and hadn't been properly socialised. Loud barking from an adjoining room announced his foreboding presence.

'Be warned, he's a force to reckon with,' cautioned his keeper, before he opened a locked door and 120 pounds of dynamic dog strained on a choke chain to approach Ross for an investigative sniff, his big nostrils flaring from a wide black nose set on his short muzzle. Ross scratched his broad skull and gave his dense coat a hearty rub. Spice turned a furrowed brow to face him, opened his mouth and licked his hand.

'He'll need a firm master!' warned his owner, looking surprised.

'I think I can manage that,' replied Ross with a determined smile and took hold of the chain.

I drew back in alarm when the eager mutt charged through our kitchen door, with Ross being dragged along at the other end of the taut chain.

'Don't worry I'm sure he's going to be fine! Just needs a bit of training and attention,' he said, and spent the next hour patiently and painstakingly inspecting his coat and ears for ticks. Spice succumbed to Ross's gentle ministrations of Vaseline, tweezers and a sterilising rub of surgical spirit and they bonded. It became a ritual over several days because Spice still had dozens of ticks in his ears waiting to be found, he'd been so neglected. Intelligence didn't shine out in his eyes as it did in Sheba's, his character being more of an opportunist nature. Most people recoiled as I had done when they looked at him, an advantage for our security, so he served our purpose well.

As a guard dog his looks were his greatest asset, but for a determined burglar he would have been easily distracted from his job by a lump of meat, or a bitch on heat. His forbidding appearance proved to be deceptive. Sheba was the one for intruders to fear, but their combined efforts kept us well-guarded with their fearsome growls and display of fangs, which I held as a reassuring thought whenever Ross went out in the evenings to work or rugby practice.

When we discovered Spice had dug a hole under the fence for night-time wanders, Ross wanted to teach him a lesson. A recent rugby injury in the form of broken ribs prevented his usual approach of dragging the dog over to the scene of crime by his collar. Any movement hurt his chest, so he grabbed the dog's ear instead and little force was needed to pull him along to the newly excavated escape tunnel.

'Bad boy,' he shouted in admonishment several times, twisting his ear.

Spice whimpered and swivelled large brown penitent eyes at his master.

'Now, don't do it again,' he roared, giving the ear another tweak and letting him skulk away while Ross addressed the gap under the fence to prevent further nocturnal forays.

'I would never have dared to punish a dog like that,' said Arthur, Ross's father who was visiting at the time. 'I'd have been scared of him taking my hand off!'

But the mastiff knew who was boss.

Both dogs behaved well around children, and sometimes licked salty baby toes. They'd sometimes take up a protective and proprietorial position near their pram or chairs, looking ready to defend them to the last. Later they tolerated pokes and tail pulls, and simply stood up with a sigh and a grunt to walk away when they'd had enough.

Spice had a weakness, which was bad news for Mowgli because he chased cats, and if he caught them it would be the final curtain for his poor victim. Our original cat Sassi had this worked out from the outset and could brave the thunderous charge of any dog stoically, refusing to run. This would confuse the mutt, who would screech to a stop in a cloud of dust for a face-off with our apparently unruffled feline, and Sassi would rub his much smaller form against the dog's front legs with a flick of his tail under a slobbery chin before stalking slowly away. Mowgli showed no such bravado and my intervention with shouts and screams in an effort to save him during the mad cat-dog sprint around the garden fell on deaf dog ears. The proximity of a mango tree helped. So Mowgli had to suffer a dozen near-death experiences and frantic tree-climbs before he learnt Sassi's art. Spice adopted his puzzled expression every time I scolded him for cat-chasing.

On the first evening in our new house we invited Cecil, Gloria and their two girls to return to their recently departed home, which was now ours, and share a simple supper with us. Everyone was weary from the day's disruptions, and a quiet evening at the poolside seemed like a good idea. We'd agreed to take on their two dogs Prince and Tammy, as well as their kitten along with the house, a fairly standard practice in the swift turn-over culture of the Copperbelt.

'We can't guarantee the kitten's safety,' warned Ross, 'Spice is really bad about chasing cats! And it wouldn't stop at chasing.'

'Okay, well perhaps if she's kept indoors for the first few weeks until things settle down? He's an outdoor dog isn't he?' suggested Gloria.

Their girls and ours were inventing games outside the kitchen door, and the kitten trailed around Gloria's ankles begging for some of the food we were preparing in the kitchen. Having suffered the trials of moving out of the home they'd loved so much, Gloria's nerves had reached breaking point and she had no patience left for the scavenging feline. Forgetting about the agreement to keep her indoors out of harm's way, she picked up the furry nuisance, yelled 'will you stop tripping me up!' and flung her out of the door towards the grass. The little cat hadn't hit the ground before Spice, alerted to the fracas, caught her mid-flight. One shake in his jaws and she was gone. Claire burst into tears, and we rushed to remove the poor little body in an attempt at damage limitation as far as the children were concerned, because our two didn't realise what had happened. Then it was Gloria's turn to burst into tears.

'I'm a murderess,' she wailed, 'and the girls saw it all…'

'It was an accident,' I consoled her

'I should have known!' she insisted, 'Ross warned me! He told me the dog was a cat-killer! Oh I can't wait to leave Zambia! Everything's going wrong!'

In all the commotion no one had time to punish the real perpetrator who watched with his puzzled expression from the side-lines. He'd just got away with murder. It wasn't an auspicious start to our life in the dream house.

In the unfamiliar surroundings of our new property, we became aware that Spice was back to his old tricks and absconding from his guarding duties every night, but reappearing the next morning. We searched the full length of the perimeter for gaps or tunnels and found none. Since the plot was surrounded by six-foot fencing, and the gate was an equal height, this must have taken some determination on his part. We assumed he went looking for girlfriends in the night, until one morning he came back covered in blood.

Horrified, Ross set about washing him down to remove the evidence. Dogs in Zambia all related to their owners' race, and would attack other races, so white-owned dogs might attack black people if defending their property, and a Zambian-owned dog might attack white people. Ross had imagined the worst case scenario and thought that Spice had been attacking the occupants of the nearby compound. It turned out there had been a murder, and Spice proudly showed us his victim which he must have dragged home over the same six-foot fence to show us, panting as drool dripped from his jowls. A cat, someone's pet, lay lifeless between his paws with Spice's slobber smeared over its matted fur. Before he left for work Ross buried the sad body, but not deep enough. By lunch-time the wretched dog had dug it up again, so proud was he of his conquest, to display the muddied corpse once again. Ross buried it again deep under the vegetable patch and lay a heavy stone on top to deter the canine grave-robber and before an angry neighbour came knocking.

A month after our move we still hadn't seen much of our new neighbours who kept to themselves. It was late morning, Mary was busy in the bedrooms and as I mixed some orange squash for the girls in the kitchen, I could see Kirsty singing happily outside the window. I jerked my head up when Sheelagh started screaming. Standing rigid by the path, she had thrown back her head bawling for no apparent reason. I rushed out to see an army of Matabele ants covering her legs, and frantically brushed them off her before carrying her indoors to calm her down. I'd ask Ross to pour some petrol and oil down the antholes and set light to them, as he'd done before.

I glimpsed Kathy coming out of her back door.

'Hi Kathy,' I waved at my neighbour on my way in, and mentioned the ants.

'Sis man,' she replied, 'those ants can be a real nuisance. Pour some boiling water on them! I hope the baby is all right!'

'She seems to have a couple of bites,' I replied checking Sheelagh's legs again, 'I'll put something on them now. It happened before and she didn't take long to recover. Why don't you come round for a coffee?'

'Oh thanks Sara, but I'm going into town to meet someone. Perhaps another day, hey?'

Sheelagh recovered with the help of a biscuit, and I put the kettle on to boil. Kirsty was still involved in her game, but a different kind of trouble was brewing outside the kitchen door.

The next-door cat underestimated Spice. Before we moved in she was accustomed to her own dogs which she domineered to her satisfaction along with our other dogs, taunting them as she looked down on them in every sense. Her favourite stance was on top of the car port which bordered our garden on the kitchen side of the house at the back. Spice would bark furiously at her while she looked down smugly at his antics, leaping up at her deliberately trailing tail. His leaps got higher, having been well practised with surmounting the high fence, and he made a grab for her tail. She twitched her tail back in a tantalising arch as he bounced up and down in rage, and on the next leap she flattened her ears and reached down to scratch his nose. Her footing faltered, she'd over-reached in her eagerness to teach him a lesson, a frantic grab for the corrugated iron roof failed with a scraping noise of claws and she fell into his jaws. He tossed her back up into the air and nothing could be done to help her.

I came running out to Kathy's cries.

'She was my baby!' she wailed, cradling the limp body which I'd had to pass into her arms, 'I was on my way out to the car when all that racket started, and I saw everything from here but couldn't do anything about it.'

'Sorry' didn't seem to be adequate but I mumbled it anyway.

She never came round for that coffee afterwards, and never seemed to be available for a passing chat either.

CHAPTER NINETEEN

Ailish

No matter where you live, brothers are brothers and sisters are sisters. The bonds that keep family close are the same no matter where you are.

TAKAYUKI IKKAKU, ARISA HOSAKA AND TOSHIHIRO KAWABATA,
ANIMAL CROSSING: WILD WORLD, 2005

'Are you still here?' asked Rowena.

I'd been avoiding visits to town because of this question. What people really meant was, 'Is your baby not here yet?' My due date of 24th October, Zambian Independence Day, had long passed and having an impatient nature I found this hard, not to mention uncomfortable. To be nine months pregnant in the humid heat of suicide month with two toddlers to chase is not an ideal situation, and made me wish we'd arranged things better. Long-term we'd planned our family to make the best use of Mary's help while we could, as we didn't expect to stay indefinitely in Zambia and hadn't considered the climate.

'It would save a lot of work to get the girls out of nappies before we go back,' had been my suggestion at one of our family planning discussions, with their ages so close together.

The prospect of a siesta during the sultry heat after lunch enticed me to put the twins to bed with optimism, although it usually meant them wrecking the room before they fell asleep exhausted on the concrete floor among the debris. Having to pick their mattresses and sheets tangled with teddies back off the floor and remake their beds was worth an hour's peace. Then we'd set off with a tray of drinks and an animal entourage into the pool area to cool off. I immersed myself in water, which felt more like a bath than a refreshing dip, while Sheelagh and

Kirsty splashed on the steps, climbing in and out, then out and in, busy with their experiments and games. They had watched Ross diving into the water every time he went for a swim. Sheelagh decided she'd do the same, and went through all the motions of stretching out her arms with her head down, then launched herself into the shallow water on the top step. I watched in horror expecting her twenty-month old skull to collide with the concrete under the surface, but she lifted her head mid-flight and entered the water unscathed.

'NO! Don't do that!' I instructed, 'you'll hurt yourself!'

She lay on her belly in the water and looked at me with toddler defiance, then climbed back to the edge, raised her arms and launched herself back into the water. Kirsty had been watching her sister with big blue eyes, and proceeded to go through the same motions, but to my relief jumped in instead with her arms still up around her ears. Kirsty's enthusiasm often outpaced her body, so she always had sticking plasters on her knees, and if either of them were to get hurt it would be her.

In the pool I could reach them quickly if they needed to be rescued from drowning, and my cumbersome floating shape, still in the same blue home-made maternity costume, was an effective barrier to them venturing into deeper waters. But this new danger of suicidal dives into shallow water was a different concern, although Sheelagh performed them many times and never hurt herself or even suffered a redness where she'd hit the water.

A couple of hours later we'd waddle back to the house that Mary had just vacated at the end of her working day, and I scooped *mealie-meal* out of the sack to boil up some *nshima* for the dogs. After stirring in half a packet of frozen *kapenta* (small oily fish) I spooned dollops of it into metal bowls, ordered the drooling dogs to 'sit' and set down their bowls for the daily bolting session. Feeding the girls demanded more care and persuasion, and involved considerably more mess, which the dogs willingly help to clear up afterwards. Then it was pyjama time, a story before bedtime, and back to the kitchen to prepare supper. This was the rhythm of our days. Baths seemed superfluous after all that time in the water, so they didn't get one very often in the run-up to the rains.

'That sounds like thunder,' said Ross peering through the burglar bars.

'Thank goodness,' I replied, 'Carrying this extra weight around I couldn't take much more of October's swelter!

Day after day we looked up at clouds expectant with rain, until finally they burst in a noisy cleansing vertical shower. The red earth exuded its African smell, and we adjusted to a change of season. Humidity dropped, and cooling winds and cloud-cover made life more bearable, but on most days a downpour terminated our pool time. Swarms of flying ants, a nuptial frenzy of insects mating, came and went. Africans collected up piles of their spent bodies wherever they could, and took them home to fry or sometimes ate them live as a delicacy, laughing at the grim fascination of squeamish Brits. They savoured them as much as grasshoppers, caterpillars and cicadas, and called them *nakapalele,* looking forward to the free bounty falling from the air at the onset of the rains. One of the Africans in the Open Pit came to work with a row of grasshopper heads attached to his lapel one night shift, lined up like scalps to show his conquests. He'd kept some in his pocket to have some fun with the *bwana*. The head was the least palatable part, so he let the insects latch on to his lapel, then pulled off their bodies and popped them one by one into his mouth, grinning at the horrified reaction of his expatriate boss.

Sleeping became easier but still uncomfortable for me in late pregnancy. Days turned into weeks without a twinge, Guy Fawkes Day came and went, and the doctor decided I'd have to be 'induced' to speed this baby into the world. I packed my little suitcase with the same contents as last time, but half the number of tiny clothes and we headed down Kabundi Hill to the hospital. Sheelagh and Kirsty stayed at home with Mary, and Ross would take the necessary time off work to look after them when she was not there.

So Ailish, like the twins, was born in a thunderstorm but this time three weeks overdue instead of two weeks early. It was Armistice Day, November 11th, and she became the only member of our small family to be born on a Thursday instead of a Friday. If we'd stayed in Zambia her future birthday parties would have to be moved to another date, because this was the anniversary of Rhodesia's Unilateral Declaration of Independence 1965 (UDI) and any celebrations would be viewed with suspicion by the Zambian authorities who were sensitive to expatriate festivities.

'You'll be trying for a boy, then?' everyone had asked, but as I held her in my arms for the first time I foresaw all the girlie things we could do together without the complication of catering for a different sex.

Ross visited on the first day brandishing a bunch of flowers, and introducing the twins to their new sister. 'Baby!' they said in turn, peering over the edge of her crib and pointing. Dressed by their father, and wearing their pinafore dresses back-to-front, they could see no promising reaction from their new sibling and set about introducing chaos into the ward with questions and investigations. Without a pause they climbed and poked things they shouldn't, and I wondered how I'd cope when we went home.

Childcare had been an eye-opener for Ross while I was in hospital. Nearly two years previously at the twins' birth it hadn't occurred to him to bring flowers, so suitably admonished by friends he drove to the 'Townships' nursery. He'd already made a stop at the Greek supermarket and persuaded the owner to sell him a 'new-birth-celebration' assortment of cigars from a small supply behind the counter. Choosing flowers at the nursery would only take a few minutes unassisted by toddlers, so he parked in the shade of a spreading acacia tree, opened the windows a smidgen, and left them in the car, much as he'd do with a pet dog. He expected a similar arrangement where they would wait quietly and patiently for his return, and then be delighted to see him when he reappeared. Seeing him about to leave the car they baulked loudly at confinement, so he innocently released their seat belts with warnings not to touch anything.

Five minutes later and happy with his flower selection, he returned to the car to find it locked. Small fists can easily push down those door-locking buttons, and he'd unwisely left the keys in the ignition.

'Kirsty, pull up the button for Daddy, please,' he began, 'this one here, look, there's a good girl.' But she wouldn't comply. 'Okay, Sheelagh see if you can do it for Daddy. Pull up this black button here, the one you must have pushed down before.' But persuading toddlers to undo what they didn't realise they'd done in the first place is not so easy. 'No, don't touch that please. Put it down. I SAID NO, PUT IT DOWN!'

As he performed his futile attempts at persuasion, they'd looked at him with interest, and then turned their attention to the box of cigars he'd bought that morning at no little cost. In front of his impotent eyes they took each fat cigar out of the bag in turn, and broke it into small pieces with satisfying snaps, to watch it crumble to the floor. Consumed with frustration Ross regained entry half an hour later by his own efforts, realizing the tobacco remains would have to be swept back up into the bag, inevitably along with some other car detritus, and rolled again.

Back at home after three days recovery I got on with things with Mary's help. Ross went back to work looking relieved to be returning to a man's world. In hospital I'd discovered a changed routine, apparently introduced after the Zambianisation of the matron's post, with shortcuts to the former strict rules of hygiene and a shorter stay. *Standards have slipped* I thought in a matronly way. As a result I soon had to return to the hospital for antibiotics to treat a painful infection, which marred our first days' home.

Friends who'd just had their firstborn found a mosquito in his bedroom. Relaxed measures for preventing malaria meant more frequent sightings, and being a scientist the baby's father took the now dead insect to work so that he could examine it under a microscope and determine if it was a female. Luckily it wasn't, so their fears of malaria were unfounded as only the females were carriers. *Standards have slipped,* I thought again.

Our new baby couldn't have been easier to manage and feed, so my focus for her first year was to keep an eye on Sheelagh and Kirsty's antics. A week after our return from hospital I emerged from an afternoon feed, still woozy from the birth and the antibiotics, and looked out of the window. The twins were making mud-pies in the central flower bed. Clay smothered their faces and mouths, and I prised a worm out of Kirsty's hand with a 'no! Dirty!' She opened her other hand to show me a *chongololo* curled up in her palm. But mud and *chongololos* were quite benign compared to what they'd discover in the garden a fortnight later.

An outing would do us all good, I decided, and searched my wardrobe for something to wear to a children's party that afternoon. I was desperate to get out of maternity clothes, and most things didn't fit any more, so I settled on a forgiving wrap-around skirt and tee shirt before going into the garden to find the girls and change them into new dresses I'd made.

'I'll kill that garden boy,' I exclaimed when I saw them, and ran over to repair what damage I could.

Both girls were totally absorbed in the contents of a pot of white paint which Solomon had left invitingly open, complete with brush, next to the swing frame he'd been painting. Their arms, legs and clothes were streaked white, and their hair stuck in white lumps to the sides of their faces.

Mary came out to join us, and trilled '*Ayee*, sorry, sorry,' in her sing-song voice as if it was her fault, and then ran back to the house for some rags. The scolding she proceeded to give Solomon, our young garden boy, which I could hear from around the other side of the house, was delivered like a volley of gunfire in a very different voice and language. He hadn't been endowed with the same wisdom as his namesake, and I could imagine him hanging his head and sulking as she let rip.

The paint was oil-based, so taking a twin each we sat on the lawn and wiped off as much as we could with Mary keeping up a stream of *ayee's*, and much head-shaking and muttering. We had to resort to white spirit in the end, and scissors for the worst bits of their hair. Their clothes had to be binned. Everyone at the party looked nice. Sheelagh and Kirsty didn't care about being late, or their strange new hair-cuts, or the red marks on their skin from being rubbed with white spirit, or their mother's lumpy shape. I did. I parked the baby in a corner and joined the crowd to take my mind off things.

'When is your baby due?' asked someone's dad, confirming my fears.

Ailish made waking noises, I made my excuses, and we left the party early.

We wanted to integrate our newborn into the family as quickly as possible, and at a few days old she learned to be kissed and cuddled with small clumsy arms. One evening with all three fed, bathed and in their nightdresses, we had a pre-bedtime dancing session to *Ipi N'tombi*, the new hit South African musical. To the words of '*Mama Tembu's getting married here tonight…*' sung by Margaret Simbana we had to rescue our newborn from boisterous displays of affection including being rolled on. Unsupervised they'd have killed her with love. A few months later during an ominous silence, I went into her bedroom to find all three in her cot along with every soft toy they possessed. Ailish had been woken from her afternoon rest to a bombardment of teddies and pandas followed by two hefty two-year-olds swinging over the side of the cot. A bleary-eyed smiling face appeared in the melee without complaint. In spite of the cot's side raised to prevent such an incident, they had climbed four feet to reach their goal.

'There's a New Year's do at the golf club,' announced Ross with gusto and now fully recovered from his illness. 'It's about time we got back into some sort of social life, don't you think?'

'Well we could I suppose,' I said hesitantly, thinking of the recent children's party and wondering what dress I could fit into, 'I'll have to ask Mary if she can babysit for Sheelagh and Kirsty.'

A long accommodating black dress made of stretchy material hung down below the maternity dresses piled on top of the same hanger. It fitted, and I felt like Cinderella being allowed to go to the ball. Mary agreed to stay the night and look after the twins on New Year's morning when they woke up so nothing barred our intention to have a late night and enjoy a lie-in the next morning.

Ailish hadn't yet slept through the night, and since I was still feeding her myself we brought her with us, putting her carrycot in an office and making frequent checks. Led Zeppelin and Pink Floyd belted out from the speakers, and I realized I'd become disconnected from music trends while immersed in baby care. Feeling more confident again to get back into a normal dress, I relaxed and enjoyed the novelty of a few glasses of beer, but discovered they encouraged milk-flow when we were dancing, as revealed by the damp orbs on the front of Ross's cotton shirt. I went to the office to see if the baby could help me out, but she refused to wake up until the morning. By the time we arrived back home on the first day of the New Year my dress was soaked, although it didn't show on the synthetic material, and the twins were already busy playing in the garden under Mary's watchful eyes. Ailish finally woke up for a feed, so afterwards I parked her pram in the shade where Mary could see her, and we fell into bed to recover.

Mary was indispensable, and a joy to have around the house. It would have been almost impossible for one person to take all three for the weekly shop, so Ailish came with me and I left Sheelagh and Kirsty under her care. These trips often involved a tour of all the food shops because shortages had worsened, and sometimes no butter, margarine, oil or even lard was available in any of them. Going without cheese had become a habit that wasn't too difficult, but no fats at all was challenging. Luckily I had a few weeks supply of margarine in the freezer which I used for baking, frying, spreading, and sauces. Like the baker adding mealie meal to the bread dough, CBC's had also become creative with 'Gale's' honey. It tasted remarkably like its much cheaper equivalent, syrup.

On our return one day I hauled a dormant Ailish in her carrycot and placed it on the dining room table. The motions of a car ride always sent her to sleep, and coming back into the house with the first loads of shopping I heard indignant cries coming from the breezeway. Mary's soothing voice was lilting under my toddlers' shrill protests. There was a dispute over a toy. A swift purveyor of justice, Mary picked up one pouting bundle, said some firm words and administered a sharp slap to her own thigh. Each twin imagined the other to have been rightly punished and having perceived the matter to be settled stopped crying. Mary lilted a few more words of arbitration, gave each little girl a teddy and went back to sweeping the floor around their sturdy stumbling legs.

CHAPTER TWENTY

Luangwa Game Park

Everything in Africa bites, but the safari bug is worst of all.

BRIAN JACKMAN

During his illness Ross went to see his boss, who asked how much holiday he'd been taking.

'None since our long leave,' replied Ross. Mounting job responsibilities, a growing family, and our recent move into the house of our dreams gave us no appetite for the planning and upheaval of holidays.

'You need to take regular breaks to be effective in your job,' advised his boss.

'Luangwa Game Park is well worth a visit,' suggested friends, 'you can get there by car, although the bush roads can be dodgy during the rains. You might have heard about Norman Carr, the conservationist? Well he's been working there, and turned it into a superb place for a holiday, with rondavels and a good restaurant. You won't see black rhino because they've been wiped out by poachers, but the rest of the game viewing is brilliant!'

We had heard about the two orphaned lions, Big Boy and Little Boy, being raised and returned to the wild by the much-respected Norman Carr, and his work with rhino conservation. After checking our bank balance we decided on a three-day break. Ailish was five weeks old and the twins 23 months. I packed all their nappies and bought a few of the new expensive disposables for emergencies. Trying to explain to our toddlers about the wonderful holiday coming our way, we sat on the sofa together, a twin on either side of me and a book, and leafed through the illustrated pages of African Wildlife that Ross had given me the previous Christmas. We found monkeys, lions, rhinos, zebra, giraffe, hippos and 'jumbos,' and pointed at them in turn. Then I drew a plane and talked about 'going on the aeroplane' to fly to Luangwa in the East of Zambia. We'd decided this trip would be hard enough with three under-twos without the stress of coaxing our little Datsun van along unpredictable bush roads and the risk of breakdowns. We reconsidered when we learnt that we'd have to pay for three airline seats, as only one free ticket per adult was allowed for infants, but sanity prevailed. Once in the game park itself the dangers of losing a wheel in a deep pothole and being stranded without food or water in searing heat didn't bear thinking about.

The luggage had been stacked in the car along with the wheels for the carrycot; drinks and a picnic had been packed in a bag; and with the twins belted into the back seats we locked the house and set off.

'We've forgotten the baby!' I exclaimed fifty yards down Birch Street. 'How could we!' Ailish was so easy, that we hardly knew she was there much of the time. We had her wheels but no carrycot. Ross turned the car around and full of guilt I rushed in to see if she was alright, having been left alone in the house for all of three minutes. Under her mosquito net tucked up in her carrycot on the dining room table, she was sleeping as soundly as she always did after a feed.

At Ndola airport a plane took off with a roaring scream while Ross unloaded our suitcases and slotted the baby and carrycot on to the wheelbase. Sheelagh tugged at my dress.

'No plane,' she cried shaking her head vigorously, 'no plane.' She had gone off the idea of going by plane having seen the real thing. 'No go on plane,' she insisted again. I looked at her little face full of horror and made a guess,

'We won't be going *on* the plane my love,' I said. She looked up at me with big brown eyes, 'we'll be going *inside* the plane on seats like your car seat.' I went over this a few times stressing that we would all be going *inside* the plane and not *on* it. She calmed down and I sighed with relief at guessing correctly and preventing a panic attack from a toddler refusing to get on the plane. We queued at check-in for the Zambian Airways flight and both twins ran round happy again. Once on the plane we sat all in a row with the carrycot secured in front of us and we looked through the window at acre after acre of tree-tops in the African bush as the plane headed eastwards.

'What's that?' asked Kirsty, squeezed up with Sheelagh on the window seat and pointing.

'Trees,' I replied. 'And look there are some huts, and there's a big river.'

'Er a jumbo!' shouted Sheelagh.

'Where?' I peered over their heads.

'It gone!' she answered.

This game went on for the full journey, Kirsty joined in and always the imaginary jumbo had 'gone'.

The flight was short, and soon our small plane had flown over an escarpment and was descending towards a red gash of dirt airstrip between the trees. The twins took the aircraft steps one at a time and a smiley driver helped us on to a minibus waiting to transfer us to the hotel. Birds seemed to sing in greeting and my eyes started to scan the bush for wildlife sightings straight away. A frog chorus was tuning up as we entered the rondavel which would be home for the next three nights. With the baby fed we set off to locate the dining room. A uniformed waiter flip-flopped over to our table and handed us a plastic-covered sticky menu. This was a game park, so I hadn't expected luxury and at least there was a good selection on offer, and we took our time making our choice. The waiter returned and hovered. The sleeves of his oversized white jacket had been folded back, and appeared to have been washed in swamp water.

'Can we have three lemonades, please, and one beer?' requested Ross

'Yes suh, but suh there is no lemonade.'

'Okay we'll have orange juice, please.'

'Sorry suh, there is no orange juice.'

'Well what do you have apart from beer?'

'We have only tonic or bitter lemon. Or milk if you want,' he added with a generous smile.

There were no shops for miles, and tap water wasn't worth the risk so we had no choice but to make do. At least the baby would not be disrupted as I was feeding her myself.

The food was not much better,

'I'd like the fish please, with salad and chips,' I ordered.

'Oh, the fish eet is off. And there is no salad, sorry,' said the waiter smiling apologetically.

'Okay I'll have chicken and chips with vegetables,'

'Er, sorry there are no chips.'

'Well tell us what you do have on offer,' suggested Ross.

'There ees pork cutlet and vegetables,'

'And potato?' I asked

'Yes, there is potato.'

Sad plates of dry pork cutlets, no gravy and a tiny boiled potato each arrived.

'I don't know why you bother with a menu,' said Ross, 'and where are the vegetables?' asked Ross, trying to rein in his frustration.

The waiter pointed at the potato. 'That ees the vegetable.'

We'd have to fill up on bread, but there was nothing to spread on it. Luangwa's reputation evidently didn't extend to its food.

'I suppose we can put up with this for a few days,' said Ross philosophically savouring his Lion beer which he could enjoy again being off medication. 'We're here for the game, and not the food.'

The next morning after a crack-of-dawn breakfast of dry toast and jam washed down with milk, grey chicory coffee or weak tea, we set off. A cheery driver and guide welcomed us aboard the open-topped Land Rover, where a middle-aged Italian couple already sat. They had won their holiday in a competition.

'Er a jumbo,' started Sheelagh, kneeling on the seat to peer and point.

'Where?'

'It gone!' and they played the game again for a few miles. Then the driver stopped the vehicle, and an elephant swayed majestically out of the bush, closely followed by another. The twins with mouths agape fell silent. Only ten yards away the two elephants swung their trunks like pendulums across long grass and fed bundles of vegetation into their mammoth pink mouths set between creamy tusks. Enormous feet swished delicately through the grass, and both beasts kept a wary long-lashed eye on us. Cameras snapped, the Italian couple whispered to each other, while Sheelagh and Kirsty stared in awe and remained quiet and still for miles after our guide had quietly steered the vehicle away. They never played the 'Er a jumbo!' game again.

Back in the restaurant that evening, there was a large party of new Zambian guests. We gasped at mounds of vegetables, dishes of butter, French wines and cheeses, which we'd never seen at any price in the supermarkets, a large selection of meats, hot and cold sauces, and bowls of fruit carried by a procession of waiters to their table. A contingent of government ministers and their acolytes were visiting. They gathered around a big table and spoke in loud important voices.

Freed from the usual restraint of their high chairs at home, our toddlers squirmed down off their chairs, bored with waiting for their food, but the staff had no time for us while they attended to the needs of the VIPs. Women, who looked much younger than the men, jabbered, posed and flirted. These were not wives or girlfriends. In the ladies toilets they spread themselves out in front of the mirrors to reapply thick make-up and readjust garish tops and brash jewellery, while I struggled for space to change the baby's nappy. Back at the table our mouths were watering and the twins stood up on their chairs banging the cutlery. Festivities at the big table had cranked up a level, and raucous laughter accompanied their banquet. I naively imagined there might have been fresh food supplies brought in for all the guests, but again we looked down at dry pork chops and tiny potatoes with no improvement in the choice of drinks.

'Why can't we have some of what they are getting?' Ross shouted to a waiter transporting a large plate of steaming roast lamb past our table. Another waiter followed with dishes of carrots, peas and courgettes.

'Ah, suh, those people are impo'tant men from de gove'nment. They bring food and drinks with them.'

'Perhaps this is how Africans felt before Independence,' I whispered after the waiters had gone.

Our game drives continued the next morning and again we watched a huge variety of game, pointing and trying to identify as many as we could. Another vehicle, carrying some of the obviously hung-over government men, overtook us. Presumably they'd left the women behind for a lie-in. Two of the passengers were asleep and the others slumped with frowns and yawns. They showed little enjoyment of the wildlife our eyes were feasting on.

The Land Rover arrived at a viewpoint and our driver cut the engine. If it wasn't for the animals we could have been looking at an English pastoral beauty spot on a sunny summer's afternoon. In a languid curve of the wide Luangwa River five hippos wallowed, emitted a few short lusty grunts and twirled their ears, then plunged down in a circle of ripples. A volley of spear-like swallows skimmed over their heads. Upstream a bull hippo yawned as if his jaw was hinged, and displayed fearsome teeth, the longest being the length of a baby's arm. Our twins' mouths opened less impressively to mimic them, and although fascinated they both inched closer to us on the seat. On the opposite bank a herd of wildebeest stared back at us looking at them, their huge heads and shoulders looking mismatched to their bodies, A life of flight occupied their whole lives. Big cats and wild dogs could strike any time of the day or night, and drinking held the perils of crocodiles or the snap of an irritable hippo's jaws. Their long stupid faces looked wary and threatened, and their hooves skittish, unlike the heavy inertia of the buffalo we'd seen earlier, who were all dark aggression and moodiness, as though their rounded heavy horns gave them a headache. In the middle of the wildebeest herd a wobble-legged baby stuck close to his mother, the remains of his umbilical cord still dangling. He stumbled and fell in a heap of stick-like legs, and his mother turned her heavy striped neck to lick and nudge him back to an upright position. That raw smell of birth would alert predators and made this a dangerous time for their smallest and weakest members. Ross had hopes of spotting some big cats, on this our first official game-viewing holiday, but it was a relief to me that we didn't with the lure of three tender and juicy little girls on board an open vehicle radiating their sweet milky smell.

Flying insects swarmed above the herd. A large fly with a long nose landed on the back of the Italian lady's shirt and folded its wings neatly back on top of each other. I was watching it when suddenly she let out a cry, holding her shoulder. It must have bitten her. Something small and hard hit the back of my neck, and I swatted at it then saw Ross doing the same.

'What was that?' he exclaimed, looking around. 'Whatever it was I hope it doesn't bite!'

'I think it was probably a tsetse fly,' explained our guide. 'They are a problem in this part of Africa, spreading 'sleeping sickness' which is a parasitic disease, like malaria. It can be fatal if left untreated, and infects cattle herds as well as humans. Like mosquitoes they feed on the blood of vertebrates, and not all tsetse flies carry the disease. They're attracted to moving vehicles, so we have to spray underneath them regularly.'

I checked the baby's mosquito net for gaps around the sides, and eyed the twins' vulnerable young exposed flesh dressed as they were in little sleeveless shifts with sandals. Ross put their hats on, but instantly small chubby hands flung them aside. He shrugged.

On our return to camp, we walked around thatched *rondavels* enjoying the shadowy cool of late afternoon and trying to work up an appetite for that evening's offerings. A flock of weaver birds flew out from the trees in a twittering yellow cloud, followed by a heavy rustling and twanging of branches. A dozen baboons descended twenty metres in front of us like thugs with malevolent intentions and we all froze.

Except Kirsty who screamed in delight, and with her little bare arms thrust out in welcome tottered in their direction as fast as her terry nappy would allow, looking intent on joining their gang. A large male with the longest teeth made a feint towards her, but she was undeterred. They took sideways glances at this unaccustomed reaction from a small human, and before Ross could run to grab her, they'd grabbed their own babies and shot back up into the trees to better assess the situation from above.

'They could have torn her apart,' panted Ross after his rescuing sprint, 'have you seen their teeth, they're vicious?'

Shaken we took our family indoors, vowing to keep Kirsty in close reach at all times. Sheelagh had cowered back behind the safety of my skirt with an instinct for self-preservation, and baby Ailish slept on, safely tucked up in her carry cot.

'Can you please be ready with your bags packed ready for Jonas to take you to the airstrip tomorrow morning at 9am,' asked the receptionist on our last day, 'your plane should be waiting for you.'

After a short flight to Ndola we expected to be home around lunchtime, allowing for delays and an hour to drive up to Chingola. In our room I had surveyed our bag of dirty washing, and reckoned there were just enough nappies between the three girls to get us back home. Potty training for the twins had been delayed until our return. Laundry services never came cheap, and disposables were expensive and hard to get hold of, so I'd packed most of our supplies for three days use. Washing them by hand was out of the question because of getting them properly clean, and we hadn't brought an iron to destroy any possible *putsi* eggs, so I piled them into plastic bags to take back with us. They'd go straight into a bucket of Napisan to soak, and then Mary would deal with them in the morning.

After breakfast we knew our holiday had ended, and headed for the minibus with a pang of regret. The bouncing journey made the twins chuckle as we headed back towards the long dusty airstrip cut out of tangled bush about a mile from the safari lodge, and my thoughts brightened at the prospect of being home in a few hours. We climbed out on to dust when we reached the clearing and Jonas helped Ross with our suitcases. There was no sign of the plane we expected to be waiting for us.

'The plane eet will be here soon,' said Jason, 'you can just wait here with the others. Then he waved a cheery 'goodbye,' and disappeared with his minibus down the red bush track to the cool sanctuary of the game lodge.

We felt abandoned, but didn't yet realise how badly, and gazed around at bare bush edged with tree stumps, still within the boundaries of the game park. Elephants, monkeys, buffalo wouldn't be far away. Lion, snakes, hyena…

I fixed the pram hood in the upright position, and draped a thin blanket over the insect gauze to keep the sun's rays off the baby's sensitive skin and eyes which always watered in bright sunlight. Ross picked up our suitcases while Sheelagh and Kirsty grabbed the sides of the pram handle and we bumped our way over rough ground in the hope of discovering some shade. We'd paid little notice to our place of arrival three days earlier in our eagerness to look for game, and searched up and down the borders of the airstrip for some kind of building or shelter which might serve as a departure lounge where we could wait. There was nothing. Our fellow passengers had settled at the side of the red ribbon of dust, including the government party, now subdued and still looking hung-over. Scrubby trees offered some shelter but also a resident population of insects and the possibility of snakes, and toilet facilities consisted of one small basic and smelly 'long drop.' But refreshments and proper facilities promised to be available on board, so we resigned ourselves to wait. For ten minutes I battled, coaxed and cajoled the twins to wear sunhats, and as usual failed. Forty minutes went by, and our tolerant cheery twins had become hot, thirsty and tearful.

'I wish we'd brought some drinks with us!' I sighed and started to wonder about dehydration affecting my milk.

This was exactly the situation we expected to avoid by paying for expensive flights instead of driving. Then Kirsty fell over and grazed her knee. I fumbled in my bag of hot belongings for a tube of liquefying antiseptic cream and some clean tissues. Baby wipes had yet to be invented. We'd been playing a clapping game which everyone had tired of, and were trying to think of more ideas for entertaining toddlers whose small dramas were becoming more frequent and insistently loud. Another hour had passed and the government party looked disgruntled, and as hot, bothered and dusty as we felt. They seemed to have exhausted their private supplies of luxuries and lounged on rocks making down-faced conversation that bore no resemblance to the raucous tone of their evenings. Scowling women perched on their bulging bags in sullen groups, fanning themselves with some big leaves they'd found. The glad rags draped over their slouching forms had become creased and limp with perspiration. An African sun rose towards its midday climax with no cloud relief, and shade from the trees contracted to a minimum. No one knew why we were waiting, and no one knew how much longer we'd have to suffer. The hotel staff had dumped us here and attempted to offer neither comforts nor information, but the lodge was beyond walking distance. I picked up Ailish to feed her under the shrivelled shadow of a tree, while balanced on one of our suitcases. Her cotton sheet bore a halo of damp radiating out from under her head, and I noticed a strip of sweat had soaked the back of his shirt as Ross tried to comfort the twins, whose indignant cries had been replaced by resigned grizzling. They were hungry and thirsty but we had nothing to offer them. Tear tracks marked their dusty faces. I'd just changed them into the last of their nappies hoping to make them more comfortable, and tried to seal our plastic bag of dirty and heat-ripened nappies with a firm knot. Damp flannels for face and finger-wiping lay grimy from overuse in another plastic bag. I'd soon have to resort to spitting on a hanky to wipe their faces, like a 1950s mother, if my dry mouth could muster up the saliva.

At last a vehicle arrived from the camp and two waiters hauled out crates of bitter lemon and tonic bottles, and the news that President

Kaunda had requisitioned our Zambia Airways plane back in Lusaka just before it was due to take off. Until a replacement could be found we'd have to keep waiting, and how long that might be was anybody's guess. The party of ministers had an unpalatable reminder of their place in the government pecking order, and we felt some justice had been administered, although we had to suffer too. Sweltering in the sultry bush, our creased clothes clung to our backs and legs, dust found every way to stick to damp skin so our toddlers were filthy, and still we had no choice but to wait, try to be patient, and make the best of things. The girls still hadn't mastered the art of sucking through straws and when they'd chewed them beyond repair we poured small amounts into their parched mouths to prevent spills of the precious liquid. Once they were happy we could drain our own drinks, and the hydration helped to relieve our headaches.

So it was with great relief that after four hours of entertaining and consoling two toddlers as well as attending to a new-born in the bush, we boarded the plane. Having the baby allowed me the privilege of a 'bulkhead' seat again, where the carrycot had to be housed. I stretched out my legs and looked out at the scorching dust patch we were escaping without any of the pangs of regret I'd had earlier. Ross, Sheelagh and Kirsty shared two seats in the row behind us, as the other front seats had already been allocated to VIPs. We didn't make a fuss about not being together, feeling grateful just to be on the aircraft at last, and sank back in the comfort of a soft seat to savour the chill of air-conditioning. The plane took off, we soared up and away towards relative civilisation, the seat belt light went off, and I lifted Ailish out of her cot. At that moment the levelling of the plane caused a rush of water from the air-conditioning to flow back along the pipes, it somehow found an outlet above me, and cascaded in a waterfall over my head. There must have been a leak or a part missing, and no one else seemed to be suffering the ignominy of this deluge. I grabbed a blanket to protect the baby, and with a soaked dress and dripping hair over one side of my head looked over at Ross.

'What next?' I moaned shaking my rats' tails, then surprised myself with a laugh because I was so immensely relieved for us to be winging our way back home. The 'next' thing proved to be a nappy crisis. Ailish still had one clean muslin nappy left in the bag, but the twins both needed changing. The only solution was to rinse the ones they were wearing in the confines of the tiny airline toilet, put on masses of nappy-rash cream, wring out the rinsed towelling nappies, and put them back on wet with plastic pants to cover them. Our easy-going girls didn't seem to mind too much, and I wouldn't have got away with it in a cold climate, but it saw us through our dilemma until we arrived back in Ndola and could buy fresh supplies.

CHAPTER TWENTY-ONE

The Snake

Love your neighbour as yourself; but don't take down the fence.

CARL SANDBURG

In February 1977 Ross found himself selected to join a group of twenty on a three-week tour of various Caterpillar operations in the United States with a view to purchasing new equipment for the Open Pit. They hoped to fit in a visit to Disneyland while they were there, and Ross would also have a short detour back home to see his parents. I was left on my own, with Mary and Solomon, twin two-year-olds, a baby of twelve weeks, and the animals for company. It would be a good break for Ross with no responsibilities except to review new mining equipment, and I didn't mind being left behind. I had plans to rid myself of that stubborn extra weight gained during pregnancy which I expected to be easier on my own.

Before he left Ross arranged for a security guard to patrol our grounds every night from six o'clock, the time when our African days extinguished themselves in a fiery orange glow. Although the thought of someone hanging around outside our bedroom windows in the darkness seemed quite creepy, it offered reassurance in the gloomy hours as most break-ins happened at night.

Mary's week finished on Saturday lunchtime, and after she'd gone with her customary 'bye bye Kir'ty, bye bye S'eelagh,' we went about our usual mundane activities which mainly involved keeping us all clean, fed and safe with a little entertainment thrown in if I was lucky. The sun shone as it usually did, the baby was taking her early afternoon nap, and the girls pottered in and out of doors while I did some sewing in the cool of the 'breezeway' between the front and back doors.

Sheelagh pointed at the veranda, 'look Mummy, 'nake!'

After their ''er a jumbo!' games at Luangwa I never paid much notice to her observations and glanced out at the shiny red concrete square of veranda. Then I did a double-take. A dark snake was winding its way towards the wall.

'Be a good girl and stay here, nasty snake,' I said throwing down my sewing, then I ran out of the door giving our unwelcome visitor a wide berth to reach Kirsty who I scooped up away from danger. She had a fascination with wild life and might easily try to pick it up, as she'd done before with bees, handing them to me like a present with a 'here y'are, Mummy!' She'd been pushing her toddle truck around the grass in the front garden, and had strayed into the flower bed with the agapanthus plants. The door slammed as I pulled it closed behind me, and we looked out at the sinister coil with me pointing at it and repeating again and again, 'Nasty snake, don't touch! Snake bites you!'

Cecil had once unfurled a snakeskin to show us. He'd skinned a ten-foot python which he'd found and killed with a handy shovel in their vegetable garden, which was now our vegetable garden. A discussion on snakes had ensued.

'I was driving out on the bush road to the game plot outside town after work one day when I saw what I thought was a branch lying right across the width of the road,' said Ross, 'then just as I went over it, I realised it wasn't a branch but a python! Must have been a big one because it had reared up its head at one side of the road but the end of its tail was out of sight at the other side! So I braked, but didn't fancy getting out so reversed back to take a better look. There was no sign of it! I was paranoid that it had wrapped itself around the axle. You hear these stories. It made me really wary about getting out of the cab when I arrived.'

'This one in the garden was relatively small, maybe a young one, but a python like the one you saw can easily swallow a duiker. That bush road must be... what? Six or seven metres wide?' asked Cecil.

I thought of our Dixie who used to leap around the garden in 11th Street, and wondered if a python had taken her, but it was rare to find snakes in town, let alone a huge python. Her abductor had more likely been a predator with two legs.

'You know it's always important to identify a snake,' he continued, 'especially if it bites you, so that they can inject you with the right anti-venom at the hospital,' he'd advised, 'it's the first thing the doctors will ask so they can give you the right antidote. Some of them are deadly and there's no time to hang around trying to find the right anti-venom. Ideally you should kill it and take it with you, just to be sure. Puff adders are the worst because they rely on camouflage for protection and don't move out of your way like other snakes so it's easy to stand on them. Their markings are more horizontal.'

'Yes we found one the other day wound round a hessian sack in the Open Pit workshop,' said Ross, 'my section boss was digging into the sack looking for nuts and bolts when two of the men pushed him away. He hadn't noticed it! They killed it with hammers, then slit it open to find a huge rat which must have been the last thing it ate. Fortunately for the section boss it had been sleeping off its big meal.'

I peered through the window to try and see if this one had horizontal markings, and could only make out blurred shapes in shades of brown.

'Another time,' continued Ross, 'we were moving an ore stockpile out at Mimbula and Fitula and disturbed loads of snakes. There were all types; it was like a biblical nest of vipers! They were coming out everywhere and men were trying to kill them any way they could, mainly by the machine-operator banging the bucket down on top of them as no one would risk getting too close. Anyway, I threw two dead cobras and a puff adder into the back of the truck to show to the safety officer, because they were a danger to the workers. On the dirt road there was this *medulla* (old man) walking in my direction so I stopped to offer him a lift. I opened the passenger door so that he could get in beside me, but he jumped in the back. He was like a cat when he saw the snakes and jumped straight out again, then ran up the road and never stopped!'

Apart from in a zoo or as road-kill I'd never seen a snake. Spiders and mice I could just about deal with, but snakes were another matter. We'd visited a snake park in Rhodesia and watched boomslangs (Afrikaans for tree snake) in a snake pit hurling themselves at the walls trying to get out, and didn't think it could be one of those. Vague memories of first aid for snake bites in the Girl Guides came to me. It involved a sharp knife which had to be sterilised in a flame, and sucking out the venom then spitting it out. But catching or killing a snake would be completely beyond my know-how. The alternative of incarcerating all of us indoors for the rest of the weekend as a safety precaution didn't appeal. We watched a forked tongue slick out of its mouth, and I shuddered.

'Spitting cobras can spit over two yards if they're cornered,' said Cecil, 'and always aim for the eyes. Dogs or cats sometimes disturb them in the flower beds. We had a dog it happened to twice in a row, and he went blind for a day or two each time but he recovered both times. We never found that damn cobra! Then there are black mambas which are *really* venomous. I haven't seen one in Zambia but that's not to say they don't get them here. A bite from one of them will kill you in twenty minutes. The inside of their mouths is black, but their skin's actually brown, and boy, can they move!'

Sheba had once been blinded by a cobra, and we never found that one either. I must stop the girls from wandering into the flower beds! Why do these things always happen when there's no one here to help? Snake worries mounted higher and higher in my imagination, and I closed both doors to the back of the house as well for good measure. My only assistants were the animals so I called the dogs to the veranda hoping they might somehow scare it off. They had been lying on the grass outside the kitchen door, shaking off the flies which tormented their ears, and occasionally rolling over to chew an old bone, or drag themselves upright to plod over to a spot under the Cassia tree for its cool shade. They arrived at the veranda with a desultory obedience, and watched me with curiosity as I tried to convey the presence of an alien. I'd imagined they see it straight away and at least bark to scare it away, but they didn't seem to register its existence at all. Afraid to get too close to the creature myself to show them with a stick, they didn't understand what I wanted of them, so I gave up and went in search of Mowgli in the hope that he would know what to do. He was curled up on our bed and gave a languorous stretch when I woke him. His wide yawn revealed the sharp teeth I envisaged plunging into the snake's neck after a brief tussle. I carried him to the front door and pushed him out in the direction of the snake sunbathing against the wall then closed the door and watched through the side window. Mowgli was still half-asleep and sat down for a wash, oblivious of the reptile only a few feet away and now stirring into life. I opened the door again, picked up our bemused cat again and skated him across the concrete to slide to a halt only inches from the snake, but still he refused to see it and sat looking blearily back at me standing behind the safety of the window and the closed door. He hadn't got the message either, and his attitude conveyed that afternoons were for siesta and not his hour for hunting. After considering the option of simply ignoring the creature, and keeping everyone indoors for the rest of the day, with the knowledge it would always be preying on my mind, I decided to go for assistance next door. With points and smiles and 'be good girls' I told the twins where I was going and closed the door without locking it so that I could get back in, but neither could small people get out as the handle was too high, or so I thought.

Kathy's husband John was South African and often went on hunting trips into the bush at weekend so I was sure he'd be able to identify the snake and know what to do. Kathy answered my knocks,

'He's having his lunch right now, so he'll come round later, okay?'

I went back to the house feeling that things weren't okay at all, not since Spice had killed her 'baby'. Kathy had no good reason to do me any favours. I got back to our house to wait, and tried to open the door I had recently left. It resisted. I gave it another shove but still it wouldn't open; I noticed a stool had been pulled alongside the door and one of the girls must have reset the latch. I shouted to them through the reinforced glass door, and Sheelagh climbed up on the stool making me think it was probably her. They had locked Ross out of the car a few months earlier and too late I realised this was a trend to be wary of.

Kirsty was busy with her toys at the back of the room. I tried to instruct Sheelagh to turn the key back again, but like the cat and the dogs she couldn't understand what I was trying to communicate.

'Key,' she kept repeating with a wise nod, 'turn key…'

Since I'd efficiently locked all the other doors, and burglar bars covered every window, I was stuck. There were now three under three's locked in the dream house, and a snake of unknown variety close by. This had turned into a nightmare. Mary and Solomon would not return until Monday morning, and no one else, apart from Ross who was in America, had a house-key. I traipsed back to knock on Kathy's kitchen door, trying to suppress my rising panic. This time she held a mauve and green doily which she was crocheting. I didn't share her taste.

'I'll let him know. He's still eating. He'll come round soon, okay?' she didn't seem to understand the urgency of the situation, and looked more interested in her doily.

I sat on our doorstep after checking on the whereabouts of the snake which by now had disappeared. My imagination ran wild as to where it might be, and I considered the possibility of it circling the house to come and find me. Paranoia was setting in. Tammy came to slump at my feet and gave me some comfort. Kirsty and Sheelagh came to the window and waved,

'Hello Mummy, wot you doin?'

I waved back. For what felt like an hour I used all my powers of persuasion to get them to turn the key in the lock or to pass it to me under the door, but without success. The baby would be waking up soon and need attention, but it seemed pointless to go knocking on Kathy's door yet again.

Eventually John appeared with their nine-year old daughter, Myleen, presumably to prevent any funny business with me, a woman on her own. A few minutes later he'd returned with the tools to force open my door and I was back with the girls in a jiffy. I gushed with gratitude, and hugged my girls as though we'd been apart for hours. Presumably a burglar could have opened the door with the same ease, but I blotted out that thought knowing we had a security guard and turned my attention to the problem in hand. The snake had disappeared. John and I then went round the area of the garden close to the house, tentatively poking in bushes and amongst dry leaves with long sticks in search of our unwelcome visitor. Myleen stayed to play with the twins indoors, oblivious of her duties as chaperone.

'What did it look like?' he asked. 'Did it have any patterns on its head or body?'

'Um, I'm not sure. It was brown with sort of diamond patterns, but it was all kind of blurry.'

'Did you notice a V shape at the back of its neck? '

'Er, no,'

'How long would you say it was?' he persisted, 'did it have a white underbelly?'

'No, I think I would have noticed that. I reckon it was about, what, twenty inches long?' I said trying to imagine it straightened out and estimating the length between my hands wishing I'd taken a better look.

'Well it's unlikely to be a mamba and it doesn't sound like a cobra or a puff adder, they're the ones you need to worry about. It could have been a young house snake, or a thread snake and neither of them are too bad, but obviously with toddlers around you can't be too careful. Let me know if it comes back, and try to get a good look at it next time.'

I was beginning to understand the importance of this information in an emergency. John gathered up his tools, and they went home. Still shaken, I filled the kettle for a calming cup of tea before Ailish woke up for her feed. The mess made indoors by the twins would have to wait for my attention later, as would a locksmith to fix the broken lock. I was still able to snib the door, but now felt uneasy about my fragile defences against intruders on top of the hidden dangers lurking in the greenery of our flower beds.

A lone woman was seen by other women, like Kathy, as a threat and by some men as an opportunity, even when she had three charges under three years old and was still feeding one of them herself. A husky voice telephoned me one late afternoon,

'Hi Sara, how are you getting on without Ross?' asked Graham, one of the 'single guys' who sometimes played golf with Ross. 'I just wondered if you'd like some avocadoes, because our tree is laden?' He was slightly breathless.

'Ooh, yes please I love avocadoes, and so do the twins. They make great baby food.' I was still quite naïve, so didn't work out the real reason for the call until I'd thought about it later, and was glad I hadn't given him any more encouragement. He'd never offered us avocadoes in previous seasons when Ross had been around. We found a bag of avocadoes at the front door the next afternoon on our return from visiting a friend with a new baby, but no sign of Graham. My response hadn't encouraged him to linger. The next enquiry was from a married man whose wife had gone back to the UK for a family funeral.

'Are you managing all right on your own?'

'Fine,' I replied, again taking his enquiry at face value, 'I managed to fix the broken washing machine myself yesterday.'

He laughed. 'That's not quite what I meant.'

What he really meant dawned a little quicker this time, but I still feigned ignorance. In spite of my efforts to have an innocent conversation, he arranged a visit but I persuaded him to bring his eight-year old son along with him. A trick I'd learned from Kathy.

CHAPTER TWENTY-TWO

Leaving it all behind

When you leave Africa, as the plane lifts, you feel that more than leaving a continent you are leaving a state of mind. Whatever awaits you at the other end of your journey will be a different order of existence.

FRANCESCA MARCIANO, "RULES OF THE WILD"

Ross returned buoyant from his travels. Regaled by hours of catching-up talk, we went to bed in the early hours, which I knew I'd regret a few hours later at the first baby cries for a morning feed. I had vivid dreams of Disneyland where they'd chosen to take a trip down the 'Zambezi' with wildlife displays which included tigers. Much amused at the Hollywood interpretation of the real thing they all knew so well, they'd still been impressed by all the new technology in spite of alien tigers.

He brought back a large chunk of Cheddar cheese bought in Harrods food hall, which accounted for my vivid dreams but was a great treat since there had been no cheese at all in Chingola for years. The temptation to eat more than I should threatened to put back all the weight I'd recently and painfully shed.

His main piece of news came from a short visit to The Royal School of Mines where he bumped into one of his old lecturers. They were on the look-out for someone with recent mining experience to take on a lecturing post.

'Would you be interested?' asked the professor. 'You must be near the end of your contract now, and the only person we have in the department with mining experience has been lecturing for over thirty years. It's time we got updated!'

Everyone we knew was searching for better opportunities. Sundowner after sundowner celebrated their moves to South Africa, Australia,

Canada, Papua New Guinea, Guyana, Chile and even troubled Rhodesia to work in other mines or industries. Few signed up for another term.

'I'll think about it,' replied Ross.

Endless discussions ensued between us and anyone else who knew of job vacancies. The pay wasn't great considering what we'd become used to and the cost of living in London would be much higher. Boosting his salary with consultancy work could help and the hours were short. We'd have to decide soon before renewing or terminating our contract due to end in six months. Sunshine, a dream home and a growing love of Africa held us back. A stressful work situation, increasing food shortages, being closer to our families and health care pushed us forward. In the end it was our children's health that made us decide, because Kirsty still worried us. Two of our friends had lost babies; one to measles and then our neighbour's little girl to an infection connected to hydrocephalus. It probably wouldn't have happened back home, but on the Copperbelt even the privileged like us were subject to fierce viruses and a dearth of drugs and specialist care.

Random events still unsettled us with their unpredictability, like Kenneth being hauled out of his car and tormented by soldiers while his wife, son and in-laws watched. They were all heading to Victoria Falls for a break, and had been stopped at a road block. Like the single guys on their jaunt into the Congo he'd ended up weeping and begging on his knees. And then I heard about the woman I'd chatted to on the plane from London having a nervous breakdown.

'The offer is on the table, all we need to do is accept it. I'll be in a perfect position there to find another situation as and when we want to move on,' Ross reasoned, still undecided.

The circularity of our lives was taking us back to The Royal School of Mines. We'd sell our flat in Dewar Place and start house-hunting in London with the proceeds to put down as a deposit and arrange our first mortgage. The next day he put in his notice to leave.

'You know I think it has been the best decision of our lives to come to Zambia, but now I feel we're making our next best decision to leave,' he said. 'No regrets. Cheers and here's to whatever's next!' He leaned back in the wobbly basket-work chair and raised a bottle of Lion beer to his mouth.

Heroes' Day on the first Monday of July arrived for Zambians to commemorate those who struggled for Independence in 1964. To celebrate ten years of independence President Kenneth Kaunda had presented a gift to the nation in honour of its heroes. It was a bronze statue of a man without a shirt or shoes and the metaphorical broken chains of colonialism held defiantly in his raised fist. It became a rallying point in Lusaka for marches and remembrance parades. We used the public holiday to fill our packing cases before we left the house we'd enjoyed for less than a year. They didn't amount to much as we sold most of our household effects, and felt duty-bound to pass on the girls' toys to Lorna's nursery as it was hard to source toys of reasonable quality. Although sturdy, they were much bashed, a state that worried our toddlers not-at-all, and soon they would reclaim almost identical replacements from church bazaars and charity shops in Britain.

For our last month in August we moved into a leave house in town, complete with their houseboy, and never missed the pool we'd just left as it was winter. I gave Mary a glowing letter of recommendation to help her find employment. Newcomers had stopped coming, and many of our friends were leaving, so we couldn't find her another job, and to tide her over Ross gave her extra money. She came back with this letter to 'Mr Danny' as she could never say just 'Dunn,' hand-written by a scribe:–

Miss Mary Musomba
House No D.33
Kaspisha Compound (Section)
20th August, 1977

Dear Mr Danny.

The first thing to say before I start thanking you is this; how are you sir? With me here, with my family we are very well indeed, only that I am very sad or I am very sad of you going back to your mother-land.

Sir, I will not and ever forget for all what you have done together with mrs. Danny I thank her very much indeed for all what she did and helped me and tell her that may God help you and her wherever you will be and may God help you two together with your family have a good and enjoyable journey to wher-everyou will be going especially when going home.

My second thing is this; I thank Mrs. Dan for her kindness of giving me such a nice and good Tesmonial (a character letter) I was very happy to receive it or to get it from her. I shall be more happier if my tesmonial was a typed one. And another thing which I say thank you sir, is the money you gave me also I was very happy when I got it.

My third thing is just a help from you and as I know there is no one who can help me at this time apart from you my former employer, please mr. Dan will you please kindly help me to give me some nails, cement and some piece of wood for making a roof (amapulanga in bemba) I need this help before you leave because if I can't cover my house it will be or the rain will destroy my new house as I don't have enough money to all what I have mentioned. Please mr. Dan help me before the rain comes and before you leave. I shall be very pleased indeed if you will help me before the rain comes.

Pass my greeting to mrs. Dan and all the children.

Yours faithfully:

Mary Musomba

She must have paid for this to be written, and it made us smile. I duly found someone to lend me a typewriter, and Ross gave her all the things for her roof, so she was happy. I missed her extra pair of eyes and ears because Sheelagh and Kirsty explored the interestingly different property with a determination that kept me on my toes, and I once found them wandering across the road at the front. When the nights weren't too cold Ross and I sipped beers on the jasmine-scented patio to the sound of crickets under a scarlet roof of cascading bougainvillea. Silent fruit bats flitted like shadows through the trees; the girls slept indoors after another busy barefoot day; the houseboy had left everything clean and laundered, and would return the next day to do the same; and the dependable sun had shone all day until sudden tropical darkness enveloped us. But trouble and danger lurked. The frogs stopped abruptly and we heard a faint but insistent pulse of drums in the distance sending out an ancestral message. This was not our homeland, we were outsiders and had three children to consider. We needed to go somewhere more stable, away from this collision of cultures and races, and the possibilities for our future proffered both excitement and regret.

September 1977

We couldn't leave without another sundowner. Dancing to a disco after the buffet and a few glasses we all chorused '*On a blanket on the ground,*' to Billie Jo Spears song. Lena sang along next to me and I wondered if she used a blanket on the ground for her alleged assignations in the golf club grounds. Rumours still ran rife in the small community.

'It's not enough for her to keep a husband happy and to take part in tennis, golf and squash,' said Val, 'she still has energy left for affairs! What stamina, it makes me tired just thinking about it!'

We danced around the pool as if we were in an Elvis movie, but to seventies songs.

'*Get me a ticket for an aeroplane,*

Aint got time to take a fast train.

Lonely days are gone, I'm a goin' home…' Sang Jefferson, and I looked forward to starting our new life.

On our last day I shopped in town with the twins holding on to the pram handles, looking for snacks to take with us. Ailish was sitting up harnessed into the pram, and I'd tucked my purse behind her. When I got to the counter it had disappeared along with my last few coins, so we left the shop empty-handed. I didn't really mind. Zambia hadn't broken our hearts, but seeped into our souls. Our marriage and our children had survived. We still loved Africa, but the time had come for a separation.

ACKNOWLEDGEMENTS

Thanks to the Phoenix Writers Group, who deliver a constant source of encouragement.

To the 'Chingola' Facebook page whose pictures stirred so many memories.

To those who read and checked the script:–Diana and Ian Dey, Nikki Burrows, and Penny Hanson.

To Mike and Anna Nott, who also lived in Zambia in the seventies and advised on nursing and mining.

And most of all to Ross who shared anecdotes, advised on mining, and tirelessly analysed every chapter over and over again.